D0909336

ATLA Monograph Series
edited by Dr. Kenneth E. Rowe

1. Ronald L. Grimes. *The Divine Imagination: William Blake's Major Prophetic Visions.* 1972.

2. George D. Kelsey. *Social Ethics Among Southern Baptists, 1917-1969.* 1973.

3. Hilda Adam Kring. *The Harmonists: A Folk-Cultural Approach.* 1973.

4. J. Steven O'Malley. *Pilgrimage of Faith: The Legacy of the Otterbeins.* 1973.

5. Charles Edwin Jones. *Perfectionist Persuasion: The Holiness Movement and American Methodism, 1867-1936.* 1974.

6. Donald E. Byrne, Jr. *No Foot of Land: Folklore of American Methodist Itinerants.* 1975.

7. Milton C. Sernett. *Black Religion and American Evangelicalism: White Protestants, Plantation Missions, and the Flowering of Negro Christianity, 1787-1865.* 1975.

8. Eva Fleischner. *Judaism in German Christian Theology Since 1945: Christianity and Israel Considered in Terms of Mission.* 1975.

9. Walter James Lowe. *Mystery & The Unconscious: A Study on the Thought of Paul Ricoeur.* 1977.

10. Norris Magnuson. *Salvation in the Slums: Evangelical Social Welfare Work, 1865-1920.* 1977.

11. William Sherman Minor. *Creativity in Henry Nelson Wieman.* 1977.

12. Thomas Virgil Peterson. *Ham and Japheth: The Mythic World of Whites in the Antebellum South.* 1978.

13. Randall K. Burkett. *Garveyism as a Religious Movement: The Institutionalism of a Black Civil Religion.* 1978.

Garveyism as a Religious Movement

The Institutionalization of a Black Civil Religion

by

RANDALL K. BURKETT

ATLA Monograph Series, No. 13

The Scarecrow Press, Inc.

and

The American Theological Library Association

Metuchen, N.J. & London

1978

Library of Congress Cataloging in Publication Data

Burkett, Randall K
    Garveyism as a religious movement.

    (ATLA monograph series ; no. 13)
    Bibliography: p.
    Includes index.
    1. Afro-Americans--Religion. 2. Garvey, Marcus,
1887-1940. 3. Afro-American clergy. 4. Universal
Negro Improvement Association--History. 5. McGuire,
George Alexander, 1866-1934. I. Title. II. Series:
American Theological Library Association. ATLA mono-
graph series ; no. 13.
BR563. N4B88   261. 8'34'5196073   78-15728
ISBN 0-8108-1163-4

Dedicated to my wife

Nancy H. Burkett

CONTENTS

LIST OF ILLUSTRATIONS

ACKNOWLEDGMENTS

Among the many individuals who provided assistance and encouragement during the preparation of this manuscript I would like especially to thank my wife, Nancy, whose careful reading has immeasurably improved it, and without whose energy, spirit, and affection it would not have been completed.

Emory J. Tolbert, already hard at work on his own dissertation on the Garvey movement when I began my research, was extraordinarily generous in sharing with me the many primary sources he uncovered. For this I am deeply grateful.

My dissertation advisor, John B. Orr, offered invaluable assistance in sharpening the theoretical framework through which I have sought to analyze the Garvey movement.

David W. Wills provided my first systematic introduction to the history of the Black church in America and spent many hours reading and discussing with me the material presented herein. His influence, if not his wisdom, may be found on every page.

Finally, George Huntston Williams has served, since my days at Harvard Divinity School, as a model of the meticulous scholar and compassionate teacher to which I continue to aspire.

I would also like to thank the Ford Foundation for awarding an Ethnic Studies Dissertation Grant which permitted me to devote a full year to research.

Worcester, Massachusetts
January 1978

EDITOR'S NOTE

Since 1972 the American Theological Library Association has undertaken responsibility for a modest dissertation publishing program in the field of religious studies. Our aim in this series is to publish two dissertations of quality each year at a reasonable cost. Titles are selected from studies, in a variety of religious and theological disciplines, nominated by graduate school deans or directors of graduate studies in religion. We are pleased to publish Randall K. Burkett's splendid study of Marcus Garvey as number 13 in our series.

Following undergraduate studies at American University, Professor Burkett studied church history at Harvard and took the doctorate in social ethics at the University of Southern California. Several of his articles and papers have appeared in print. In addition to this study of Garvey, Dr. Burkett is preparing two other titles scheduled for publication soon: Black Redemption: Churchmen Speak for the Garvey Movement (Temple University Press) and Black Apostles: Afro-American Clergy Confront the Twentieth Century (G. K. Hall), which he is editing with Richard Newman. He currently directs the special studies program at the College of the Holy Cross in Worcester, Massachusetts.

St. Clair Drake is best known as co-author with Horace Cayton of Black Metropolis (1945, revised 1962, 1970). He was on the faculty of Roosevelt University in Chicago for 23 years during which period he was granted leave on two occasions to teach and carry out research in Liberia and Ghana. He has written extensively on race relations and Pan-Africanism as a social movement, and has served as Professor of Sociology and Anthropology at Stanford University where he organized the program in African and Afro-American Studies from 1969 through 1976. He is currently completing a book on Africa and the Black Diaspora.

Kenneth E. Rowe
Series Editor

Drew University Library
Madison, New Jersey 07940

FOREWORD

by St. Clair Drake

The young author of this important book, still in his thirties, studied International Relations at the American University in Washington, D.C. and when the "Black Power" movement was cresting in the United States was putting these crucial current events into perspective while completing work for an M.T.S. in Church History at Harvard Divinity School. He then spent four years at the University of Southern California assisting in curriculum development while studying for the Ph.D. in the field of Social Ethics. During that period he began to reflect seriously upon the life and works of a controversial Black leader whose fame was world-wide in the years immediately following the First World War, Marcus Garvey.

In this book, Professor Burkett makes his second significant contribution to the once neglected but now rapidly expanding field of what is sometimes called "Garvey scholarship." (His first was Black Redemption: Churchmen Speak for the Garvey Movement, a valuable presentation of documentary evidence on a subject where misinformation prevailed.) This analysis is unique, considering as it does the religious implications of Marcus Garvey's Universal Negro Improvement Association (UNIA). No detailed knowledge of the man and the movement is required for understanding and appreciating this straightforward, well-documented and lucidly presented scholarly work. However, it can also serve as an indispensable companion volume--supplementary and corrective--to the standard popular sources: E. David Cronon's Black Moses (1969), Theodore G. Vincent's Black Power and the Garvey Movement (1971), and Tony Martin's Race First (1976). It will be especially valuable, too, in providing partial context for studying the Garvey papers which Professor Robert Hill of the University of California, Los Angeles will begin to publish next year. The American Theological Library Association has been responsive to some significant signs of the times in selecting Professor Burkett's book for inclusion in its monograph series. Scholars and non-professional readers, alike, will profit from the choice.

This important study presents the Black "race leader," Marcus Garvey, to us in the unfamiliar role of "theologian" attempting to "create a form of civil religion"* among the people of the Black Diaspora in the Western Hemisphere-- what he once called "the beloved and scattered millions." His hope was that this "civil religion" would, someday, become the religion of the African Homeland, too. This conception of Garvey and Garveyism is startling when we first confront it, but that is because over half a century lies between us and the days when the New York press was regularly reporting the details of the faithful gathering in Harlem's Liberty Hall (and sometimes in Madison Square Garden) to listen to sermons and speeches and to sing such inspirational numbers as the UNIA hymn which contained the lines:

> Ethiopia, thou land of our fathers ...
> Ethiopia, the tyrant is falling ...
> Jehovah, the Great One, has heard us
> Has noted our sighs and our tears,
> With His spirit of love he has stirred us
> To be one through the coming years.

And, even the metropolitan reporters probably did not know that, at one point in its history, the UNIA required its chaplains, when baptizing a baby, to ask the god-parents to pledge that it be "... diligently instructed in the Holy Scriptures" and that it be taught the Creed, the Lord's Prayer, the Ten Commandments, and the Catechism of the Universal Negro Improvement Association. Professor Burkett explains the meaning and function of the hymns, the rituals, and the Catechism--and much more--pointing out that they were not mere strategies conceived for mobilizing the Black masses, but were, rather, a serious attempt to provide "a coherent way of viewing the world" for a people whose old certainties had been shaken by the Great Migration from the South,

---

*The author is applying, with modifications, a concept that proved useful in Robert N. Bellah's "Civil Religion in America," in The Religious Situation 1968, ed. by Donald R. Cutler (1968).

World War I, and a series of devastating race riots, as well as a post-War depression. They were in the process of rejecting the view of society and themselves that "White Christianity" had imposed upon them for centuries.

Millions of Black people throughout the world hailed the name of Marcus Garvey during the early Twenties because he imbued them with a new sense of self respect and held before them the vision of a future when Black men everywhere would no longer be powerless. Many who did not actually join the UNIA were sympathetic to some or all of what they thought Garvey stood for--this energetic and very eloquent and very black West Indian. But, between 1927, when the United States government deported the Jamaican immigrant who became a charismatic mass leader, and the Black Power upsurge during the mid-Sixties, only small scattered groups of devoted followers kept the Garvey dream alive. Though memory of his name never died out, knowledge of the details of the movement did. Professor Burkett now brings back to consciousness a particularly neglected phase of the Garvey movement, previously ignored because, as he notes, early students of the movement had a tendency to "minimize," or "trivialize," or "ridicule," the role of religion in the UNIA.

Few white historians have felt that Garvey and the UNIA were worthy of more than a line or two when they were writing about the Twenties, and, for reasons that Professor Burkett discusses, Black historians and social scientists were not inclined to emphasize Garvey's role in Afro-American affairs, although they usually mentioned the movement. However, 30 years after Garvey's deportation and a decade after his death, the Black Muslims in the United States, the Rastafarian Brethren in Jamaica, and most nationalist leaders in sub-Saharan Africa were referring to Garvey as the "forerunner" of Pan-Africanism or, metaphorically, as an "Elijah" or "John the Baptist." Yet, for most Afro-Americans, living as a minority in a country where the Civil Rights Movement was interracial and "integrationist" and where its participants sometimes sang a paraphrased spiritual, "Black and White Together, We Shall Not Be Moved," a Black Nationalist remembered primarily for his slogans, "Africa for the Africans, At Home and Abroad" and "One God! One Aim! One Destiny!" could not be a revered heroic figure of the past.

By the mid-Sixties, however, militant Black youth

were wearing the UNIA colors even when they didn't know
their origin or what the official interpretation of the meaning
of the red, black, and green had been. When Malcolm X
became the alter ego of the ghetto youth and pointed out that
his father had been a UNIA organizer as well as a Baptist
preacher, the circle of Garvey admirers widened and the
desire for knowledge about him increased. Those who read
Muhammad Speaks and the Black Panther, as well as occa-
sional Black Nationalist booklets, gradually learned discon-
nected facts that were not inconsistent with the ideologies
espoused by these groups. The young Black militants were
impressed by the fact that one of their contemporary heroes,
Kwame Nkrumah, first prime minister in de-colonized Black
Africa, wrote in his autobiography that Garvey had been his
inspiration. And they did not fail to note that he named
Ghana's shipping company The Black Star Line after the
UNIA's ambitious but disastrous venture. The facts sur-
rounding Garvey's arrest and deportation became, for them,
a stick with which to beat what they defined as "house niggers"--past and present--who cooperate with the Establishment to destroy the leaders of "the field niggers." Garvey
had prophesied that he'd return "in the whirlwind." The
young new believers saw his spirit abroad in the northern
ghetto rebellions that set fire to the cities. By this time
their elders were rediscovering Garvey, too, and some of
them later discerned his spirit in the program of govern-
ment-subsidized Black Capitalism. Garvey would have certainly repudiated both groups who invoked his name.

Black Nationalism was viewed as a threat by the Civil
Rights Movement which had gained momentum under the auspices of the Southern Christian Leadership Conference after
the famous Montgomery bus boycott in which Rev. Martin
Luther King became involved. The SCLC was organized by
well-educated preachers whose loyal constituency was made
up of not-so-highly-educated adult lower middle class church
members and their far-flung group of local pastors. The
allies who supplied funds and moral support to the non-violent
breakers of Jim Crow laws included committees of the major
white denominations cooperating with liberal labor unionists
of all races and with human relations committees, public and
private. Later, as CORE and SNCC became active in the
South, younger interracial groups "laid their bodies on the
line" and at the peak of movement northern white adults, too,
came South and sometimes went to jail. The list of martyrs
included whites who gave their lives in Mississippi as well
as Blacks.

Most leaders of a broad-based movement such as this would have felt uneasy about according a place of honor to Garvey as a symbol of the struggle for equal rights in the United States. Not only was he compromised by having been adopted as a hero by the Black Nationalists, but most civil rights leaders also had an oversimplified and stereotyped image of the man. To them he was something of a Black Fascist, an opponent of integration who hated white people, and a misleader who tried to lure Afro-Americans into a flight to Africa instead of leading them in a fight for their rights at home. And worst of all, he had been accused of co-operating with the Ku Klux Klan. Much of the available documentation seemed to confirm this image--his Philosophy and Opinions, which had been reprinted, and scattered quotations in propaganda literature. Only now is full documentation of Garvey and the UNIA becoming available, so periodized that we can speak of the Garvey of the Twenties in the U.S.A., of the Garvey of the late Twenties and early Thirties in Jamaica, and of the five London years before his death. When a context for interpretation is provided and specific statements are related to time and place, and his poetry and reflections as well as his oratory are studied, the Garvey that emerges is not a "hate-monger" nor a proponent of immediate whole-sale emigration to Africa, and the commercial implications of the UNIA assume a prominence that has been ignored until recently. The civil rights leaders were not in a position to make any such detached assessment of Garvey and Garveyism.

Many of Martin Luther King's followers must have been disconcerted when, while he was visiting Jamaica in 1965, he spoke at the Garvey memorial shrine in a Kingston public park. He implied that Garvey had prepared the way for the success of the Civil Rights Movement; "Marcus Garvey was the first man of color in the history of the United States to lead and develop a mass movement.... He was the first man on a mass scale and level to give millions of Negroes a sense of dignity and destiny, and make the Negro feel he is somebody...." King--whose biography bore the title, Crusader without Violence--King who opposed racism in all its forms; how could he praise Garvey who exalted "Blackness" and who organized the African Legion as the prototype of the military forces that would someday drive "the White man" out of Africa? The answer to the "How could he?" is very complex. It is tied up with the fact that King's variety of non-violence was really not Gandhian in the final analysis and that he was keenly aware of the fact that behavior that could be expected of a Black minority in the United States was not necessarily realistic behavior for Africans and West Indians seeking to establish nations on their own soil. Although he never made his position clear on the armed liberation struggles, King never repudiated the establishment of armies and navies in the new African nations. At home he did not oppose the use of the United States army or the national guard to protect the rights of Black Americans. Disorderly mob violence, not state-legitimated violence, seems to have been the real target of his opposition, and to him, hate and vengeance were the most unChristian of evils that emerge in group struggles.

But laying aside speculation for a firm clue that appears in Professor Burkett's book, there is a quotation from a Harlem clergyman who opposed the UNIA, the father of Congressman Adam Clayton Powell and a "Black" man who could pass for white. He said upon one occasion, "I am not writing a brief for Marcus Garvey ... but he is the only man that ever made Negroes who are not black ashamed of their color." Rev. Powell was giving the negative side of a positive fact, that Garvey made the darker-skinned Afro-Americans not only accept their "negroidness" but even feel proud of it. King knew that until all Afro-Americans could say "Black is beautiful" and mean it, the kind of movement he, himself, was leading was impossible. Everyone who has studied the Garvey movement cites one enduring legacy-- "race pride." King certainly did not agree with much of what Garvey taught, but he recognized his great contribution to Black Liberation. He was willing to say, in effect, "Wisdom is justified of all her children." (Garvey, fighting for the very existence of his organization in the Twenties, could not have conceded as much.) It was in this spirit, too, that scores of Black preachers supported Garvey during the early Twenties--a fact not generally known, and, indeed, previously denied with a dogmatism born of ignorance. Professor Burkett has retrieved this facet of truth as a participant in the ongoing scholarly effort to present a rounded picture of the Garvey movement.

By the late Sixties neither the historians nor the sociologists--Black or White--could ignore Garveyism. So, the academic conferences on the subject were called, professors began to approve the dissertations when they would have previously said "No," and publishers found that good books on Garvey and the UNIA merited serious consideration. The opportunity had come to set the record straight on Garvey and his influential movement, to fill in the gaps, and to rectify distortions, as well as to consider the movement in relationship to existing bodies of philosophy and social science theory. But myths and misconceptions about Garvey's views on God, and of the relationships between the UNIA and the Black churches, had never been subjected to scrutiny and tested against the facts until Professor Burkett chose to do so. His book makes a contribution to the field of Garvey research on three important levels. First, it assembles a body of previously neglected fact which refutes the myth that Black churchmen presented a front of monolithic opposition to Marcus Garvey and his Universal Negro Improvement Association. That widely held erroneous opinion is proved false. Second, it analyzes the beliefs and rituals of the UNIA and interprets their significance boldly and imaginatively in terms of one contemporary theoretical approach in the field of the sociology of religion. And, finally, the author presents the material in a format that stimulates constructive criticism as well as additional research and comparative analysis.

Many of the ministers who expressed approval of some aspects of Garvey's work, like most of the competing race leaders of the time--and most of the journalists--used what Professor Burkett calls the "omnipresent conjunctive"--that ubiquitous "but" or "yet." But not all of them had reservations serious enough to prevent active cooperation, and it is with those who didn't that the book is concerned. By patient analysis of the content of the UNIA newspaper, The Negro World, and by industrious searching through biographies and autobiographies, the columns of the weekly Negro press, and fugitive materials in several library collections, he has proved beyond the ability of any skeptics to refute him that the UNIA attracted the support of some of the leading Black churchmen in the United States. Some joined while others only preached or spoke from UNIA platforms or lent moral support from time to time. He found that "Every independent Black denomination with a membership of more than twenty-five thousand in 1920 had clergymen who were actively working on behalf of the UNIA, as did many of the smaller independent Black denominations...." The personal ideology of some of these ministers that brought them to the movement was simply one of "race loyalty," but there were also university trained theologians among them who saw the UNIA as an additional vehicle for realizing some of the aims of the Social Gospel movement of which they considered themselves a part. As a child I was in close contact with Afro-American ministers who could not avoid the impact of the Garvey movement. Some became active members. (My father served as International Organizer for a period of three years.) But until I read Professor Burkett's book I had no conception of the full extent to which the Black clergy was involved. As I saw familiar Baptist names appearing in unfamiliar contexts along with unfamiliar names from other denominations, my curiosity was aroused. I began to think of project after project that I would be suggesting to students for term papers and master's theses were I still teaching in the field of African and Afro-American Studies. I fantasied, too, about the grant proposals that ought to be written so that we will have a definitive history compiled of every Black denomination, and in-depth biographies written of the outstanding clergymen who were active during the first quarter of the Twentieth Century. Professor Burkett has performed the pioneer service of lifting the veil. Let us hope that he and others will complete the unveiling.

What will surprise readers most, perhaps, and excite the greatest amount of controversy, is the author's conclusion that Marcus Garvey was "the foremost Black theologian of the early 20th Century," seeking continuously to provide "a coherent theological framework" within which UNIA rituals "could be interpreted and understood." (Garvey's close associate for a time, Rev. George A. McGuire, was a well-trained Anglican clergyman and they discussed and debated theological and philosophical questions together.) Garvey, however, denied any pretensions to being a theologian. The author contends, despite Garvey's own disclaimer, that Garvey developed consistent, although gradually evolving ideas, which he as a scholar finds significant when he "... imposes categories of systematic theology ..." upon them: doctrines of God and of Christ and his work; an anthropology; and a doctrine of salvation closely articulated to his eschatology; and a definite ecclesiology. Professor Burkett presents an analysis of, and excerpts from, sermons and speeches that were printed in, or reported upon, in UNIA publications. The Universal Negro Ritual and the Universal Negro Catechism, that Chaplain McGuire wrote but which Garvey influenced, are discussed in detail. But the most illuminating material comes from a source seldom drawn upon, the confidential Lesson Guides for the School of African Philosophy that Garvey developed after deportation from the United States.

The author makes a convincing case for his appraisal of
Garvey as a theologian concerned with the "big" questions
of Evil and Free Will as well as with more partial perspec-
tives concerned with race. Citations as well as quotations
make it possible for the reader to test the conclusion for
himself. Garvey was less sophisticated than the trained
theologians of today who are striving to develop a consistent
"Black Theology," but he avoids the crude racial chauvinism
of some of the less scrupulous ministers and uninformed laymen who argue that the historical Jesus and the Madonna
were indubitably Black, or that Jesus was a Black Messiah
sent to redeem a Black nation. Some varieties of modern
Black Nationalists who put Garvey in their pantheon will, no
doubt, be disappointed to discover how tenaciously he clung
to the Judaeo-Christian tradition in developing a theology for
Black people. It is fruitless, however, to speculate about
how he would have reacted to the new myth and ritual that
is invented to replace Christmas with Kwanza and to an ethical code based upon the seven Swahili principles (Kawaida):
UMOJA (unity), UJAMAA (family style cooperative produc-
tion), UJIMA (collective work and responsibility), KUUMBA
(creativity), IMANI (faith), NIA (purpose), KWICHAGLIA
(self-determination). This generation of Black Nationalists
which rejects Garvey's God does applaud him for the fight
he put up against the racism that infected his white co-re-
ligionists, and it still adheres to a secularized version of
his eschatology.

The "redemption of Africa" is a phrase that had wide
currency during the 19th Century among Afro-Americans who
supported the missionary movement as well as among Black
Nationalists. They based their hope upon a Biblical prophecy
which Professor Burkett informs us became the most frequently used rallying cry in the UNIA: Psalms 68:31--
"Princes shall come out of Egypt and Ethiopia shall soon
stretch forth her hand unto God." (When the Ethiopians de-
feated the Italians at the Battle of Adowa in 1896 the event
was widely interpreted as the beginning of the fulfilment of
the prophecy.) Garvey believed that God was "no respecter
of persons" but also that Black people would eventually be
vindicated and their enemies punished for the unjust suffering
they had inflicted. Professor Burkett comes to a conclusion
that others have held tentatively, but have never assembled
the source material to give it a high level of plausibility:
namely, that Garveyism was able to strike deep root in
Black communities primarily because it was firmly grounded

in Afro-American religious traditions, particularly in those eschatological beliefs with apocalyptic overtones, about an inevitable "African redemption." There are two additional facets of this fertile soil on which the seeds of Garveyism fell. The idea of developing trade relations with Africa as an aspect of the "redemption" had surfaced in Black Baptist circles long before Garvey landed in the United States in 1916, as Shepperson and Price document so well in their book, Independent African. The reasons for the readiness of African religious groups to accept the movement have not yet been systematically explored. A few years ago some of my Kenya friends presented me with a pamphlet written in English and Kikuyu that was published to commemorate the arrival of a bishop of the African Orthodox Church in the late Twenties to train and ordain preachers for the independent churches that had split away from the missions because they believed in "Africa for the Africans" and in the preservation of some of their customs to which the missionaries objected. I was told that Jomo Kenyatta, who read The Negro World, had advised the Kikuyu elders to contact the Garvey movement, and a bishop came up from South Africa. (They didn't know that the African Orthodox Church wasn't the official UNIA Church but only had close relations with the movement.)

Marcus Garvey's seriousness of purpose, as well as his statesmanship, is revealed in Professor Burkett's thorough analysis of a conflict between him and the first Chaplain-General of the UNIA, his friend Bishop George A. McGuire, who either wished to make the UNIA itself a religious organization or to have the African Orthodox Church which he had founded declared its official church. Garvey opposed him even to the point of dropping him from the UNIA for a time, because the concept of a "civil religion" demanded a powerful motivating myth that could reconcile partial interests and unite Black people in "nation building." It had to be at a sufficiently high level of generality to allow members of "the nation" to retain membership in Christian denominations, sects, and cults, and even to non-Christian faiths, while still belonging to the Universal Negro Improvement Association. This was the concept that relaxed the fears of many leaders of Black churches and provided a basis for cooperation with them. The UNIA failure, when it did come, was not due to problems with Black churchmen, but the circumstances were such that they could not save it from the disintegrating forces either. Professor Burkett's book becomes the definitive work on relations between the UNIA and churchmen during the period of the movement's greatest growth and influence. It provides a basis for a sequel on how churchmen reacted when the difficult days came, how they interpreted the decline of the movement if they did so, and what residue of influence from the movement affected their subsequent activities. The point has been proved beyond doubt that the most outstanding of the Black clergymen supported Garvey, or at least did not oppose him. The sequel might well tell us something about which ones opposed him, and how, and why.

Professor Burkett's systematic treatment of the religious dimension of the UNIA and of Garvey's thought and action will be very useful in developing a framework for interpretation of other Garvey research--completed, in process, and contemplated. I have tried to utilize it for taking a fresh look at the Kraus-Thomson reprints of The Black Man, a magazine Garvey published during his period of self-imposed exile in London for the decade before his death. Professor Robert Hill of UCLA, whose knowledge of the UNIA and of Garvey is perhaps unrivalled, has provided a perceptive introductory essay and a group of explanatory footnotes, but this thorough study of the religious aspect of Garveyism provides us with an additional lens for scrutinizing the primary source material. For instance, one of Professor Burkett's many richly informative footnotes tells us that when Garvey's newspaper, The Negro World, went out of existence after October 17, 1933 when it published Vol. 32, No. 11, its presses and remaining supplies were purchased by a religious organization, Father Divine's Peace Mission, which proceeded to publish World Peace Echo. Interracial in membership and aggressively "integrationist," Father Divine's Peace Mission stood at the opposite pole from Garveyism in these and many other ways--including its insistence upon celibacy. Yet the evidence presented by the author indicates that the World Peace Echo modeled some of its journalistic practices on those of The Negro World. Professor Burkett suggests that "a careful study of the relationship between these two historically contiguous movements should be undertaken." Let us hope that someone will accept that challenge, asking such questions as, "Is it possible that the Peace Mission adopted some of Garvey's economic programs, too?" and "Were there any relations between Father Divine's 'angels' and the members of UNIA splinter groups in Harlem?" These and numerous other questions come readily to mind, but a very modest goal might be an examination of what Garvey had to say about Father Divine and his movement in the pages of The Black Man.

In the December 1935 issue of The Black Man Garvey blasted Father Divine for "outraging his race" by the blasphemous claim to be God. (The author has pointed out that Garvey was essentially Arian in his theology and may have doubted the Divine Incarnation. Therefore Divine would be doubly culpable.) Also, Garvey referred to a paternity charge that had been made against Father Divine by a woman who said she had borne a "god child," and noted that although some people might find it humorous, "... to us as a race it is serious for a man to so disgrace us before man and before God." Three months later Garvey criticized the Jamaican Pocomania cult and Father Divine's Peace Mission in the same article, on the grounds that both encouraged Negroes to express the "lowest of their animal natures and dispositions." Within another three months, a UNIA conference held in Canada passed a formal resolution that Garvey printed in The Black Man under the caption, CONDEMNS FATHER DIVINE AS A RELIGIOUS FAKE. Garvey also printed a long letter from a former UNIA member appealing to him to recognize Father Divine as "the very same CHRIST of 1900 years ago" and flattering the UNIA founder by saying that "... 'Garveyism' was the highest grace this so-called race had, according to the division among the sons of earth. But today a greater than Garvey is here. Shiloh has truly come...." She stressed the point that Divine has made "... 'one man at Jerusalem' out of races, creeds, colours, denominations, nationalism, theories, and doctrines, recognizing only that sacred duty, 'THE BROTHERHOOD OF MAN'--and the 'FATHERHOOD OF GOD'." There was something strangely contemporary about her boast that "tens of thousands had received Evangelical names and discarded those cursed slave names...." Garvey poured ridicule upon Divine in a note at the end of the letter.

Garvey's master slogan was the psalm that referred to the empowerment of Egypt and Ethiopia. Only after that had taken place could brotherhood be egalitarian and thereby acceptable. Achieving "brotherhood" by celibate isolation from the mainstream and showering of orgiastic praise upon "Father" was as bizarre as it was premature, to Garvey's way of thinking. Yet, to completely understand the intensity of the condemnatory resolution that referred to Divine's claim to divinity as "vile" and "blasphemous" and as "being worse than paganism and heathenism and idolatry, " one must understand Garvey's Doctrine of God, his Christology, and his concept of anthropology. The author of this book carefully explains them. Following the suggestions to search out relations between Garveyism and Divine's Peace Mission leads on to considering both movements in relation to the Nation of Islam which, like the Divine movement, abandoned "slave names" (but not for evangelical names) and which claimed Garvey as a spiritual predecessor. Mr. Muhammad, like Garvey, tried to institute a "civil religion" but his demand that Blacks accept Islam limited the membership drastically. Father Divine's "kingdoms" were in the world but not of it. Race was "abolitionized" (as Father phrased it) within them, but the break with Afro-American culture, secular and religious, was too great to allow the Peace Missions to become more than cult houses. The Nation of Islam was very much of this world, but was too exclusive.

The idea of Garveyism as an attempt to institute a "civil religion" is a challenging one that should lead to continuous reflection and comparative study. It raises a question as to whether a segment of a larger society can ever be so organized and as to whether or not a land base in which all the inhabitants are members of the single spiritual and civic community may not be necessary to achieve such a goal. To Garvey, a base in Africa was deemed an absolute necessity to be acquired as soon as possible. Parallels with the Church of Jesus Christ of Latter Day Saints as led by Brigham Young almost a century before Garvey immediately come to mind. The frontier was still open and the Saints left the East, where they were a usually tolerated but sometimes persecuted minority, and headed to the West where they founded the state of Deseret, a theocracy. They ended up, however, as a denomination popularly known as the Mormons; their communities were forcibly incorporated into the state machinery of Utah; and the church was forced by the Federal Government to give up one of its central tenets, polygyny. But important legacies of that charismatic Utopian period remain--a community-minded church that takes care of its own, produces highly disciplined individuals and has world-wide extensions although it has less than 5,000,000 members. The frontier was closed by the time the UNIA was founded. Garvey never visualized Utopia in the West. It is significant that one of the last hopes for all-Black communities, those in Oklahoma, was destroyed around 1914 when whites surrounded the Blacks and disenfranchised them. A back-to-Africa movement burgeoned in the wake of this failure that actually carried a shipload of people to the Gold Coast. This kind of action was "in the air" when Garvey arrived in the United States. Nevertheless, two decades after Garvey's deportation, the Nation of Islam revived the quite unrealistic dream of building a community like that of the Mormons', composed of the people of "the Lost Found Nation in this Wilderness of North America." Like the Mormons, the Black Muslims were pressured back into mainstream conformity. The World Community of Islam in the West is its new name and it is now accepting as members those it once abused as Devils. Like the Mormons it was willing to pay the price necessary for survival as a viable economic entity and a sect within the larger society, but it never secured a "land base." In the 1970s, the Garveyites were managing a few farms in Liberia under sufferance from a Black government subservient to the USA just as the Black Muslims were farming in the American South under the rule of whites. Meanwhile, over 40 African nations had emerged as sovereign independent states, but not through UNIA action.

Another comparison that merits serious attention involves a well known contemporary religious group. Whether or not Garvey was ever influenced by it directly is not clear, but its existence may have made the atmosphere somewhat more favorable to his message than it otherwise would have been. Reference has been made to an apperceptive mass that included the "redemption of Africa" tradition which had been conserved by the Black church. That church had fostered a more general Protestant eschatological tradition, too, one which made church people interested in the application of Biblical prophecy generally to contemporary events. Garvey made the call for a Black International with "One God! One Aim! One Destiny!" in 1917. The Russian Revolution occurred that same year and the Red International appealed to the workers of the world--regardless of race--to unite because they had nothing to lose but their chains. This was also the year the United States entered World War I. One year before this, the great migration to the North on a massive scale had begun, and the year before that the greatest of the Black leaders--Garvey's initial inspiration, Booker T. Washington--had died. Garvey arrived on the American scene in the fullness of time, for after race riots erupted in over 30 cities in 1919, Black Americans who had tried so hard to prove their patriotism during the War were disillusioned and ready to listen to a leader with a comprehensive plan for racial salvation. The UNIA, two years old, now became attractive. Talk about a League of Nations and of national rights for Irishmen and Indians raised hopes that Africa's liberation was near. And, if this were so, an "Africa for the Africans at Home and Abroad" was relevant to their fate.

Throughout the period of the first World War, from 1914 on, Black preachers were certainly alert to "the signs of the times"--war, famine, pestilence, and death. Many Black church people were familiar with one interpretation of what was going on, that of Pastor Charles Taze Russell of the Watchtower Society whose "Bible Study" books were very widely sold and discussed. The teaching was apocalyptic and the eschatology involved an intricate theological mathematics and had "predicted" the end of the world for 1914, at which time all nations would pass under the judgment of Jehovah and God's "righteous kingdom" would be established on earth. According to Russell, the way had already been prepared for the millenium by the anarchist and socialist forces of the world which functioned as one of God's instruments of judgment. As has happened so often in history when adventists set a specific date, the faithful were in disarray when the messiah and the millenium did not appear at the appointed time. However, an adjusted Watchtower doctrine carried by Jehovah's Witnesses under the leadership of Charles Rutherford began to spread rapidly after the war.

The Witnesses had a profound effect on central Africa, where the doctrine was known as Kitawala. It was somewhat less influential among Afro-Americans, who were not prepared to say that all governments--including those of the only three Black nations in the world, Haiti, Liberia, and Ethiopia--were the Devil's Kingdoms, just as those of the imperialist powers were, or that no earthly kingdom was worth striving for since the only true Christians were citizens of the Righteous Kingdom, invisible but ready to break through out of eternity into time at any moment. The pre-War Watchtower movement had been acceptable to Afro-Americans; the post-War Witness movement was less so. The vindication of Black people through the "redemption of Africa" was the expected outcome of the terrible war and the shattering riots as they saw it. It is understandable why many Black preachers and their congregations, even if they didn't agree with every jot and tittle of Garveyism, could visualize Garvey and his movement, during the early

Twenties, as God's instruments in the latter days when young men would dream dreams and old men would see visions.

San Diego, California
February 20, 1978

INTRODUCTION

There is a growing if belated awareness that Marcus Mosias Garvey was a pivotal figure in the twentieth-century Afro-American experience. The meteoric rise to national prominence in the decade from 1917 to 1927 of his Universal Negro Improvement Association and African Communities League (UNIA) as the largest mass-based protest movement among Black people in the history of the United States is a phenomenon which one might have expected to receive the most intensive and detailed investigation on the part of both scholars and Black activists. Nearly every analyst or commentator on twentieth-century Black history has made at least passing reference to the Garvey movement, but until recently there has been surprisingly little work done to discern its inner logic or appeal.

The reasons for this neglect are complex. Although there is much to attract advocates of Black power, Black pride, and Black nationalism to Marcus Garvey as the vanguard of their cause, he has not appeared unqualifiedly as a patron saint. In the first place, his economic theory was all wrong. He was, after all, a Bookerite. His first inspiration to action came not while reading the Communist Manifesto or Das Kapital but, of all things, Booker T. Washington's autobiography, Up From Slavery.[1] The most scathing of the Garvey critics were the leaders of the "Garvey Must Go!" campaign, spearheaded by the socialist-inspired Messenger, under the editorship of A. Philip Randolph and Chandler Owen. Although Randolph at an early point in his "radical" phase was sufficiently open to Garvey to appear on the same platform at Harlem political rallies, by mid-1920 he had become convinced that Garvey was unalterably dedicated to a capitalist economic policy (then anathema to Randolph) and generally alienated by the style and character of Garvey's movement.[2] The transfer to the Messenger staff of the former editor of the Negro World, Warner A. Domingo, insured that the ensuing anti-Garvey campaign would have benefit not only of an inside knowledge of the workings of the

1

UNIA but also the special passion of an ex-believer whose
personal mission was to enlighten those who had not seen
the error of their ways.[3]   There were others who joined in
the "Garvey Must Go!" chorus, typified by such diverse figures as businessman Harry H. Pace, clergyman Robert W.
Bagnall, Communist Cyril V. Briggs, and conservative columnist George S. Schuyler.   In fact, as has been frequently
pointed out, a large portion of those generally recognized as
composing the Black intelligentsia of the day, including a
wide range of Black radicals, was hostile to Garvey.[4]

   Second, there are distinct religious overtones to the
Garvey movement which, at least in the "blatant" form expressed in Garveyism, remain suspect.   Black radicals have
long criticized the "escapist" and "otherworldly" character
of twentieth-century Black religion for contributing to the
quiescence and acceptance of oppression among the masses
of Black Christians.   Thus, to the extent that the Garvey
movement has been perceived as a quasi-religious cult analogous to the Father Divine Peace Mission Movement, Black
radicals (and for different reasons, conservative middle- and
upper-class Blacks as well) have looked askance at the UNIA.

   Numerous hypotheses can be advanced to explain the
scholarly neglect of Marcus Garvey.   Foremost among these
has been the tendency of latter-day interpreters to rely on
the perceptions and frames of reference of a rather select
group of men who were firsthand observers (and often active
opponents) of the UNIA.   Among these we can count W. E.
Burghardt DuBois, who commented on Garvey frequently in
the editorial pages of the Crisis and elsewhere, and who was
both a consistent critic of the UNIA and the recipient of some
of Garvey's most vituperative invective and embittered denun-
ciation.[5]   Another influential interpreter was Claude McKay
who, like Garvey, was a Jamaican by birth, and who was at
least for a brief period sufficiently interested in the UNIA to
serve as foreign correspondent for Garvey's paper, the Negro World.   McKay was quickly disillusioned, however, and
in subsequent years he devoted a long chapter in his book
Harlem-Negro Metropolis to a rather unflattering analysis of
his compatriot.[6]   A similar, if slightly less critical, account
was provided in James Weldon Johnson's Black Manhattan,
while the chapter in Roi Ottley's widely read New World A-
Coming described Garvey as a "squat, ugly black man with
intelligent eyes and big head," and portrayed him as an energetic but finally incompetent leader of a mass movement
which had mushroomed beyond his capacity to guide it.[7]

This chorus of criticism of Garvey by his contemporaries, combined with the fact that a large number of his detractors survived him and were thus able to canonize their earlier assessments with more "objective" evaluations written after the heat of battle, has meant that a revisionist perspective has been a long time in coming. That such a new perspective was inevitable, however, is discernible even from the pages of the critics who treated him so harshly in the past. If one takes from the shelf any dozen books dealing however briefly with Garvey, one can discern what might be termed the phenomenon of the "omnipresent conjunction" or qualifying clause with which each of those discussions ends. Adam Clayton Powell, Sr., pastor of the prestigious and influential Abyssinia Baptist Church in New York City during the Garvey era, and one of the UNIA's harshest critics, provides a classic example in his autobiography when he concludes, "I am not writing a brief for Marcus Garvey, but it is recording the truth, and perhaps for the first time, to say that he is the only man that ever made Negroes who are not black ashamed of their color."[8]

Writing in his autobiography of 1940, W. E. B. DuBois observed of the Garvey movement,

> It was a grandiose and bombastic scheme, utterly impracticable as a whole, but it was sincere and had some practical features; and Garvey proved not only an astonishingly popular leader, but a master of propaganda.[9]

Roi Ottley, at the end of his generally unsympathetic treatment of Garvey in New World A-Coming, nevertheless concludes:

> Concretely, the movement set in motion what was to be the most compelling force in Negro life --race and color consciousness, which is today that ephemeral thing that inspires "race loyalty"; the banner to which Negroes rally; the chain that binds them together. It has propelled many a political and social movement and stimulated racial internationalism.... It accounts for much constructive belligerency today.[10]

In similar fashion, James Weldon Johnson wrote, "Garvey failed; yet he might have succeeded with more than moderate success.... He stirred the imagination of the

Negro masses as no Negro ever had. "[11] Claude McKay persisted in his assessment of Garvey as a "West Indian charlatan, " and "yet within a decade he aroused the social consciousness of the Negro masses more than any other leader
ever did. "[12] This pattern can be replicated in most of the
secondary literature as well as in the writings of those who
knew the movement firsthand. It indicates an irrepressible
awareness, even from the early days of the movement, that
Garvey's was a unique organization--one whose significance
would continue to be felt in succeeding generations.

Another concrete factor in the scholarly neglect of
Garvey and the UNIA, in addition to the tendency to rely on
a limited number of interpreters, has been the general un-
availability of primary source materials, and the assumption
among researchers that copies of the official news organ of
the Association, the Negro World, were either not extant or
not useful for research. Recently, however, something ap-
proximating a complete run of the paper, from May 1920 to
its final issue in October 1933, has become available.[13]
What renders this so significant is the extraordinary value
of the paper in recording events of the period, including the
UNIA's own history. Garvey deemed it of major importance
to interpret international events to Black persons in the
United States and around the world, and for this reason considerable space was given to world-wide news. Similarly,
national news, including discussion of bills before Congress
that would affect Black Americans; election of local, state,
and national officials; and any events of special importance
to men and women of African descent were reported or discussed.[14]

Clearly, then, we are in a new position with respect
to resources for Garvey research, and it is no longer necessary to rely solely on the observations of those hostile critics
who opposed the movement. It is this fact, combined with a
new ethos or ideological climate with respect to interracial
relations and the great interest in a search for bases for
Black unity, that spurred the considerable attention to Garvey
and the UNIA which we are presently witnessing.[15] A flurry
of articles on Garvey has already been published; several
monographs are either already in print or forthcoming; and
a number of dissertations have been completed or are presently underway on various aspects of both the man and his
movement. In the very near future we should be in a much
better position to understand both the successes and the
failures of the UNIA.

nalytical approach of the present study is sharply
__u. It seeks to describe and to clarify the religious
dimensions of the Garvey movement. While this may at
first glance appear to be a rather narrow perspective, the
fact is, as Gayraud S. Wilmore has recently and most in-
cisively made clear, there has been an integral relationship
throughout American history between Black religion and
Black radicalism.[16] This historic relationship is nowhere
more clearly seen than in the UNIA. Garvey had from the
outset conceived the organization as a missionary religious
association espousing "The Brotherhood of Man and The
Fatherhood of God, " and he explicitly committed the UNIA,
in its original statement of aims, to promoting "a conscientious Christian worship among the native tribes of Africa."[17]
The organization was suffused with a religious ethos which
was reflected in the variety of rituals and symbols that Garvey developed, as well as in the paraphernalia and regalia
of nationhood that were displayed on the platform of Liberty
Hall. The task of the first chapter will be to describe the
ethos in which the work of the UNIA was carried forth and
to delineate the rituals which were unique to it.

It has been the tendency of Garvey's critics to minimize or trivialize or to ridicule the prominence given within
the UNIA to religious issues. On the basis of careful reading of the numerous Garvey speeches and editorials published
in the Negro World, however, there is good evidence to suggest that Garvey himself took these issues very seriously.
Indeed, these speeches reveal that Garvey was concerned not
simply with the articulation of an array of symbols and
elaborate religious ritual, but also with the explication of a
coherent theological framework within which these rituals
could be interpreted and understood. One finds Garvey, for
instance, struggling with the problem of theodicy, and en-
deavoring to define God so as not to make Him responsible
for a suffering world (and especially a suffering Black people),
yet insisting that God's purposes were being achieved in the
world and that His chosen Black people were marked for a
special destiny in Africa. Garvey groped for an anthropology
which could interpret the evil of which man (and not merely
the white man) was capable, while insisting that man is essentially free to choose his own destiny and determine his
own future. Garvey's conceptualization of Jesus portrayed
Him as both the perfect model of (Black) manhood and as one
who empowers man to action against injustice. He spoke of
salvation which was by faith and by work(s), though the redemption which he sought was invariably social rather than

individual. The resurrection to come was of the Negro people as a whole: that which was to be redeemed was Africa, the promised land. The task of the second chapter will be to examine these motifs in some detail, and to make the case for seeing Marcus Garvey as the foremost Black theologian of the early twentieth century.

In addition to the rituals and beliefs endemic to Garveyism as a religious movement, there was also a carefully worked out organizational structure which finally emerged in viable form by 1922. While there was considerable enthusiasm for the UNIA among Black churchmen, this sentiment was by no means unanimous, and the fears of many churchmen were exacerbated precisely by the organizational structure which the UNIA assumed in the early 1920s. At least for a brief period of time the UNIA moved in the direction of assuming explicit denominational status, and this move was consciously fostered by the organization's second Chaplain-General, George Alexander McGuire. He compiled, at the behest of the High Executive Council (the UNIA's governing body) a Universal Negro Ritual and a Universal Negro Catechism, complete with baptismal ceremonies by which infants were simultaneously welcomed to the Christian faith and initiated into the Universal Negro Improvement Association. As will be argued in the third chapter, McGuire, a brilliant orator as well as an astute theologian, was to move so far in the direction of making the UNIA into a religious denomination, or, barring that, making his African Orthodox Church (AOC) into the official church of the UNIA, that Garvey had finally to replace him as Chaplain-General. The considerable confusion that has surrounded discussions concerning the relation of the UNIA and the AOC stems in part from the failure to understand the differing personalities and purposes of the remarkable men who were leaders of the two organizations.

It seems that it was only over a period of time that Garvey became clear in his own mind as to the appropriate form that religion should take in the UNIA, as he sought to determine the proper relationship between his own organization and the Black churches. His problem was complicated by the fact that there were Black Jews, Black Islamicists, practically every variety of Christian group, plus numerous vocal and articulate anticlerical if not atheistic spokesmen to be found in his organization. Finding a solution to the "religious question" (which was posed, for example, at each of Garvey's annual International Conventions of the Negro Peoples

of the World) was by no means an easy task. Garvey was
not able to implement in any systematic way his resolution
of the religious question due to the collapse of the UNIA,
under the attack of the Black press, a goodly portion of the
Black intelligentsia, numerous colonial powers, and the
United States government.

Yet, the outlines of Garvey's program seem clear.
It will here be argued, drawing upon a category articulated
by Robert Bellah and others, [18] that Garvey was self-consciously working to create a form of civil religion. The
present study could well be conceived, in fact, as a case
study in Black civil religion. Bellah's argument, briefly
stated, is that (for the most part white) America's self-
interpretation as a people chosen by God to be a "light unto
the nations"--as either exemplar or savior or both--is not
simply a meaningless or a sacrilegious invocation of divine
sanction for its own perceived interests. The civil religion
"has its own seriousness and integrity";[19] indeed, at its best
it is a "powerful motivating myth" predicated on a shared
historic experience, and it possesses the capacity of calling
the nation itself first into being, and then into judgment, in
the name of the higher ideals to which it is dedicated.
Further, the civil religion always stands in a somewhat
ambiguous relationship with respect to particular religions;
it can stand alongside of, exist in tension with, or subsume
or at least seek to incorporate them. [20]

It is the thesis of this study that without ever using
the term, and with no explicit statement of intent, Garvey
was attempting to fashion a Black civil religion. He unabashedly set out to create a new/old mythos, a coherent interpretation of reality which, while clearly building on elements long established in the tradition of the Black church,
yet moved to a new level of self-consciousness and con-
sciousness-formation. He boldly posited a coherent theological system complete with a doctrine of God--a Black
God, the express designation of which was to shatter old
patterns of belief and to demonstrate the fact that all men,
all Black men, are created in His image. The panoply of
symbols, the theology, the pomp and ceremony, the use of
music, as well as the adumbration and explication of the
theme of nationhood (from the creation of dukes and knights,
the issuing of passports and establishment of a civil service,
to creation of a flag, motto and national anthem) were advanced to demonstrate to all men and women of African descent their essential oneness in the struggle for survival in

a hostile, white-dominated world. Garvey also demonstrated the power which would be theirs if that oneness could be actualized via self-respect, self-reliance, and faith in one another and in one's God.

The themes that Garvey used were drawn from the Old and New Testaments, as well as from the (white) civil religion that Bellah has specified, but with a twist: Negroes are the chosen people; Africa is the promised land. Destiny under God, human rights guaranteed by God, necessity of sacrifice and martyrdom--these themes he incorporated as well. The beliefs, rituals, and symbols of the UNIA's civil religion--especially after Garvey's controversy with McGuire was settled--were at a sufficiently high level of generality that they would allow members of the "nation" to continue to participate in their particular religious organizations, and at the same time be part of the Universal Negro Improvement Association. The beliefs and rituals grew out of a shared experience of oppression and were predicated on the solid foundation of the religious faith of Black folk. Finally, Garvey's Black civil religion had the capacity to be judgmental, both with respect to particular churches, which were continually chided for their inclination to otherworldliness; and with respect to the people as a whole, who Garvey believed were too often guilty of blaming others for their shortcomings, or of seeing fate rather than themselves as controlling the present and future.

The litmus test for the success of Garveyism as a Black civil religion is the level of acceptance it would achieve among the most influential segment of mass Black leadership, the clergy. The Black church, well into the twentieth century, has played a unique role as bearer of culture and molder of values, and the clergy have historically been at the center of that process. Any efforts at articulating and institutionalizing a Black civil religion must necessarily, therefore, be tested against the hard rock of clergy dubiety and jealousy, for it was moving to the very heart of the Black church's understanding of its special task with respect both to its people and to Africa. This is the task of Part II of this book.

In the face of the widespread assumption that the Black clergy as a whole--or at least the educated and institutional elite among them--stood firmly in opposition to the Garvey movement, it is necessary to chronicle in some detail the participation of a broad spectrum of clergy from every denominational, geographic, and educational background who actively participated in or verbally supported the UNIA. The names generally cited include the Episcopalian George Alexander McGuire (Chaplain-General, later founder of the African Orthodox Church); John E. Bruce "Grit" (popular journalist and active AME Zion layman); and William H. Ferris (active AME clergyman and author, for three years editor of the Negro World). In addition, there are such figures as William Yancy Bell, an ardent defender of Garvey in Liberty Hall who later served as a CME bishop from 1938 until his death in 1962; the widow of Bishop Alexander Walters, Lelia Coleman, who week after week appeared on the platform at UNIA meetings; the father of an AME bishop, R. R. Wright, Sr., who was founder of the Citizens and Southern Bank in Philadelphia and an active AME churchman; Dr. William W. Lucas, Field Secretary of the Board of Foreign Missions of the Methodist Episcopal Church and a nationally recognized pulpiteer; and Baptist churchmen such as Willis W. Brown, pastor of the prestigious Metropolitan Baptist Church in New York City; Junius C. Austin, pastor of enormous churches in Pittsburgh and later in Chicago; and William H. Moses of the National Baptist Church in New York City, Field Secretary of the National Baptist Convention, USA, Inc., and a candidate for the office of president of the NBC at the same time he was actively supporting the UNIA.

Due to the paucity of historical research on the Black clergy in this period, considerable biographical data has been provided along with the evidence of involvement in the UNIA. It is hoped that this material, presented in Part II, will provide the basis for further study of the history of the Black church in this period, as well as demonstrate the range and depth of clergy support for the UNIA. It is this support for the UNIA (rather than the opposition) which seems to be the remarkable fact. It is evidence that the Black civil religion which Marcus Garvey was creating resonated positively among a segment of Black leadership that has historically served as a sounding board for the pivotal notion that "Blacks in America view themselves as a people, an ethnic community, and their religion as the source, together with color, of their social cohesion."[21] This perception was at the core of Garvey's Universal Negro Improvement Association, and on this basis he was widely supported by many of the most articulate and thoughtful Black church leaders.

Notes

1. Though it is true that on one occasion the American
   Marxist Rose Pastor Stokes spoke from the platform
   of Liberty Hall in Harlem, Marcus Garvey was a
   persistent foe of Communism and of Marxism, both
   of which he believed to be ideologies antithetical to
   the interests of Black Americans. Pragmatically,
   he feared that a Communist government in the United
   States would strengthen the power of what was in his
   opinion the most racist segment of American society,
   the white working class.

2. Theodore G. Vincent, Black Power and the Garvey Movement (Berkeley, 1971), esp. pp. 44-46, 62-72.

3. Although the first articles on the UNIA in the September
   and October 1920 issues of the Messenger were critical in tone, they were at least "civil" as well. As
   the months passed, the note of civility was dropped,
   culminating in a January 1923 reference to Garvey as
   a "supreme Negro Jamaican Jackass." Meanwhile, in
   his speeches Randolph was characterizing Garvey as
   the "little half-wit Lilliputian," Messenger 5 (January
   1923), 561. Garvey was never one to take such attacks lying down, and when he replied in kind via the
   Negro World, the result was an unseemly spate of
   charge and counter-charge that could never redound
   to the favor of any of the participants. The "Garvey
   Must Go!" campaign is analyzed in Theodore Kornweibel, Jr., No Crystal Stair: Black Life and the
   Messenger, 1917-1928 (Westport, Conn., 1975),
   chapter 5.

4. Harold Cruse in The Crisis of the Negro Intellectual
   (New York, 1967), pp. 115-146, calls attention to the
   fact that many of Garvey's harshest critics were
   West Indian by origin and further, that much criticism of Garvey was motivated by "anti-West Indian
   bias."

5. DuBois's Crisis editorials on Garvey include the following: "Marcus Garvey," 21 (December 1920), 58-60,
   and 21 (January 1921), 112-15; "The Black Star Line,"
   24 (September 1922), 210-14; "The U.N.I.A.," 25
   (January 1923), 120-22. Other of DuBois's comments
   on Garvey may be found in his essay "Back to Africa,"

Century 105 (February 1923), 539-548; Dusk of Dawn (New York, 1940), pp. 277-78, etc. Garvey's hostility to DuBois antedates his first visit to the United States, as evidenced by a letter Garvey sent to Robert R. Moton, then head of Tuskegee Institute. In that letter, written to advise Moton of conditions prevailing in Jamaica, Garvey observed: "Black men here are never truly honoured. Don't you believe like coloured Dr. DuBois that the 'race problem is at an end here' except you want to admit the utter insignificance of the black man." The letter, dated 29 February 1916, is included in the appendix to Daniel T. Williams, "The Perilous Road of Marcus M. Garvey: A Bibliography," which is published in his Eight Negro Bibliographies (New York, 1970), p. 7, and now reprinted in Carl S. Matthews, "Marcus Garvey Writes from Jamaica on the Mulatto Escape Hatch," Journal of Negro History 59 (1974), 170-76 quoting at p. 175.

6. Harlem-Negro Metropolis (New York, 1940), esp. pp. 143-180. See also McKay's article, "Garvey as a Negro Moses," Liberator 5 (April 1922), 8-9 and his autobiography, A Long Way from Home (New York, 1937). Although McKay does not there mention Garvey by name, it is clear that his reference to "a West Indian charlatan" (p. 354) was directed to the UNIA leader. Garvey lost no love for McKay, either, and the pages of the Negro World joined in the general chorus of condemnation among the Black intelligentsia that greeted publication of McKay's novel Home to Harlem. See, for instance, Garvey's lead editorial in the Negro World (henceforth NW) 24:34 (29 September 1928), p. 1.

7. James Weldon Johnson, Black Manhattan (New York, 1930), pp. 251-59. George E. Kent indicates in his "The Soulful Way of Claude McKay," Black World 20 (November 1970), 37-51, that McKay was actually dependent for his conclusions with respect to Garvey upon Johnson's work. Roi Ottley's New World A-Coming (Boston, 1943), ch. 6, devoted to Garvey, contains numerous errors of both fact and interpretation. His discussion of Garvey in The Negro in New York (New York, 1967), jointly written with William J. Weatherby, is likewise plagued with factual inaccuracies.

8. Against the Tide: An Autobiography (New York, 1938),
   p. 71. Emphasis added. Powell, incidentally, was
   himself of very light complexion. For Powell's
   anti-Garvey position, see, for instance, his denun-
   ciation of Garvey in the Baltimore Afro-American,
   3 September 1920, p. 1.

9. Dusk of Dawn, p. 277. Emphasis added. It should be
   noted that DuBois never indulged in the unrestrained
   recriminations characteristic of many of Garvey's
   opponents.

10. Ottley, New World A-Coming, p. 81.

11. Johnson, Black Manhattan, p. 256. Emphasis added.

12. McKay, A Long Way, p. 354. Emphasis added.

13. Three hitherto generally unknown collections of the
    Negro World have recently become available for
    scholarly research. In 1970, a nearly complete
    run of the paper from 1923 to 1933 was presented
    to the Schomburg Branch of the New York Public
    Library by the University of Minnesota. Gaps in
    these holdings are considerably filled by the collec-
    tion retained by the Minnesota Historical Society.
    In addition, the University of California at Los An-
    geles has secured on microfilm an extremely valu-
    able collection of early Negro Worlds. This collection
    includes sporadic issues from 1920 and 1921, a com-
    plete run for the year 1922, and a few issues from
    1923. Most recently, nine issues dated May through
    August 1920 (including reports of the crucial First
    International Convention of Negro Peoples of the
    World), turned up on a reel of "Radical Newspapers"
    preserved in the Library of Congress. While there
    are still significant gaps remaining, we are now in
    a much better position to analyze the Garvey move-
    ment as viewed from the "inside" by those who were
    writing for the organization. In addition, missing
    issues of the paper continue to be discovered, along
    with a variety of extremely valuable memorabilia
    which have been retained by old-time Garveyites. A
    variety of such materials is available on microfilm
    at UCLA.

14. In terms of the history of the Garvey movement itself,

detailed reports of each week's meetings at Liberty
Hall in Harlem were made in the paper, including
verbatim texts of many speeches. The fact that the
constitution of the UNIA required each local chapter
or division to send to national headquarters written
monthly reports of the unit's progress, and the
further fact that many of these reports were published in the weekly section "News and Views of
UNIA Divisions," means that extensive local studies
of UNIA activities may be pursued via the Negro
World. These local studies can be augmented by
the long lists of contributors to the "African Redemption Fund" or the "Marcus Garvey Release Fund,"
or one of the numerous other special causes for
which money was solicited. The contributors are
listed by city and state, and the amounts of the
contributions, ranging from three cents to one hundred dollars or more, are itemized.

Finally, the wide range of articles and editorials, both signed and unsigned, as well as Garvey's own weekly address to "Fellow Men of the
Negro Race," taking all of the front page of each
issue, render the paper an invaluable tool to discern
issues that were deemed important to UNIA officials
from the period of the movement's greatest success
to the paper's demise in the early 1930s.

Other of Garvey's publications include the
briefly published daily Negro Times, appearing in
New York City during 1922 and 1923; The Blackman,
"A Daily Newspaper Devoted to the Uplift of the
Negro Race and the Good of Humanity," published
in Kingston, Jamaica, between 30 March 1929 and
14 February 1931 (a complete collection of which
may be found in the archives of the Institute of
Jamaica, Kingston); and a monthly periodical The
Black Man, published irregularly in London between
1934 and 1939, which is now reprinted by Kraus-
Thomson (Millwood, N.Y., 1975).

15.   Ironically, until very recently the only two full-length
      scholarly treatments of Garvey were written by
      whites: Edmund D. Cronon, Black Moses: The
      Story of Marcus Garvey and the Universal Negro Im-
      provement Association (Madison, 1955); and Theodore
      G. Vincent's Black Power and the Garvey Movement,
      cited previously. A very important new study is
      Tony Martin's Race First: The Ideological and

Organizational Struggles of Marcus Garvey and the Universal Negro Improvement Association (Westport, Conn., 1976).

16. Gayraud S. Wilmore, Black Religion and Black Radicalism (New York, 1972), p. xii, et passim. Wilmore is also one of the few scholars who has taken seriously the religious dimensions of the Garvey movement.

17. Emphasis added. See the text of "General Objects" of the Association as stated in 1914, found reprinted in Daniel T. Williams, ed., "Perilous Road," Appendix. The wording was only later changed to read "to promote a conscientious spiritual worship," presumably to accommodate the increasing religious diversity of UNIA membership.

18. Robert N. Bellah, "Civil Religion in America," in The Religious Situation 1968, ed. Donald R. Cutler (Boston, 1968), pp. 331-356. See also Conrad Cherry's further amplification of the theme in God's New Israel: Religious Interpretations of American Destiny (Englewood Cliffs, 1971).

19. Bellah, "Civil Religion," p. 331 and Cherry, God's New Israel, pp. 8-24, esp. p. 21.

20. Cherry, God's New Israel, pp. 14-16.

21. Preston N. Williams, "Towards a Sociological Understanding of the Black Religious Community," Soundings 54 (1971), p. 267. Italics deleted.

CHAPTER 1

RELIGIOUS ETHOS OF THE UNIA*

Several insightful Black intellectuals contemporaneous with Marcus Garvey have at least alluded to the religious motifs which were to be found in the program and propaganda of the Universal Negro Improvement Association. One of the first of these was Claude McKay, one-time correspondent for the Negro World, who wrote an article for the April 1922 issue of the radical magazine, Liberator, in which he suggested that the essence of the appeal of this new "Negro Moses" was Garvey's imitation of one Alexander Bedward, a West Indian cultic leader who flourished in Jamaica between 1891 and the early 1920s. The Bedwardites constituted "a religious sect ... purely native in its emotional and external features," which was "the true religion of thousands of natives." McKay hypothesized that perhaps "the notorious career of Bedward, the prophet, worked unconsciously upon Marcus Garvey's mind and made him work out his plans along similar spectacular lines."[1]

McKay's readers, familiar with Bedward's career, were aware, of course, that he had recently been placed in a Jamaican mental institution. He was committed for having prophesied that as the Black incarnation of Jesus Christ, he would on a given day be whisked off to heaven in a white throne, returning after three days to wreak destruction upon the (white) non-elect.[2] Presumably McKay's implication was that the same fate might be appropriate for Garvey, or at least that Garvey, like Bedward, was best understood as an impostor and a fraud.[3]

---

*A revised version of this chapter appeared in the journal Afro-Americans in New York Life and History I:2 (July 1977), 167-182, under the title "Religious Dimensions of the Universal Negro Improvement Association and African Communities League."

A more suggestive, if still cursory, analysis of the religious aspects of the Garvey movement was made in a brief article by E. Franklin Frazier published in 1926. Writing in the Nation, Frazier called for a "closer examination of the ideals and symbols which Garvey always held up for his followers," and suggested that precisely this symbolism was the basis of Garvey's unique appeal. He pointed specifically to resonant religious themes such as the "redemption of Africa," which Frazier saw as formally analogous to the syndicalists' myth of the general strike. The "redemption of Africa" had become for the UNIA a central motivating mythos, an equivalent to the idea of paradise which had been lost, but which was "always almost at hand." Formative events of the Judeo-Christian tradition were likewise re-symbolized:

> Garvey who was well acquainted with the tremendous influence of religion in the life of the Negro proved himself matchless in assimilating his own program to the religious experience of the Negro. Christmas, with its association of the lowly birth of Jesus, became symbolic of the Negro's birth among the nations of the world. Easter became the symbol of the resurrection of an oppressed and crucified race. [4]

Such "naive symbolism," as Frazier termed it, ought not to blind one to the power which the symbols possess in evincing commitment and devotion; nor need one conclude that Garvey was simply a "common swindler" capitalizing on the superstitions of a people for selfish gains, "when the evidence seems to place him among the so-called cranks who refuse to deal realistically with life."[5] Whether in spite of or because of his lack of realism, however, Garvey had achieved a dramatic goal: sustained grass roots support on a mass basis. As Frazier concluded, "He has the distinction of initiating the first real mass movement among American Negroes."[6]

It is not insignificant that whereas the editors of the Negro World relegated to the back pages of their paper a brief reply to the "Bedwardism" charge leveled by McKay, they reprinted the full text of Frazier's article and reserved their own corrective assessment of certain aspects of his critique to a subsequent editorial column.[7] Evidently Frazier's intuition concerning the importance both of the movement itself and of the religious elements within it was in much closer agreement with the UNIA's self-understanding than was McKay's perspective.

Unfortunately, no one developed the suggestions advanced by Frazier, by way of a systematic investigation into the religious framework around which the UNIA was organized. Instead, the typical application of the "religious" interpretation was made in a pejorative sense, the point being that Garvey's was but another in a long string of "escapist" or "utopian" cultic movements which have had the net effect in the Black community of siphoning off effective protest into an "other-worldly" and apolitical realm. James Weldon Johnson provided an example in his condescending description of the UNIA:

> The movement became more than a movement, it became a religion, its members became zealots. Meetings at Liberty Hall were conducted with an elaborate liturgy. The moment for the entry of the "Provisional President" into the auditorium was solemn; a hushed and expectant silence on the throng, the African Legion and Black Cross nurses flanking the long aisle and coming to attention, the band and audience joining in the hymn: "God Save our President," and Garvey, surrounded by his guard of honour from the Legion, marching majestically through the double line and mounting the rostrum; it was impressive if for no other reason than the way in which it impressed the throng. [8]

While such men as McKay, Frazier, and Johnson were thus aware of the presence of religious motifs within the UNIA, they were mostly content to use this knowledge as a club with which to attack Garvey. One suspects that for all of these men religion was basically understood as synonymous with "escapism," or as compensation in another world for material rewards denied in the present world. [9] Simply to conclude that Garveyism was a religion was therefore to go a long way towards discrediting it, or denying the need to take it seriously. [10] Where religion is viewed more broadly, however, as that universal phenomenon endemic to the human enterprise whereby one attempts to make sense of the world in face of the meaning-shattering events by which one is continually bombarded, a more careful examination of these "religious elements" within the UNIA appears to be justified. The question then becomes whether these are

isolated and/or extrinsic elements, adopted only for their
instrumental value, or whether they have a larger significance. If the latter is the case, then it will become important to see how these elements are woven into a coherent
view of the world.

This chapter provides a careful descriptive analysis
of the religious ethos of the UNIA, examining the structure
and format of its meetings, noting the vocabulary with which
members addressed issues, clarifying the role of chaplains
within the organization, and elucidating the religio-political
symbols of nationhood by which its purposes were embodied.
This discussion should therefore provide a foundation for the
"closer examination of the ideals and symbols" of the UNIA
which was called for by Frazier a half century ago.

Typical UNIA Meetings

From the descriptive point of view alone, one can
scarcely help being struck by the fact that meetings of the
Universal Negro Improvement Association possessed many
of the characteristics of a religious service. This was true
of special rallies that were held in Madison Square Garden,
of the regular Sunday evening meetings in Harlem's Liberty
Hall, and of local division and chapter meetings that were
held throughout the United States and the Caribbean. A typical example of the special rallies is one held in Madison
Square Garden on March 16, 1924, on the occasion of the
return to the United States of a delegation which the UNIA
had sent to Europe and Africa "to Negotiate for the Repa-
triation of Negroes to a Homeland of Their Own in Africa."[11]
More than ten thousand persons attended the evening program.

The festivities opened with a colorful procession of
officers of the Association and a parade of units from the
numerous auxiliary organizations of the UNIA, including the
Black Cross Nurses, the Royal Guards, the Royal Engineering
Corps, the Royal Medical Corps, and the Universal African
Legion. During the procession, the officers sang "Shine on
Eternal Light," one of the official opening hymns used by the
Association. It had been written by the bandmaster of the
UNIA, Rabbi Arnold J. Ford. Next, the audience joined in
singing the first, third and fourth stanzas of Reginald Heber's
century-old missionary hymn, "From Greenland's Icy Moun-
tains," which was also used as an opening hymn.[12] The
Chaplain-General offered a prayer, which was followed by an

Harry T. Burleigh, renowned singer who performed frequently in Liberty Hall.

elaborate and carefully selected musical program. First the UNIA band played a march and the UNIA choir offered the "Gloria." There were three solos, followed by a quartet rendering of "Heaven," written by Black composer Harry T. Burleigh; and the musical presentation was capped by a stirring solo sung by Mme. Marie B. Houston. All of the numbers were explicitly religious in terms of theme, and although this was perhaps a more elaborate musical program than usual, the UNIA meetings at both national and local levels invariably featured outstanding musical talent.[13]

Sir William Sherrill, the Second Assistant President-General, delivered the first speech of the evening, elucidating the purpose of the UNIA. Another musical interlude introduced the high point of the evening: Marcus Garvey's address, "The Negro and the Future." Garvey's speeches were always carefully timed to achieve the maximum impact and were delivered in a fiery and dramatic style that left no member of the audience unmoved. His talk was followed by a brief sermonette by Rev. Dr. William H. Moses, a New York City Baptist minister whose subject for the evening was the familiar Biblical text, "Ethiopia Shall Soon Stretch Forth Her Hands Unto God." The speeches were followed by a presentation of delegates and announcements, and the program was closed by the singing of the first verses of the African National Anthem and the Star Spangled Banner[14] and a benediction. The format of a religious service was followed even to the point of receiving an offering, which was the normal practice both at special rallies such as the one just described and at the regular Sunday evening meetings in the Harlem Liberty Hall.

While the massive rallies at Madison Square Garden were doubtless more elaborate in their planning and execution than the regular weekly programs at Liberty Hall, the spirit and tone of those weekly meetings were the same. A typical Sunday evening program is described in the following excerpt from a Negro World report:

> The meeting tonight opened with the customary religious service of congregational singing of anthem and prayer, followed by all repeating the Twenty-Third Psalm, after which the High Chancellor, the Rev. Dr. G. E. Stewart, the presiding officer, offered a special prayer for the safe return of the President-General. Then followed the musical program, the Liberty Choir and the Black Star

Line Band performing their parts well. Mr.
Samuels sang a baritone solo. Madame Fraser-
Robinson was the soloist. [15]

The speakers for this particular evening included, in
addition to Stewart, two other clergymen: William H. Ferris,
a Harvard Divinity School alumnus and editor of the Negro
World; and Frederick A. Toote, "Speaker in Convention" and
one of the founders of the African Orthodox Church. Toote's
speech was devoted almost wholly to the imminent return of
Marcus Garvey, who was just concluding an extensive trip
through the Caribbean on behalf of the UNIA. He closed
with a "fervent appeal to all friends of the movement to help
make the reception to be tendered to Mr. Garvey an unqualified success," and his appeal evidently did not go unanswered,
as the paper reported:

> This brought a voluntary response of nearly every-
> one present, who came forward and made a liberal
> contribution toward the expenses of the proposed
> welcome. Following this, the meeting closed, with
> everyone in a happy frame of mind, and elated over
> the glad tidings that had been heard. [16]

For a time Sunday morning programs were also held
in the Harlem Liberty Hall, and these were evidently strictly
worship services. On at least one occasion, the morning
worship service was reported in the Pittsburgh Courier's
regular weekly section "Among the Churches," which published summaries of sermons delivered in Harlem's most
prestigious churches. Reporting on the program "At Liberty
Hall" for Sunday, May 23, 1924, the Courier noted that an
"overflowing crowd" was in attendance at the eleven o'clock
service. The Reverend G. Emonei Carter presided, and
Bishop George Alexander McGuire delivered the sermon
based on a text from the book of Hebrews, chapter eleven. [17]

The meetings of local UNIA chapters and divisions
across the country similarly reflected the tone of a religious
service, and followed a carefully ritualized pattern. The
following item concerning the Los Angeles Division, dated
January 30, 1923, is typical of the reports appearing weekly
in "The News and Views of UNIA Divisions" section of the
Negro World:

> The Los Angeles Division, No. 156, met in
> their hall, 1824 Central Avenue, with the president,

Bishop Frederick A. Toote, UNIA official and a founder of the African Orthodox Church.

Mr. D. J. Henderson. The meeting opened by
singing From Greenland['s] Icy Mountain, the motto
being repeated by the chaplain. The front page of
the Negro World was read by Mr. Henderson.
    Mr. J. J. Stafford, second vice-president
was present as master of ceremonies. First on
the program was a selection by the choir, next
Rev. A. Brown, [on the] subject, "Love is the
Greatest Thing." A paper [was read] by Mr.
Hoxie stating what the editor of the "Los Angeles
Times" (White) said: "That the great God who we
serve is a Black Man," referring to the finding
[recently of the] Egyptian King [Tut, who died],
3000 years ago. Mr. Hoxie said we, the Negroes
that were brought to this country as slaves, never
knew of anything, not until Marcus Garvey came.
Go on, go on, Marcus Garvey, until victory shine
upon the continent of Africa.[16]

Local UNIA meetings were normally held on Sunday
evenings, though some divisions held morning services as
well. Almost always, when a division was first founded,
meetings were held in the church of a friendly (or at least
a neutral) minister in the community, though each local organization was strongly encouraged by national headquarters
to build its own "Liberty Hall" as quickly as possible. Often,
as in the case of the Los Angeles Division, the prime mover
on the UNIA's behalf was a prominent clergyman. In this instance it was the influential pastor of Tabernacle Baptist
Church, the Reverend John Dawson Gordon, in whose church
the Association held its meetings for over a year and a
half.[19] Gordon soon became a national officer of the UNIA,
and a large number of his congregation became active Garveyites.[20]

As was the case at the special rallies and in the Harlem Liberty Hall meetings, then, local UNIA meetings were
characterized by hymn singing, prayers, and sermons by
local clergymen. Special rituals were devised to give local
groups a sense of identification with the national organization,
such as public reading of the front page of the Negro World,
which was always written by Marcus Garvey. A regular
feature of the local meetings was the welcoming of new
visitors and the introduction of prominent community leaders
in the audience. The reports carried in the "News and
Views" section of the Negro World invariably concluded with
a listing of influential citizens who had attended the chapter

or division meeting, and special prominence was given to testimonials of support from any clergymen present. In addition to these regular weekly features of local meetings, there were special ceremonies prescribed for unique events such as the "unveiling" of the charter of a new UNIA chapter or division, a practice not dissimilar from the dedication and consecration ceremonies found in many churches. Mortgage burning ceremonies were likewise held by local UNIA groups.

Vocabulary of the UNIA

There is another important sense in which the UNIA reflected a religious ethos, namely, in the language and the vocabulary on which the movement drew both to describe its own purposes and to evoke commitment and loyalty amongst its membership. Unquestionably the vocabulary of the UNIA was drawn from the religious realm, as can be attested by practically every issue of the Negro World.

Garvey himself provides a classic example in a speech he delivered in February 1921 at Liberty Hall. On that occasion he stated:

> I wish I could convert the world of Negroes overnight to the tremendous possibilities of the Universal Negro Improvement Association. It pains me every every [sic] moment of the day when I see Negroes losing the grasp they should have on their own. You of Liberty Hall I must ask you [sic] to go out as missionaries and preach this doctrine of the Universal Negro Improvement Association. Let all the world know that this is the hour; this is the time for our salvation. Prayer alone will not save us; sentiment alone will not save us. We have to work and work and work if we are to be saved ... the time is now to preach the beatitude of bread and butter. I have contributed my bit to preaching this doctrine. [21]

The "doctrine" of the UNIA to which Garvey continually referred, and which he here felicitously characterized as "the beatitude of bread and butter," was a combination of faith in oneself, in one's race, and in God. It included a political and an economic, as well as a specifically religious program, though all were expressed in religious terminology. The most widely touted element of Garvey's political program, for instance, was the "Back to Africa" demand, which was most frequently described in terms of the "Redemption of Africa." This theme has a venerable place in Black American history,[22] and Garvey was by no means using the idea in ignorance of its past history.

Garvey's speeches and editorials were sermonic in style, containing extensive use of Biblical references and religious imagery. Every address was a call to commitment, determination, and sacrifice, with a not infrequent note of apocalypticism creeping in. Amy Jacques Garvey has recorded in her biography of her husband that as a boy, young Marcus learned his lessons in elocution by standing outside the opened windows of churches in Kingston--churches in which the most outstanding preachers of the day delivered their addresses.[23] Perhaps he learned more than lessons in rhetoric while listening at those open windows.

Another example of the tendency of Garveyites to express political programs in a religious vocabulary is found in this excerpt from a revivalist-style speech by the Reverend James W. H. Eason, who was the first Chaplain-General of the UNIA, and later was named "Leader of American Negroes." Speaking on the topic, "The Significance of the Life Pledge," he remarked,

> A life pledge makes a man out and out, a man all round, who stands four-square to every wind that blows. Play the man; the race demands it. Africa expects every man to do his duty. Liberia is calling to you for commercial development.
> I want everyone in this building tonight to make a life pledge, come weal, come woe. I will count one in the uplift of my race; I will count one to glorify my God; I will count one to help put over the Liberian constructive loan. I will pledge my word, my money and my sacred honor to see to it that the Liberian constructive loan is a success, that the ideas of the provisional president may be advanced and spread abroad to the world.[24]

Such calls for "life pledges," Garvey's "vision of a redeemed Africa," and his hope to "convert the world of Negroes" did not go unheeded. Indeed, numerous Garveyites have indicated that their decisions to join the UNIA were more than rhetorically analogous to a conversion experience. Some have provided descriptions of the process by which they were "grasped" and brought into the fold of Garvey's organization. One of these was William L. Sherrill, himself the son of a Methodist Episcopal minister in Hot Springs, Arkansas, who as early as 1922 accepted Garvey's call. Amy Jacques Garvey preserved the text of Sherrill's conversion experience as he recalled it many years after the event:

> Here was I, a successful business man with a family, member of a church, a lodge, and fully insured to protect them. I did not have to join anything else. I subscribed to the anti-lynching campaign every time a Negro was lynched. I did not like to hear people talk about conditions of my people, as I had overcome many of them; let everybody else do likewise. I argued this way against the persuasion of friends.
>
> One night on my way to a show, I saw a huge crowd outside a church. I went up and said, "What's going on in there?" A lady turned to me and said, "Man alive, don't you know that Marcus Garvey is in there talking? Yes, indeed, Garvey in person." "Shucks," I said, "I may as well see what he looks like." I could not get near the windows, so I had to get a ticket for standing room only. I squeezed in, until I could get a good look at him; then suddenly he turned in my direction, and in a voice like thunder from Heaven he said, "Men and women, what are you here for? To live unto yourself, until your body manures the earth, or to live God's Purpose to the fullest?" He continued to complete his thought in that compelling, yet pleading voice for nearly an hour. I stood there like one in a trance, every sentence ringing in my ears, and finding an echo in my heart. When I walked out of that church, I was a different man--I knew my sacred obligations to my Creator, and my responsibilities to my fellow men, and so help me! I am still on the Garvey train. [25]

It was not only the magnetism of Garvey's personality that was capable of eliciting such total commitment to the movement. Richard Hilton Tobitt, for instance, an African Methodist Episcopal clergyman in Bermuda, felt the call of the UNIA when reading the Negro World. As he observed in a biographical essay some years later,

> It was while giving a public lecture in St.

Paul's A.M.E. Church, Hamilton City, Bermuda, on the subject, "Is Education Necessary to the Negro?" that a copy of "The Negro World" was placed in my hands for the first time. . . . Having carefully analyzed the program of the UNIA as set forth by its founder, Marcus Garvey, and believing in the integrity of the man and the righteousness of the course he espoused, I caught his vision and became a ready disciple of Garveyism, which I discovered was the "Master Key" . . . to the correct solution of the vexed race problem of the world and a sane and practical exposition of true religion. Without delay, I set to work to organize the Bermuda Division of the UNIA . . . and "left the court of Pharaoh, choosing rather to suffer affliction with my people than to dwell in the land of Goshen."[26]

Such conversions often came at a high price. Tobitt, for instance, in his reference to the "Court of Pharaoh" was no doubt alluding to his disbarment from the ministry of the AME Church in Bermuda as a consequence of having joined the UNIA. In addition, government funds for the school over which he presided were withdrawn, the governor of the island declaring that Tobitt had clearly demonstrated by his action that he was "no longer a fit person to be entrusted with the education of children."[27]

Religious vocabulary was consistently used by Garveyites in their Sunday evening speeches in Liberty Hall. A typical headline in the Negro World for February 26, 1921 quoted William Ferris, who "Says Gospel Message of UNIA Has Swept Over the World Like a Tidal Wave, Giving Hope and Inspiration to the Negro Everywhere."[28] One A. S. Gray spoke to an audience in Oakland, California, on the "Righteousness of the UNIA."[29] Marcus Garvey called upon his followers to "act as living missionaries to convince others,"[30] and on another occasion referred to the UNIA as "the great ark of safety."[31] Such language persisted in the pages of the Negro World to the paper's very last issue. In an editorial by Mme. M. L. T. De Mena, published in that issue on October 17, 1933, the paper's editor described "Garveyism as the guiding star of Ethiopia's restoration."

The Sacred few, the noble few, the gallant few, who . . . from a burning heart and languishing soul . . . felt the true zealousness and sublimity of race consciousness, the fundamentality of nationhood, the

Negro World began to take on the quality of a sacred text.

> infancy of a great commonwealth, operated and
> goevrned [sic] by Negroes in yonder fragrant
> Africa's sunny fields; yea a modern heaven and
> refuge, a substantial environment, a solace where-
> in all Negro generations will be called blessed.
> This is our abiding faith, the eternal creed, the
> renovated religion, that now appeals and aches
> within the breast of our hundred million Negroes
> under the ethics of the Universal Negro Improve-
> ment Association. [32]

The Negro World itself was referred to as the "Testament of the UNIA" because, according to one official, it
"has been the greatest missionary in building up divisions
and making converts to the cause outside of New York
City."[33] Indeed, one could go so far as to say that the
Negro World began to take on the quality of a sacred text.
As earlier noted, part of the ritual of each Sunday evening
program in the local "Liberty Halls" outside of New York
City consisted in reading aloud the lead editorial which com-
prised the entire front page of each issue of the paper. The
public reading of this editorial gave Garvey regular access
to all UNIA members and insured that all would receive inspiration and information directly from their leader.[34]

Chaplains in the UNIA

The religious ethos of UNIA meetings, which was set by the formal structure of the regular programs and by the language used by its officials, was further reinforced by the presence of chaplains at both local and national levels. Each chapter or division was required by the UNIA constitution to select a chaplain, whose duty it was to attend to the spiritual concerns of the members. All chaplains were under the direction of the Chaplain-General, who was a member of the High Executive Council, the UNIA's ruling body.

By far the most able of the Chaplains-General was West Indian-born George Alexander McGuire,[35] who was elected to the post at the first annual International Convention of the Negro Peoples of the World in August 1920. Under his leadership, the religio-political nationalism which was present in the UNIA from its earliest days was made ever more explicit and pervasive. One of his first deeds as Chaplain-General, for instance, was to compile the Universal Negro Ritual, published in 1921. The Ritual was modeled after the Book of Common Prayer on which McGuire was raised as a member of the Church of England and which he later used as a priest in the Protestant Episcopal Church.

All chaplains were obliged to follow and all members were encouraged to acquire and study the Ritual, which prescribed the standard order of service to be followed in UNIA meetings. The standard format, exemplified in the three services described earlier, opened with the hymn "From Greenland's Icy Mountains" and with one or more of the special prayers which McGuire compiled. These were to be followed by singing of either "O Africa Awaken" or "Shine on Eternal Light" (both hymns especially composed for the UNIA), prior to presentation of the featured events of the program. "These preliminaries," it was remarked on one occasion, "lend a religious air to the meeting, and the audience responds and participates with a fervor and zeal that is highly commendable."[36] The meeting closed with additional prayers and the African National Anthem.[37] As will be detailed in a later chapter, in addition to standardizing the order by which meetings were to proceed, McGuire included in the Ritual a baptism and a burial service for UNIA members. On occasion, marriages also took place under Association auspices. Clearly, in McGuire's conception, the UNIA was an all-embracing institution ministering to the spiritual needs of its members from the cradle to the grave.

Under McGuire's leadership the role of the chaplains was broadened and clarified, and efforts were made to upgrade the standards required of those who sought the post. At the time of his election as Chaplain-General, McGuire was able to effectuate changes in the UNIA constitution in order to accomplish these goals. One such revision concerned Section 63 of the Book of Laws, which henceforth required that all chaplains of local divisions or chapters "must be ordained ministers or have their first license."[38] The implementation of this section presumed, of course, the membership of at least one ordained clergyman in every UNIA division in the country as well as the willingness of each division to grant a significant leadership role to that person. McGuire may have encountered some resistance to this rule, as is suggested by the following notice made in the "Chaplain-General's Department" column in the Negro World:

> The Chaplain-General hereby announces that in accordance with Section 63 that [sic] no Chaplains in the various Divisions will be recognized as qualified for such office unless they meet the requirements as laid down. Evidence must be sent to this office of the ordination of Chaplains to the ministry, or credentials of license as lay-readers or local preachers. There can be no excuse for lack of qualification as His Grace the Chaplain-General is ready to issue a license to any layman who can pass a fair and reasonable examination in English and religious knowledge.[39]

Opposition to the ordination requirement apparently persisted, and in the 1922 revision of the General Laws, the relevant section was made simply to read, "All Chaplains of the UNIA and ACL shall be intelligent persons versed in reading and interpretation of the Universal Ritual and the Scriptures."[40]

Another constitutional revision which McGuire discussed in the Negro World, and which required action by local UNIA chaplains, concerned the necessity of creating youth organizations in each UNIA division. The relevant section of the General Laws required "That in every Division of the UNIA, a juvenile branch be formed and only teachings of spiritual and racial uplift be taught."[41] The Rules and Regulations for Juveniles, which were published as part of the Constitution and Book of Laws, indicate the type of training envisioned for children of UNIA members. A variety of classes were to be formed. The Infant Class included all children, ages one to seven, and they were to be taught the following:

> Bible Class and Prayer. Doctrine of the UNIA and ACL. Facts about the Black Star Line Steamship Corporation, the Negro Factories Corporation, and History of Africa (in story book fashion). [42]

Children aged seven to thirteen composed the Number Two Class, and they were divided by sex for their program. For the girls this included:

> Taught to make Souvenirs with cloth, needle and thread, for sale for Juvenile Department. Ritual of Universal Negro Improvement Association. Write Negro stories, taught Race pride and love. Taught Negro history and Etiquette and be given disciplinary training by the Legions. [43]

Boys received the same training, except that they were to make souvenirs from wood rather than by needle and thread.

The "Cadets" class consisted of youths aged thirteen to sixteen, who were required to study the Ritual, military training, flag signals, and Negro history. Books specifically recommended for study included J. A. Rogers's From Superman to Man; Sydney H. Olivier's White Capital and Colored Labor; Hubert H. Harrison's When Africa Awakes; and the book, African Lure and Lyrics. It was specified that the class was to be taught by a member of the Universal African Legions "who is acquainted with military tactics." [44]

Finally there was a Preparatory Nursing Class under the direction of the Black Cross Nurses, for girls aged fourteen to eighteen. Their responsibilities included:

> Making uniforms for Juveniles; Negro History; Etiquette; Talk on latest topics of the day; Elementary principles of Economy; Negro Story Writing; Hygiene and Domestic Science. [45]

A Lady Vice-President was placed in charge as superintendent of the Juvenile Department, and teachers were to be appointed by the division president. There is no indication as to how often classes were expected to meet, though it seems clear that the intent was to supplement rather than to replace the public education system. Coming out of the tradition of the Protestant Episcopal Church, in which confirmation classes and catechetical training were long established, McGuire was aware of the importance of providing a mechanism whereby Negro youths could regularly and from an early age be taught the spiritual and racial values of the organization. In all cases it was the responsibility of the chaplains to provide religious training for juveniles. Not surprisingly, on completion of the Universal Negro Ritual McGuire turned to the task of devising a Universal Negro Catechism for use in the juvenile branches to assist in this task.[46]

Finally, in one of his columns in the Negro World for the "Chaplain-General's Department," McGuire set forth the model of chaplaincy to which he hoped all would aspire, and listed the duties of the office as he perceived them. They were:

> a. To conduct Divine Service according to the Universal Negro Ritual on Sunday mornings or afternoons where it is the desire of the members of the Division to have such Sunday service.
> b. To conduct the Ritual as prescribed in the Ritual Book in connection with Mass Meetings or Members' Meetings.
> c. To instruct the members of the Juvenile Branch in his Division in the knowledge supplied in the Universal Negro Catechism.
> d. To see that every member of his Division purchase the Universal Negro Ritual and the Universal Negro Catechism.
> e. To visit the sick and afflicted members of his Division and report to the proper officers any case needing charity.
> f. To govern his own life and conversation in such manner as may prove him worthy to be a moral and spiritual guide to his fellow members.[47]

In brief, McGuire hoped that the chaplains would function as spiritual leaders to members, inculcators of racial and moral values for the young, counselors and comforters to the sick and needy, and models of the moral and righteous life for the entire community. Their presence in each local chapter or division was meant to insure that the religious ethos established as normative by the national organization would be carefully followed in every UNIA gathering across the country.

Garveyite Regalia and the Paraphernalia of Nationhood

We have thus far examined the rituals, both implicitly and explicitly religious, to be found in meetings of the UNIA; described the language, drawn primarily from the religious realm, by which its programs were presented; and observed the role of the "religious virtuosi" (to borrow a term from Max Weber) who were specially designated to inculcate the values and norms of the Association. What remains to be noted, in this essentially descriptive discussion concerning the religious ethos of the Garvey movement, is the multitude of religio-political symbols of nationhood by which the UNIA fostered the idea of peoplehood and self-identity.

Nationhood was the perdurable motif around which much of the activity in the UNIA revolved. The constitution, first adopted in 1918 and amended in succeeding years, set forth the constituent elements of the nationhood motif in systematic fashion. The list of officers, for instance, included a President-General who was at the same time Provisional President of Africa (the chief administrative position, which Garvey held himself). Assistant Presidents-General also held the titles of "Titular Leader of American Negroes" or "Titular Leader of the West Indies, South and Central America." There were appointed Ministers of African Legions, of Education, and of Labor and Industries, as well as Ministers Plenipotentiary, who were designated as ambassadors "to all regular governments" and to the League of Nations. [48] In addition to enumerating these titles of officials modeled after that of a national government, the constitution also authorized a variety of agencies to perform quasi-governmental tasks. These included a Civil Service, which gave regular exams and offered limited positions to be filled by UNIA members in good standing; a Passports Bureau, which issued passports to facilitate travel of members from one branch to another; and a Bureau of Justice, to insure the rights of Negroes wherever they might reside throughout the world. Even taxes were levied: in addition to the one dollar annual membership tax, there was a ten cent per month levy as a "death tax," in exchange for which members were to receive free burial by the Association. [49]

Garvey took care to integrate religious imagery into his conceptualization of the "new nationality." The official motto of the UNIA was "One God! One Aim! One Destiny!" The motto was to be found emblazoned on the official banner, on UNIA stationery, and on the letterhead of the Negro World,

and it was repeated at every meeting of the Association.
The notion of a unified religious faith for all Black persons
implied by the words "One God" was a perennial topic for
discussion at International Conventions and was a theme to
which Garvey frequently returned in his speeches. The official slogan, "Pro Deo, Pro Africa, Pro Justitia, " was
less widely used than the motto, although it also contained
a God referent.

On the official letterhead of UNIA stationery was also
printed the Biblical injunction from Acts 18:26, "He created
of one blood all nations of man to dwell upon the face of the
earth. " To be sure, Garveyites were unabashed in proclaim-
ing the goals of their organization as being the uplift of one
particular racial group, but this was always presented in the
context of a demand for respect of the rights of all mankind
and a commitment finally to the brotherhood of man and the
Fatherhood of God.

The most frequently cited Biblical passage by far,
and the one which most often served as a text for sermon
topics in Liberty Halls around the country, was the one
from Psalms 68:31, "Princes shall come forth from Egypt;
Ethiopia shall soon stretch forth her hand to God. " This
Biblical prophecy has been cited by Black churchmen in
America at least since the eighteenth century, to specify
God's special concern for men of African descent. [50] The
concern for Africa that was so central to the UNIA, and the
conviction that God was working in history through the in-
strumentality of the UNIA to create a nation, Africa, as a
part of His larger purposes, rendered this verse from the
Psalms uniquely appropriate to the Garvey movement. The
meaning of the passage, as understood by Garveyites, was
explicated in the Universal Negro Catechism:

> Q. What prediction made in the 68th Psalm and
> the 31st verse is now being fulfilled?
> A. "Princes shall come out of Egypt, Ethiopia
> shall soon stretch forth her hands unto God. "
> Q. What does this verse prove?
> A. That Negroes will set up their own government
> in Africa, with rulers of their own race. [51]

Here was Biblical warrant and ultimate grounding for the
Association's political program, and irrefragable evidence
that the UNIA's work was indeed of God.

Note the "Psalmist's Prophecy" inscribed on the pillars
of this Sunday School quarterly.

The Psalmist's prophecy concerning Ethiopia was also incorporated in the "Universal Ethiopian Anthem," another basic element in the UNIA's paraphernalia of nationhood. Written by Ben Burrell and UNIA Choirmaster Arnold J. Ford, it again illustrates the mixture of religious and political elements which was so characteristic of Garveyite rituals and symbols. The text of the hymn, which was officially adopted as the anthem "of the Negro race," is as follows:

> Ethiopia, thou land of our fathers,
> Thou land where the gods loved to be,
> As storm cloud at night sudden gathers
> Our armies come rushing to thee.
> We must in the fight be victorious,
> When swords are thrust outward to glean;
> For us will the Vict'ry be glorious
> When led by the red, black and green

Chorus

> Advance, advance to victory!
> Let Africa be free!
> Advance to meet the foe
> With the might
> Of the red, the black, and the green.

> Ethiopia, the tyrant's falling
> Who smote thee upon thy knees;
> And thy children are lustily calling
> From over the distant seas.
> Jehovah the Great One has heard us,
> Has noted our sighs and our tears,
> With His spirit of love He has stirred us
> To be one through the coming years.

Chorus

> O Jehovah, Thou God of the ages,
> Grant unto our sons that lead
> The wisdom Thou gav'st to Thy sages
> When Israel was sore in need.
> Thy voice thro' the dim past has spoken,
> Ethiopia shall stretch forth her hand,
> By Thee shall all fetters be broken
> And Heav'n bless our dear Motherland. [52]

In sharp contrast to the much more familiar "Negro National Hymn," written by James Weldon Johnson some twenty years earlier, Ford's anthem was a call for military preparedness in anticipation of an inevitable conflagration which would be demanded before God's promise of freedom could be realized. Johnson's hymn, "Lift Every Voice and Sing," had breathed an air of determined hopefulness reflective of faith in the "harmonies of Liberty" which were working gradually but certainly toward a victory that was all but won. The God of whom Johnson had spoken was a benevolent if stern God, who has guided and is guiding the destiny of Black people to justice and to their promised land, to "the place for which our fathers sighed," which for Johnson was surely not Africa, but a just and truly democratic United States of America.[53] For Ford, however, it was Ethiopia which was the object of the people's affection, and it was the God of retribution, Jehovah, who would insure that just as He had long ago led His people, Israel, to freedom, so now would He work through the instrument of the Universal Negro Improvement Association to achieve the redemption of His people and of their homeland, Africa.

It should be evident from the foregoing that the religious ethos of the UNIA was pervasive, embracing nearly every facet of its organizational life. The religious elements we have described were not isolated or random occurrences, but are to be found everywhere one looks within the movement. And just as recent students of religion in America have insisted that the God-references, the ceremonial and the religious symbols of nationhood developed over the past two hundred years of this nation's existence cannot simply be dismissed as insignificant "ritualistic" expressions, but are "indicative of deep-seated values and commitments"[54] worthy of careful examination, so can it be argued that the rituals and symbols developed by the Universal Negro Improvement Association are constitutive of a coherent way of viewing the world which deserves to be taken seriously. In order to make that case, it is essential to lay bare the theoretical framework out of which these rituals and symbols were developed. This will be the task of the next chapter.

Notes

1. Claude McKay, "Garvey as a Negro Moses," Liberator 5 (April 1922), p. 8. In his autobiography A Long

Way, pp. 55, 67, 87, McKay reports it was on the urging of his good friend, Hubert H. Harrison, that he started sending articles to Garvey's paper from Europe. Harrison was at the time an active Garvey supporter and columnist/editor for the Negro World.

2. Bedward had specified December 31, 1920 as the date of his ascension. On Bedward, see Leonard E. Barrett, The Rastafarians: A Study in Messianic Cultism in Jamaica (Rio Piedras, Puerto Rico, 1968), pp. 55-57; Martha Warren Beckwith, "Some Religious Cults in Jamaica," American Journal of Psychology 34 (1923), 32-45, esp. pp. 40-45; and Roscoe M. Pierson, "Alexander Bedward and the Jamaica Native Baptist Free Church," in Randall K. Burkett and Richard Newman, eds., Black Apostles: Afro-American Clergy Confront the Twentieth Century (Boston, 1978).

3. McKay, "Garvey as a Negro Moses," p. 8. McKay does temper his judgment of Garvey by remarking on the UNIA leader's "energetic and quick-witted mind." As McKay goes on in the article to make clear, the real basis of his objection to Garvey was the latter's persistent anti-union and anti-socialist economic program.

4. E. Franklin Frazier, "Garvey: A Mass Leader," Nation 123 (August 18, 1926), p. 148.

5. Ibid.

6. Ibid.

7. The Negro World reply to McKay is found in NW 12:16 (June 3, 1922), p. 12. Frazier's article was reprinted in NW 21:2 (August 21, 1926), p. 5, with an editorial reply in NW 21:3 (August 28, 1926), p. 4.

8. James Weldon Johnson, Black Manhattan, p. 255.

9. For a discussion of James W. Johnson's attitude towards religion generally, see the comments by Benjamin E. Mays in his book The Negro's God as Reflected in His Literature (New York, 1969), pp. 234-36. Frazier's negative assessment of the religion of the Negro, which he said has "cast a shadow over the entire

intellectual life of Negroes and has been responsible
for the so-called backwardness of American Negroes,"
was summarized in his influential essay The Negro
Church in America (New York, 1963), p. 86. Stanford M. Lyman, in his recent study The Black
American in Sociological Thought (New York, 1972),
places Frazier's critique of the Negro church in the
context of his sociological framework developed out
of the Chicago school of sociology under the tutelage
of Robert E. Park. See especially his discussion in
ch. 2, pp. 55-67.

10. A similar association is made by August Meier in his
Negro Thought in America: 1880-1915 (Ann Arbor,
1966), where he concludes that "The escapist Utopian
character of the Garvey movement as a response to
economic deprivation is revealed in the fact that a
large number of ex-Garveyites joined the Father Divine movement during the depression of the 1930's,"
p. 315, n. 39. Interpreters more sympathetic to
Garvey have also been chary of calling attention to
the religious elements for fear of lending credence
to the earlier associated notion that Garveyism was
simply "an oversized sect or cult, an escapist pseudo-
religion of which Garvey was God while many of his
followers were only a cut above fools." Theodore G.
Vincent, Black Power and the Garvey Movement, p. 1,
et passim, is typical in this respect.

11. The text of the speech delivered by Marcus Garvey on
this occasion is printed in Philosophy and Opinions
of Marcus Garvey (henceforth P&O), ed. Amy Jacques
Garvey (New York, 1969), II, 118-123. A copy of
the evening program guide is preserved in Vol. 32 of
the "Alexander Gumby Collection on the American
Negro," housed in the Department of Special Collections, Columbia University. See also the account in
the New York Times, March 17, 1924, p. 2.

12. The significance of the UNIA's use of this hymn is discussed in detail in chapter 3.

13. Amy Jacques Garvey, writing in her biographical study
Garvey and Garveyism (London, 1970), observed concerning the place of music in the UNIA, "Our people
love to sing; it is said they sang their way out of
slavery, through their spirituals, which expressed

their sorrow, and their firm belief that God was
leading them, as He had led the children of Israel
through the Wilderness, and Daniel out of the lion's
den. So Garvey outlined a set of meaningful hymns,
and [Ben] Burrell and [Arnold J.] Ford of the music
department put them into proper verse and set them
to music." p. 47. Most of these hymns were published in Ford's Universal Ethiopian Hymnal, which
is discussed below.

14. Garvey always insisted that the UNIA was not a subversive organization intent on the overthrow of the
United States government, and inclusion in the program of the Star Spangled Banner was meant to un-
derscore this point.

15. NW 10:22 (July 16, 1921), p. 1.

16. Ibid.

17. Pittsburgh Courier, May 31, 1924, p. 13.

18. NW 14:2 (February 24, 1923), p. 7

19. Gayraud S. Wilmore's characterization of the Black
church as "the NAACP on its knees" might thus just
as accurately be applied to the UNIA during the
early 1920s. See his Black Religion and Black
Radicalism (Garden City, 1972), p. 197. The practice of allowing protest organizations to utilize facili-
ties of Black churches as a forum for debate and a
base of operations has a long history, extending from
the anti-slavery period to the present day.

20. On occasion, when a minister was won over to the UNIA,
his entire congregation would join the Association.
See for example the statement of one R. H. Cosgrove
of Natchez, Mississippi, who reported at an International Convention of the UNIA that "he pastored a
little church of about 500 members, and everyone
was a member of the association, as he was of the
opinion that if he was to be a spiritual leader he
should also be able to lead them in their temporal
affairs. He attended the convention to see things for
himself so that he could take back to the people who
trusted him a true report of the work of the movement." NW 17:1 (August 18, 1924), p. 2.

21. NW 10:2 (February 19, 1921), p. 4. Emphasis added.

22. See St. Clair Drake, The Redemption of Africa and Black Religion (Chicago, 1970), and also below, chapter 2.

23. Amy Jacques Garvey, Garvey and Garveyism, p. 5.

24. NW 9:12 (November 6, 1920), p. 8. On Eason, see my Black Redemption: Churchmen Speak for the Garvey Movement (Philadelphia, 1978), chapter 3.

25. Amy Jacques Garvey, Garvey and Garveyism, p. 266. See also the biographical sketch of Sherrill in NW 15:5 (September 15, 1923), p. 4 and George Alexander McGuire's remarks in introducing Sherrill at the Fourth International Convention, NW 13:3 (September 2, 1922), p. 12.

26. NW 15:10 (October 20, 1923), p. 10.

27. Reported by William F. Elkins in "Marcus Garvey, the Negro World, and the British West Indies: 1919-1920," Science and Society 36 (Spring 1972), p. 71. All was not loss for Tobitt, however, for his conversion opened new horizons for the expression of his social and religious conscience. He was one of the signers of the famous "Declaration of Rights of the Negro Peoples of the World" in 1920, and was elected leader of the Eastern Province of the West Indies. He subsequently held numerous posts within the UNIA.

28. NW 10:2 (February 26, 1921), p. 3.

29. NW 13:18 (December 16, 1922), p. 8.

30. NW 10:2 (February 26, 1921), p. 4.

31. NW 30:22 (December 26, 1931), p. 1.

32. "Are We Discouraged?" NW 32:11 (October 17, 1933), p. 4.

33. NW 10:7 (April 2, 1921), p. 3. The speaker was George Alexander McGuire.

34. The point should not be pushed too far, however, so
    as to suggest that the Negro World literally replaced
    the Bible as the sacred text for UNIA members. An
    instructive comparison is available in the pattern
    followed in the Father Divine Peace Mission Move-
    ment, where, according to Arthur Huff Fauset, "The
    sacred text ... is not the Bible, but the New Day,
    a weekly periodical issued by the organization. Fol-
    lowers invariably refer to this book [sic] rather than
    to the Bible when they wish to speak with authority."
    Black Gods of the Metropolis (Philadelphia, 1944),
    p. 60. Divine, who gained prominence in Harlem in
    the years shortly after the decline of the Garvey
    movement, appears here to have radicalized an idea
    found in more moderate form in the UNIA. Simi-
    larly, Divine seems to have taken to an extreme
    other journalistic ideas originated by Garvey: where-
    as the Negro World published verbatim texts of many
    speeches delivered at Liberty Hall and most of the
    speeches delivered elsewhere by Garvey, the New
    Day published verbatim transcripts of practically
    every word uttered by Father Divine at his famous
    banquet meetings. And whereas the Negro World
    contained a regular Spanish column and (briefly) a
    French column, due to the circulation of the paper
    in Latin America and French-speaking Africa and
    the Caribbean, the New Day regularly carried trans-
    lations of Divine's speeches in French, Spanish, Ger-
    man, and Russian. It is significant that when the
    Negro World at last folded, on October 17, 1933,
    with publication of Vol. 32, No. 11, its presses and
    remaining supplies were purchased by none other
    than Father Divine, who published as a predecessor
    to the New Day his World (Peace) Echo. At least
    the first fifteen issues continued to number their
    papers with a dual system: Old Series, Vol. 32,
    No. 12 (following the Negro World numbering); New
    Series, Vol. 1, No. 1; etc. A careful study of the
    relationship between these two historically contiguous
    movements should be undertaken.

35. Chapter 3, below, is devoted to an analysis of McGuire's
    role in the UNIA.

36. NW 8:18 (June 5, 1920), p. 2.

37. The text of the anthem is printed below, p. 36.

38. NW 10:7 (April 2, 1921), p. 7.

39. Ibid. Emphasis added.

40. Constitution and Book of Laws Made for the Government of the Universal Negro Improvement Association, Inc., and African Communities League, Inc., of the World (New York, July 1918; Revised and amended August 1922). General Laws, Sec. 62, p. 57. Coincidentally or not, McGuire by this time had been ousted from the UNIA.

41. NW 10:7 (April 2, 1921), p. 7. Emphasis added. See also Sec. 61 of the revised 1922 edition of the Constitution and Book of Laws, p. 57.

42. Ibid., p. 85.

43. Ibid.

44. Ibid., p. 86.

45. Ibid.

46. The Catechism is examined in detail in chapter 3.

47. NW 10:7 (April 2, 1921), p. 7.

48. Constitution and Book of Laws, p. 56.

49. Vincent, Black Power, p. 167, lists these and other of the "trappings of nationhood" fostered by the UNIA.

50. Absalom Jones and Richard Allen, in their brief encomium to whites who were working to improve the condition of slaves in the United States, concluded with the words, "May he, who hath arisen to plead our cause, and engaged you as volunteers in the service, add to your numbers until the princes shall come forth from Egypt, and Ethiopia stretch out her hand unto God." A Narrative of the Proceedings of the Black People, During the Late Awful Calamity in Philadelphia, in the Year, 1793, in Dorothy Porter, ed., Negro Protest Pamphlets (New York, 1969), p. 23. This is the first written evidence I have been able to discover concerning the use of this passage by Black churchmen.

51. The Universal Negro Catechism, written by George Alexander McGuire in 1921, is discussed elsewhere. The passage is quoted from p. 11.

52. The text of the Anthem may be found in P&O, II, pp. 140-41. The militancy evidenced by the anthem is typical both of the general mood of Harlem in the post-War period and also of the aggressiveness which especially in its earliest period was characteristic of Garveyite rhetoric. The circumstances of its writing are themselves indicative of the incidents which all too often were perpetrated on Black Americans and which they were increasingly unwilling to accept without resistance or retaliation. According to an article in the Negro World, the hymn was occasioned by the brutal slaying in 1919 of a young woman who had been working as a housemaid in New York City. The girl, aged 17, had been raped by the head of the household where she worked. When she reported to her mistress that she was pregnant as a result of the attack, the woman, a "Negro hater," became enraged and threw her out of the house. Soon thereafter, according to the article, "she was found dead, her body horribly mutilated." William A. Stephenson, "The Universal Ethiopian Anthem and How It Came to Be Written," NW 15:2 (August 25, 1923), p. 2.

53. In his autobiography Along This Way (New York, 1961), pp. 154-56, Johnson described the circumstances of the song's composition, the score for which was composed by his brother J. Rosamond Johnson. The second stanza of "Lift Every Voice" seems to make clear that it is the new home in America which is the Negro's rightful heritage, as a result of his centuries of struggle here.

54. Bellah, "Civil Religion in America," p. 333.

CHAPTER 2

GARVEY AS BLACK THEOLOGIAN

Garveyites frequently commented on the importance of religion to the work of the Universal Negro Improvement Association and on the imperative need to rewrite the theology which had been taught to most of its members. The remarks of the Reverend John Dawson Gordon, Assistant President-General of the UNIA, offer a typical example of this concern. In a speech to a Boston audience Gordon "compared the U.N.I.A. with religious organizations and acclaimed that the white man's religion had met its Waterloo and that the Hon. Marcus Garvey and the Universal Negro Improvement Association have found the missing link in the Christian Church." The UNIA would not simply be content with new organizational forms, Gordon declared, for "the Negro people of the world will have to reconstruct the theology of the church in order to hasten the building up of the morale of the Negroes of the world."[1]

Garvey himself frequently stated that "our theologians" are at work rewriting (white) theology so as to make it pertinent to the needs and experience of the Black man. He rarely specified who was included in this group of theologians and never explicitly included himself among them. On the contrary, he repeatedly insisted that he was neither a preacher nor a theologian nor any manner of religious leader. In spite of his denials, however, it is my contention that Marcus Garvey was the UNIA's most shrewd and perspicacious theologian.

This conclusion is based on the examination of annual UNIA convention debates concerning religious questions, in which Garvey invariably took a leading role, and on a careful reading of his countless speeches and editorials, which are replete with discussion of theological issues. Garvey was by no means a systematic theologian, in the sense of carefully setting forth a unified or definitive statement concerning his

doctrine of God, of Christ, of man, and of man's destiny.
By imposing the categories of systematic theology upon his
disparate speeches and writings, however, I hope to demonstrate that there is a palpable unity to Garvey's thought, and
that he self-consciously sought to interpret the Christian
faith which was his heritage, in the light both of his people's
experience and of the latest scientific information available.

Doctrine of God

If Garvey's theology was by temperament unsystematic,
it was also by principle nondogmatic. He insisted that religion was a phenomenon universally experienced, and that no
man ought to criticize another either for holding to religion
in general or for believing in a particular conception of the
deity. Speaking at the Sixth International UNIA Convention
(1929) he declared,

> Man is a religious being, that is to say, he
> must have some kind of belief--call it superstition
> or what not. Man who has started to think traces
> his origin beyond man; and as such has been grop-
> ing in the dark to find out the source from whence
> he came, and by our own intuition we have attribu-
> ted that source to something beyond us; and in so
> believing we accept the idea of a religion. Some
> make our God the God of Fire; some make our God
> the God of water; some make our God the God of
> the Elements and others of us accept the Christian
> belief. Man's religion is something we cannot
> eliminate from his system or destroy in him;
> therefore, it is folly for any man to go about at-
> tacking another man's religion, because to him it
> is fundamental. You may be a Christian; you may
> be a Mohammedan; that is your religion. We are
> all entitled to our own religious belief. Some of
> us are Catholics, some of us are Presbyterians,
> some of us are Baptists, and we deem it a right
> to adhere to our particular belief. [2]

While Garvey was thus content to have his followers
remain within any (Black-led) religious organization, whether
Protestant or Catholic, Christian or non-Christian, he was
not willing for them to retain the religious ideals or concep-
tualizations of another race. In the first place, he specifically and emphatically rejected the conceptualization of God

as white. As he declared on one occasion,

> If the white man has the idea of a white God,
> let him worship his God as he desires.... We,
> as Negroes, have found a new ideal. Whilst our
> God has no color, yet it is human to see everything
> through one's own spectacles, and since the white
> people have seen their God through white spectacles,
> we have only now started out (late though it be) to
> see our God through our own spectacles.... We
> Negroes believe in the God of Ethiopia, the ever-
> lasting God--God the Father, God the Son and God
> the Holy Ghost, the one God of all ages. That is
> the God in whom we believe, but we shall worship
> Him through the spectacles of Ethiopia. [3]

As Biblical warrant for rejection of the white God, Garvey
cited not only the Psalmist's prophecy concerning Ethiopia,
but also the Mosaic prohibition against idolatry. God has
declared that He made man in His own image, and since
"Every man is a pattern of God ... and all of God's crea-
tures go to make God" (all men being part of God), thus
Black men must see that it is idolatrous to make God white.
"When you bow to a graven image, when you bow to the god
of another species, you dishonor the God that is in you, and
you ... abase the God of your existence and commit a sin
against the Holy Ghost.... Therefore, the U.N.I.A. desires
every Negro to destroy the image of the white God that you
have been taught to bow to. "[4]

Garvey had much more to say about God, however,
than that He must not be conceived by Black men to be
white. In the confidential Lesson Guides written for his
School of African Philosophy, for instance, he sought to
characterize the attributes of God. God must first be understood, Garvey wrote, as Universal Intelligence:

> There is a God and we believe in Him. He
> is not a person nor a physical being. He is a
> spirit and He is universal intelligence. Never deny
> that there is a God. God being universal intelli-
> gence created the universe out of that intelligence.
> It is intelligence that creates. Man is a part of
> the creation of universal intelligence and man was
> created in the image and likeness of God only by
> his intelligence. It is the intelligence of man that
> is like God, but man's intelligence is only a unitary
> particle of God's universal intelligence. [5]

God is thus absolute mind, the sum of all intelligence of which man can see only a part. But as He has the capacity to create and control, He must also be characterized as absolute power. This is a power which no man has the ability to deny.

> There is a God.
> No man can say there is no God, because no man is like God. Man is limited in his intelligence at the most and man knows how insufficient he is between life and death--that he is born without his knowledge and dies without his will or wish; when his birth and death [occur] must logically and naturally be controlled by somebody else.
> It could not be man because man is always man whether he be a big man or small man. So power that gives birth and causes death must be greater than man's power. Whatsoever that power is, it must be an absolute power.
> Some men call it by different names but all mean the same thing and it is God. [6]

Now the perennial problem with which all theologians have had to deal, having posited an all-knowing and all-powerful God, is to explain the source of suffering and misery to which man is subjected. To Garvey that question took a particular poignancy for the Black man, who had endured more than his share of suffering. As he forthrightly queried, "If God is God, and He is God, if He is the God of love and of justice, how can He permanently permit these men [who oppress us] to rule the destiny of all mankind?"[7] In the various answers which Garvey offered to this question he identified several other attributes of God. On the one hand, God had to be a God of absolute impartiality and fairness, which was the meaning of the oft-repeated phrase, God is no respecter of persons. In an extended explication of this theme Garvey observed,

> There can be no God if there be inequality in the creation or in the creative purpose of God. And there could be no God that would create a race to be a race of slaves and another to be one of Masters. That race, this race of slaves, would reject such a God.
> There is no God who would create me a black man, to be a hewer of wood and a drawer of water. It is a lie! It is a damned lie.

If there is such a God, then I would have to look for another God. But there is no such God. The God that exists, the God that I love, the God that you also love and adore, is a God of love, a God of Mercy, a God of Charity and a God that is no respecter of persons. Such a God I worship; such a God I adore; and such a God I know would never place me here especially to be a hewer of wood, a drawer of water, a picker of cotton and a laborer in a cane field. He placed me here AS MY SOVEREIGN LORD to make of life whatsoever I desire to do. If I want to be an industrial captain, it is all left to my selection. God has no plantation; He is not an economist; He has nothing to do with the affairs of men or the economic arrangements of humanity. Otherwise he would be an unfair God. [8]

From the premise that God is absolutely impartial and is not a respecter of persons, Garvey at various times offered two different and perhaps finally irreconcilable lines of argumentation. On the one hand, he insisted that whereas God is not responsible for a race's being in or out of slavery, the responsibility and the fault had to be placed squarely on the enslaved race itself. "You take yourselves into slavery," he insisted, "and you will remain in that state so long as you lack human will."

Some of us flatter ourselves to believe that God is with us and God is a being who is taking care of us in this serfdom and peonage and slavery that we are enduring. God is vexed with you because you are subordinating the powers that He gave you. [9]

On another occasion he declared,

God is not going to save you. He has done all He possibly could: He has given you a life to live, and if you do not exercise your own will in your own behalf you will be lost. God does not interfere with the temporal things of life; He does not interfere with the political destiny of races and nations; God is concerned with the spiritual destiny of man and not the political destiny of man. [10]

And on still another occasion he said,

> There are two understandings of God ... the
> scientific and the sentimental. The Negro assumes
> the sentimental idea, and therein he makes his big
> mistake. We must not blame God for our servile
> condition, because God gave us our physical self
> and made us lords of creation on an equality with
> all other men; nor must we blame the white man,
> who is similarly using the ability given to him by
> God. We have only ourselves to blame. "The
> fault is not in our stars, but in ourselves, that we
> are underlings."[11]

It should be noted that at the heart of the "scientific" understanding to which Garvey alluded was his assumption that life
is essentially a struggle for existence in which only the
"fittest," in the Darwinian sense of that word, survive. Garvey was here drawing upon, or at least allying himself with,
the theologizing of William H. Ferris, who declared repeatedly
in Negro World editorials that a scientific God had empowered
man with a will to act, and then thrown him back on his own
resources either to survive or to be destroyed.[12]

For the most part Garvey argued this line consistently,
insisting that as absolute impartiality, God does not side for
or against one race or another; that each group and each individual receives its just deserts; and thus that one ought not
to sit around and pray to God for the help one could best
give oneself. On the other hand, Garvey occasionally argued
that since God is just and fair and since one particular race
has suffered so much, a time is coming when retribution
will be paid. Indeed, the trials through which God had put
the Negro race must reflect a special purpose for which He
is preparing them:

> If humanity is regarded as made up of the
> children of God, and God loves all humanity--we
> all know that--then God will be more pleased with
> that race that protects all humanity than with that
> race that outrages all humanity. Up to now, we
> have found no race in power that has held out a
> helping hand and protection to all humanity, and it
> is apparent that that position is left for the new
> Ethiopia. Let us, therefore, continue our journey,
> man. I believe when we reach the goal we shall
> reign forever, because we shall be the elect of
> God. He must have had His purpose when He took
> us through the rigors of slavery for more than two

William H. Ferris (from Album of the Academic Class
of 1895, Yale University).

hundred and fifty years.... [T]here must be some wonderful purpose of God in bringing us through all we had to endure in the past three hundred years, down to the present, and I attribute it to that prophecy of God that His children shall one day stretch forth their hands again unto Him.[13]

While this theme of God's special action on behalf of the Negro race was thus present in Garvey's thinking, it must be emphasized that it was a subordinate theme, and one which was much more frequently heard from other speakers in Liberty Hall. It seems to have occurred to Garvey only in connection with the "special prophecy" of the Psalmist. On one occasion he went so far as to declare, "Otherwise I would not believe in God; but I am persuaded to believe in Him because He Himself said, 'Princes shall come out of Egypt and Ethiopia shall stretch forth her hands unto God.'"[14] However, even though Garvey was willing to draw upon the "chosenness" theme, with its connotation of a God who chooses and who acts in history on behalf of justice, he much more frequently spoke of an impartial God who had created man with the capacity to act on his own behalf, and repeatedly insisted that God should not be besieged with petitions for the help that one should give oneself.

Christ and His Work

Garvey was adamant in his insistence on the indisputability of the existence of God, regardless of how He might be conceptualized. It is interesting to discover, however, that he was much less certain as to the historicity of Jesus and to claims that He was the Christ. Thus, in the chapter of the confidential Lesson Guides devoted to the topic of "Christ," Garvey began with the observation that "Christ is supposed to be the begotten Son of God," whose special mission was to take the form of man in order "to teach man how to lift himself back to God."[15] He even found it necessary to offer a defense of the very idea of a Christ, declaring that "If Christ as man never existed, but was only an assumption it would have been a glorious assumption to set man a spiritual high example of how he should live." Just as one does not doubt the existence of one's great-grandfather, though never having seen him, so one ought not to doubt the existence of Christ. Garvey thus advised his students to "Deny that positively which you know of, and not that which you do not know of."[16]

It is difficult to ascertain whether Garvey's doubts about the historical Jesus as Christ were a reaction against the "Jesus, meek and mild, " whose turned cheek was the model preached by white Christians to Blacks, or whether he simply could not accept as intellectually tenable the risen Christ of orthodox Christianity which the then-flourishing "higher criticism" was bringing into question. In any case, Garvey never discussed the question in public; and he had no difficulty in accepting as the highest ideal for all of mankind both the central teaching of Jesus, which was love, and Jesus as the model of the moral life.

It was imperative, of course, that the doctrine of Christ be properly understood. Just as was the case in his discussion of the nature of God, this meant first of all that He had to be conceived historically as a Black man. One of the most spectacular ceremonies which took place under UNIA auspices, and the event which probably caused more comment throughout the United States in both the white and the Black press than any other in Liberty Hall, was the divine service for "the canonization of the Lord Jesus Christ as the Black Man of Sorrows, and also the canonization of the Blessed Virgin Mary as a black woman."[17] It is in the Lesson Guides, however, where one finds Garvey's private assessment as to the paramount themes which would be emphasized concerning the doctrine of Christ:

> In reading Christian Literature and accepting the doctrine of Jesus Christ lay special claim to your association with Jesus and the Son of God. Show that whilst the white and yellow worlds, that is to say--the worlds of Europe and Asia Minor persecuted and crucified Jesus the Son of God, it was the black race through Simon the black Cirenian [sic] who befriended the Son of God and took up the Cross and bore it alongside of Him up to the heights of Calvary. The Roman Catholics, therefore, have no rightful claim to the Cross nor is any other professing Christian before the Negro. The Cross is the property of the Negro in his religion because it was he who bore it.
>
> Never admit that Jesus Christ was a white man, otherwise he could not be the Son of God and God to redeem all mankind. Jesus Christ had the blood of all races in his veins, and tracing the Jewish race back to Abraham and to Moses, from which Jesus sprang through the line of Jesse, you

>will find Negro blood everywhere, so Jesus had
>much of Negro blood in him. [18]

Implicit in the latter portion of this statement is a
principled universalism in Christ, for Garvey's claim was
not that Jesus Christ was of pure African descent, but that
He "had the blood of all races in his veins," and on this
depended His capacity to redeem all of mankind. The over-
all impact of the remarks, however, was to reinforce a
particularistic interpretation of Christ's significance. This
was accomplished primarily through emphasis on the centrality of Simon the Cyrenian, the Black man who had been
forced to bear Jesus' Cross up Calvary Hill. By virtue of
this unique deed Garvey argued that the Negro race stood in
a special relationship to Jesus; and on occasion this special
act of Simon's was publicly contrasted with the act of be-
trayal by the white men who, he suggested, had to bear
responsibility for Christ's crucifixion:

>Give us the standard bearer of Christ; let him
>lead and we shall follow, Christ the crucified,
>Christ the despised, we appeal to you from the
>great memories of the past; we appeal to you for
>help, for succor and for leadership.... Oh Jesus
>the Christ, oh Jesus the Redeemer, when white
>men scorned you, when white men spurned you,
>when white men spat upon you, when white men
>pierced your side out of which blood and water
>gushed forth, it was a black man in the person
>of Simon the Cyrenian who took the cross and
>bore it on heights of calvary. As he bore it in
>the past to lighten your burden as you climbed
>your Calvary, so now, when we are climbing our
>calvary and the burden being heavy--Jesus we ask
>you to help us on the journey up the heights. [19]

In terms of Garvey's use of Jesus as a model for the
present world, this passage also points to one aspect of His
life on earth, namely, Jesus the despised, the rejected, the
one who bears undeserved suffering, and who thereby has a
special affection for those who are despised, rejected, and
forced to bear unmerited suffering. This model of Jesus as
suffering servant was always balanced, however, with the
model of Jesus as great reformer or as "the greatest radical," who suffers unto death, it is true, but who does not
do so meekly. In one Easter sermon Garvey characterized
Jesus as having met the same resistance to His message to

which "all reformers and reform movements" are subject
when they cease to preach a strictly spiritual message and
demand that existing social and economic relationships be
transformed. When it became clear that Jesus' message
was both spiritual and temporal, He was quickly declared
to be an impostor, a dangerous individual who must be destroyed.

> When Jesus came the privileged few were
> taking advantage of the unfortunate masses. Be-
> cause the teaching of Jesus sought to equalize the
> spiritual and even the temporal rights of man,
> those who held authority, sway and dominion sought
> His liberty by prosecution, sought His life by death.
> He was called to yield up that life for the cause
> He loved--because He was indeed a great reformer. [20]

On another occasion Christ was characterized, like
"all great reformers, " to be a radical--one who was rough,
unyielding, uncompromising, fearing only God. "All true
warriors know no fear. Our friends are fainthearted, but
Jesus Christ was the greatest radical the world ever saw.
Jesus opposed wrong. His program was to lift up humanity
and save mankind. "[21] And on still another occasion the
theme of Christ, the One who suffers, and Christ, the
Greatest Reformer, were conflated as parts of a whole:

> If we could see the sufferings of Christ, if we
> could see the patience of Christ, if we could see
> the very crucifixion of Christ, then we would see
> the creature, the being spiritual that God would
> have us to be; and knowing ourselves as we do,
> we could well realize how far we are from God. . . .
> [T]he world derided Him; the world scoffed at Him;
> they called Him all kinds of names. He was an
> imposter; He was a disturber of the public peace;
> He was not fit to be among good society; He was
> an outcast; He was a traitor to the king. . . .
> Christ was the first great reformer. . . .
> [T]here is one lesson we can learn from the
> teachings of Christ. . . . [T]he spiritual doctrines
> of Jesus were righteous; the doctrines of Jesus
> were just, and even though He died nearly nine-
> teen hundred years ago, what has happened? After
> the lapse of nineteen hundred years His religion is
> the greatest moving force in the world today, mor-
> ally and spiritually. It shows you, therefore, the
> power of a righteous cause. [22]

Anthropology

For Garvey, as for most theologians, there are ana-
logues between one's doctrine of God and one's conception of
man. This was the point, after all, of Garvey's insistence
that God had in some sense to be Black, for it affirmed that
Black men were fully men, that they were coequal sons of
God with all other of His sons, and that they too would share
in the divine inheritance. Garvey made explicit the inter-
connection between the doctrines of God and of man, in a
speech to a UNIA audience in Cincinnati.

> Do you know what it is to be a man? To be
> a man is to bear the semblance of my Creator,
> the image of my Creator. If you are conscious of
> the fact that you were created in the image of your
> Creator, then you realize that you are a man.
> Man is the supreme lord, the supreme master of
> the world. [23]

The most definitive public statement of Garvey's doctrine of man was published in a front page editorial of the
Negro World and was entitled "Dissertation on Man." In this
statement (reproduced here only in part) one can discern
several key elements in his conception of the nature of man.

> Man is the individual who is able to shape his
> own character, master his own will, direct his own
> life and shape his own ends.
> When God breathed into the nostrils of man
> the breath of life, made him a living soul, and be-
> stowed upon him the authority of Lord of Creation,
> He never intended that that individual should descend
> to the level of a peon, a serf, or a slave, but that
> he should be always man in the fullest possession
> of his senses, and with the truest knowledge of him-
> self.
> But how changed has man become since crea-
> tion? We find him today divided into different
> classes--the helpless imbecile class, the sycophan-
> tic class, the slave class, the servant class and
> the master class. These different classes God
> never created. He created Man. But this indi-
> vidual has so retrograded, as to make it impossible
> to find him. It is so difficult to find a real man.
> As far as our race goes, I hardly believe that
> we can find one hundred real men who are able to

> measure up to the higher purpose of the creation.
> It is because of this lack of manhood in us as a
> race why [sic] we have stagnated for several cen-
> turies and now find ourselves at the foot of the
> great human ladder....
> After the creation, and after man was given
> possession of the world, the Creator relinquished
> all authority to his lord, except that which was
> spiritual. All that authority which meant the regu-
> lation of human affairs, human society, and human
> happiness was given to man by the Creator, and
> man, therefore, became master of his own destiny,
> and architect of his own fate.[24]

Man is here understood above all else as a creature
whose will is free to act as he chooses; he is a lord over
creation in his own right, who was made by the supreme
Lord of Creation to serve no other man. Distinctions of
class or intelligence are not indelible distinctions bestowed
by God, but are the manifestations of the failure to realize
the potential for which man is intended. The Creator has
stepped back from his creation to see how and what man can
accomplish with his God-given powers, and man must depend
upon his own resources to achieve what he will.

The attributes of God which Garvey describes in their
infinity are characteristic of man in his finitude. Thus, in
the passage cited earlier describing God as Universal Intelligence, Garvey observed that it was precisely in man's intelligence that he shared the likeness of God, though of course
that intelligence was only partial and incomplete.[25] Whereas
God was characterized as absolute power in his capacity as
Lord of Creation, man has also been given dominion as a
lord of creation to utilize physical, material power for his
own benefit and for the benefit of his fellow man. And whereas God is understood as absolute impartiality, so man must
recognize that he is created equal to all other men, with no
group being divinely intended to reign over the other.

While man has the capacity, then, as a free agent to
act with benevolence and charity toward his fellow man, inas-
much as he is created in the image of an impartial God, the
cruel and harsh fact is that for the most part he does not so
behave. The dark side of man's nature, his capacity for
evil, was by no means neglected in Garvey's theology. This
theme is elaborated in the eleventh of his Lesson Guides
written for the School of African Philosophy, in the chapter

entitled "Man."

Man because of his sin which caused him to have
fallen from his high estate of spiritual cleanliness
to the level of a creature, who acts only for his
own satisfaction by the gift of freewill, must be
regarded as a dangerous creature of life. When
he wants he can be good, otherwise he is generally
bad. If dealing with him you must calculate for
his vices and his damnable evils. He is apt to
disappoint you at any time therefore you cannot
wholly rely on him as an individual. Always try
to touch him with the hope of bringing out that
which is good, but be ever on your guard to experience the worst that is in him, because he is
always in conflict with himself as between good and
evil.

When he can profit from evil he will do it and
forget goodness. This has been his behaviour ever
since the first record of his existence and his first
contact with his fellows.

Cain slew Abel for his success. Jacob robbed
Esau of his birthright and down the ages of human
history man has been robbing, exploiting and mur-
dering man for gain....

The passion of man is in evidence everywhere.
It revolts against affection, kindness and even love
when it has a personal object to attain....

Seek first to know him then before you completely trust him, because you are apt to be disappointed. A man shakes your hand today and tomorrow he is chief witness against you for execution.
What is it that has caused him to do that. It is
his vileness. Know it then that he is vile, and
only when you know him sufficiently may you trust
him as far as your judgment would dictate....

It is generally evil, which gives you evidence
sufficient that man is vile and only in remote in-
stances good. If you know it then, why take the
chance of always believing before seeing? The
taste of the pudding is the proof of it. Know your
man before you believe. Never believe before you
know. Let your mission be always to make man
good, therefore talk to man always from the loftiest
pinnacle. You may convert somebdoy [sic], you
may turn a vile man good, and if you succeed in

doing this in even one instance you have accomplished a great work.[26]

It should not be supposed that this understanding of
man was only applicable to interpersonal relations and the
caution with which future UNIA leaders should approach their
fellow man, or that this insight concerning man's capacity
for evil was something which Garvey discussed only privately
with his most intimate associates. On the contrary, this
theme was the subject of frequent public comment. One of
the most notable presentations of the theme was included in
Garvey's opening address to the Third International Convention (1922), where Garvey declared

> From the fall of Adam man became a rebel-
> lious, wicked, covetous, murderous creature, yes
> man from the time of Cain and Abel coveted the
> property of his brother man, became envious of
> his brother's success, yes, it was on the principle
> of injustice that Cain killed Abel, it is on the same
> principle of injustice that England exploits Africa,
> that France exploits Africa, that Italy exploits
> Africa, that Belgium exploits Africa, that the
> stronger nations of the world exploit the weak.
> Jesus the great Redeemer came to save man from
> his fallen state, but man, because of his wicked-
> ness, because of his murderous principles, re-
> jected the teachings of Christ, and man was never
> satisfied until he nailed even the Christ to the Cross
> of Calvary. Man is wicked, man is envious, man
> is rebellious, man is murderous, and you can ex-
> pect very little of man. The only protection against
> injustice in man is power, physical power, financial
> power, educational power, scientific power, power of
> every kind; it is that power that the Universal Negro
> Improvement Association is encouraging Negroes to
> get for themselves.[27]

Garvey here illustrates the social consequence of man's
sinfulness, and makes clear that the individual man's capacity
for evil is only compounded when he organizes himself in
groups. The same covetousness of another's property which
drove Cain to slay his brother has driven nation to rob from
nation. Significantly, in the previously cited passage which
described the sinfulness of the individual man, Garvey spoke
at least of the possibility of converting him, of turning him
from his evil ways toward the good. When speaking of men

in groups, however, there is no indication that it is possible
for such a "conversion" to occur. The only appropriate
category by which races or nations can address one another
is power.

Doctrine of Salvation

Just as there is a two-fold aspect to the nature of
man, namely, man's capacity for evil on the one hand and
his creation as a free agent in the likeness of God on the
other; so there is a dual aspect to Garvey's doctrine of salvation. The persistent self-reliance which was at the heart
of his social philosophy meant that salvation had to lie within
man's own grasp and could not rest solely on the salvific act
of another. Salvation would be achieved not by faith alone,
but by the persistent work of every man. In the previous
chapter, reference was made to Garvey's "beatitude of bread
and butter," in which he had declared, "this is the time for
our salvation. Prayer alone will not save us; sentiment
alone will not save us. We have to work and work and work
if we are to be saved."[28] A corollary to this salvation by
work was his adamant rejection of "fatalism," which he repeatedly characterized as the bane of the race's existence.
In his powerful Easter sermon entitled "The Resurrection of
the Negro," Garvey declared,

> Some of us seem to accept the fatalist posi-
> tion, the fatalist attitude, that God accorded to us a
> certain position and condition, and therefore there
> is no need trying to be otherwise. The moment you
> accept such an attitude, the moment you accept such
> an opinion, the moment you harbor such an idea,
> you hurl an insult at the great God who created you,
> because you question Him for His love, you question
> Him for His mercy.... All that you see in crea-
> tion, all that you see in the world, was created by
> God for the use of man, and you four hundred mil-
> lion black souls have as much right to your posses-
> sion in this world as any other man.
> Created in the image of the same God we have
> the same common future, and tonight I trust that
> there will be a spiritual and material and a temporal
> resurrection among Negroes everywhere.[29]

If one side of Garvey's doctrine of salvation was emphasis upon work, individual self-reliance, and a rejection of

fatalism, the other (social) side of his concept of salvation was his admonition to secure power. As would be anticipated, given his basically Arian Christology, Jesus was not himself the instrument or vehicle of salvation. As the great reformer or the "greatest radical," He empowered man to act for his own and his people's salvation. The demand for power was argued most persuasively in one of Garvey's Negro World editorials:

> Gradually, even though slowly, we are getting to realize that the fight is now or never. We have to fight for a place in the world if we must exist; that place is not going to be yielded up to us by philanthropy, by charity, but only through that stronger power that will compel others to give us that which is our due. I say POWER because it is necessary. Except the individual, the race or the nation has power that is exclusive; it means that that individual, that race or that nation will be bound by the will of the other who possesses this great qualification. It was the physical and pugilistic power of Jack Johnson that kept him in the ring. It was the industrial and scientific power of the Teutonic race that kept them for years as the dictators of the economic and scientific policies of Europe. It is the military, naval, and political power of Great Britain that keeps her mistress of the world; hence it is advisable for the Negro to get power; get power of every kind, power in education, in science, in industry, in politics, in higher government, and physically. We want that kind of power that will stand out signally so that other races and nations can see, and if they won't see, feel. POWER is the only argument that satisfies man. Man is not satisfied; neither is he moved by prayers, by petitions, but every man is moved by that power of authority which forces him to do, even against his will.... The only advice I can give the Negro is to get power. [30]

In the final analysis it must be said that the salvation Garvey most earnestly sought was both social and this-worldly. He shared with the proponents of the Social Gospel who were his contemporaries a rejection both of the overemphasis on salvation of the individual soul and of an other-worldly orientation which led to neglect of man's physical and social needs. In his passionate demand for social justice, however, he had no illusion that the Kingdom was nearly at hand. In fact, a fair reading of the times indicated that things were getting worse, not better, in the present world. As Garvey remarked at the conclusion of his survey of international events during the previous year, "Those of us who lead the Universal Negro Improvement Association can interpret the signs of the times. We foresee the time when the great white race in America will have grown numerically to the point of selfish race exclusion, when no common appeal to humanity will save our competitive race from their prejudice and injustice, hence the Universal Negro Improvement Association warns the Negro of America as well as of the western world of the dangers of the future, and advises that the best effort of today should be that concentrated on the building up of a national home of our own in Africa."[31] With this pessimistic forecast of the course of racial relations, Garvey insisted that justice could be achieved only by a fair distribution of power. "Why does the white man act today as he does towards you and me?" he queried, and then answered his own question: "It is not because there is a difference between us in religion or in color, but because there is a difference between us in power."[32]

Eschatology: The Redemption of Africa

In keeping with his insistent demand that attention be focused on the present world, Garvey rarely spoke of life after death and he never spoke of it in compensatory terms so as to suggest that injustices of the present would be rectified on the other side of the grave. Death was not something to be feared but was to be welcomed, especially if it came as a consequence of fighting for the freedom of Africa. A note of apocalypticism frequently crept into his language as he spoke of the impending world conflagration that he insisted (only a year or two after the end of World War I) was bound to come.

> Keep your eyes steadfast on the object, and what is it? It is the emancipation of four hundred million souls. It is the freeing of our own country Africa and the making of it of a great United States, a powerful government, not to be controlled by alien races, but to be dominated by ourselves. This is the object, this is the vision, for this we live, and for this we will die....
> As the war clouds gather let us gird our loins and in greater numbers and stronger determination

hold fast until the hour comes, and come it surely
will.... [F]our hundred million Negroes [are]
ready for the march toward African redemption. [33]

This apocalyptic element was made even more explicit
in Garvey's long poem, "The Tragedy of White Injustice."
He regarded this poem as of crucial importance in revealing
the true character of the white man's behavior and the opportunity that his avarice would present to the Black man:

> The white man now enjoys his "Vanity Fair";
> He thinks of self and not of others care--
> Fratricidal course, that to hell doth lead--
> This is poison upon which the gentry feed....
>
> Out of the clear of God's Eternity
> Shall rise a kingdom of Black Fraternity;
> There shall be conquests o'er militant forces;
> For as man proposes, God disposes.
> Signs of retribution are on every hand:
> Be ready, black men, like Gideon's band.
> They may scoff and mock at you today,
> But get you ready for the awful fray. [34]

While Garvey repeatedly denounced those who called
for renunciation of the present world and its vale of woes in
favor of a life to come, this is by no means to suggest that
he did not articulate a vision of the future towards which his
people could look with expectation and hope. This vision
was embodied in the powerful image of the "Redemption of
Africa," one of the most enduring and potent motivating myths
in Black American religious history. As St. Clair Drake has
demonstrated, the image of the "redemption of Africa" had
served throughout the nineteenth century as "one important
focus of meaningful activity among New World Negroes," and
as "an energizing myth in both the New World and in Africa
itself for those pre-political movements that arose while the
powerless were gathering their strength for realistic and re-
warding political activity." [35] It was revitalized in the twentieth century by Marcus Garvey, who seemed to want to make
it a legitimate political goal as the specific objective of the
UNIA. Even for Garvey, however, the "redemption of Africa"
functioned primarily in a religious sense as the eschatological
goal toward which all of history was leading, and for the
realization of which all one's efforts ought to be directed.
In one of his many eloquent statements of this theme, Garvey
illustrated how the vision of Africa redeemed could empower

The journal for which Marcus Garvey wrote
while living in London, 1912-1914.

one to act on his own behalf for the uplift of the race:

> I have a vision of the future, and I see before
> me a picture of a redeemed Africa, with her dotted
> cities, with her beautiful civilization, with her mil-
> lions of happy children, going to and fro. Why
> should I lose hope, why should I give up and take
> a back place in this age of progress? Remember
> that you are men, that God created you Lords of
> this creation. Lift up yourselves, men, take your-
> selves out of the mire and hitch your hopes to the
> stars; yes, rise as high as the very stars them-
> selves. Let no man pull you down, let no man
> destroy your ambition, because man is but your
> companion, your equal; man is your brother; he is
> not your lord; he is not your sovereign master. [36]

Even when denying that his "vision of the future" was
anything more than a careful analysis of political realities,
his prophetic self-consciousness was never far from the surface. This was evident in a speech Garvey delivered to a
midwestern audience that had gathered to hear the political
program of the UNIA.

> I am sounding this second warning, and I want
> you to take it from a man who feels the conscious-
> ness of what he says. I am not pretending to be a
> prophet; I am not pretending to be a sage or a
> philosopher. I am but an ordinary man with
> ordinary common sense who can see where
> the wind blows, and the man who is so foolish
> as not to be able to see and understand where the
> wind blows, I am sorry for him.... I can see
> where the wind is blowing, and it is because of
> what I see that I am talking to you like this. [37]

The wind only bloweth, however, as the gospel writer tells
us, where it listeth, and the one who can discern where it
blows is surely a man of God. Garvey knew which way the
wind was moving, and, as he declared in one of his most
celebrated passages, its object was Africa:

> No one knows when the hour of Africa's Re-
> demption cometh. It is in the wind. It is coming.
> One day, like a storm, it will be here. When that
> day comes all Africa will stand together. [38]

Ecclesiology

The proper way in which to conceptualize the UNIA as a religious or quasi-religious organization was a matter of considerable concern to Marcus Garvey. Given the fragmentation of the Black churches and the tenacity of denominational loyalties among both clergy and laity, it was clear that the UNIA could never succeed as simply one more denomination or sect from which one might choose one's religious affiliation. As will be made evident in the next chapter, the struggle between Garvey and George Alexander McGuire (after Garvey, the UNIA's most perceptive and creative theologian) hinged precisely on this issue, for McGuire sought to establish the African Orthodox Church as the official religious organization of the UNIA, and would have had Garveyites attending the AOC on Sunday mornings in place of their own churches. Garvey worked to avoid the untenable position of forcing his followers to choose between the UNIA and any particular Black denomination.

An unsigned article appearing in the Negro World in August 1923 stated the goal for which Garvey was striving in terms of his ecclesiology:

> The churches were not doing the work undertaken by Marcus Garvey, yet some preachers are among the crusaders. A full explanation of their attitude might be pretty hard to arrive at and harder to state without entering on contentious matter. It is enough simply to point out the obvious fact that Negro churches are divided, in some cases forbidden to work together with other movements, and they furnish no convenient meeting-ground for united work. Only a movement that welcomes all people of all denominations and is officially attached to none while having its own assembly halls can spread its net wide enough to gather in all people desiring to identify with it.[39]

Garvey as Black Theologian

The last quoted statement is as close as we are likely to come to an explicit formulation of the all-embracing role into which Garvey sought to cast the UNIA. What he was struggling to institutionalize can most accurately be described as a species of civil religion, or more specifically, a Black

civil religion. It provided a common set of shared beliefs
and value commitments which sought to bind its adherents--
all those men and women of African descent who proudly
took the name Negro--into a collectivity which was divinely
called to a special task in the world. The movement possessed its own meeting halls, its own order of worship as
set forth in the Ritual, its distinctive set of beliefs, and
even special holidays of its own creation. The beliefs and
rituals of the UNIA, however, were of a sufficiently high
level of generality so that in assenting to them one could
continue to adhere to particular doctrines and practices of
the separate Black denominations; and one could still attend
those churches on Sunday mornings while participating in
UNIA activities on Sunday evenings.

    The symbols, rituals, and beliefs which constituted
the inchoate Black civil religion were, of course, not new
to Garvey's audience; indeed, had they been new they would
not have found a responsive hearing. They rather grew out
of and built upon a shared experience of slavery and of
racial discrimination, as that experience was interpreted in
the light of a transcendent goal: the uplift of the Negro race
and the Redemption of Africa. They stood as symbols of
national solidarity, binding all men who willingly accepted
the hitherto opprobrious term "Negro" into a single people
whom God had specially chosen for the task of building up a
nation in Africa--a nation capable, first, of securing that
continent's freedom and, second, of ensuring the rights of
Negroes wherever they might reside in the world.

    It should be evident that the characterization of Marcus
Garvey as Black theologian is one that is being made not simply by virtue of the fact that a considerable number of Garvey's speeches took up the subject matter of religion; nor is
it being made as a result of his insistence that God must be
painted Black. The point is rather that in an unsystematic
but nevertheless consistent manner Garvey was persistently
about the business of interpreting the world and its travails
in an ultimately meaningful way. Though rejecting any dog-
matic claim concerning the finality of his own perceptions,
Garvey was convinced of the indelibly religious nature of man.
It was precisely his relativism, coupled with his ineradicable
belief in the transcendent, which permitted Garvey to have no
qualms about defining God, man, Christ, and Providence, in
the light of the historical experiences and needs of his own
people. God was never the God only of men and women of
African descent; yet He was uniquely the God of Ethiopia who

had promised that princes would be brought forth out of Egypt and into their own inheritance. The themes were by no means new to the tradition of the Black church; what was distinctive was the uncompromising this-worldly context in which they were interpreted, and the supra-institutional structure into which Garvey sought to organize them.

Notes

1. NW 10:1 (February 19, 1921), p. 10.

2. "Speech of Marcus Garvey Outlining Discussion on Formulating of Plans to Unify the Religious Beliefs and Practices of the Entire Negro Race," The Blackman (Kingston), August 31, 1929, p. 13.

3. P&O, I, 44.

4. Marcus Garvey's address "Africa and the Negro," delivered at the Florida Avenue Presbyterian Church, Washington, D.C., January 16, 1924. NW 15:25 (February 2, 1924), p. 7. See also NW 16:26 (August 9, 1924), p. 7.

5. Lesson 6, God, "Intelligence, Education, Universal Knowledge and How to Get It." (Mimeographed, n.d.), p. 1.

6. Lesson 14, Self-Initiative, ibid., pp. 2, 3.

7. NW 11:21 (January 7, 1922), p. 1.

8. NW 14:6 (March 24, 1923), p. 7. Benjamin E. Mays finds this theme of the "impartiality of God" to be predominant among Blacks in the period following World War I. See especially chapter 6 of his study, The Negro's God.

9. NW 11:10 (October 22, 1921), p. 2.

10. NW 13:15 (November 25, 1922), p. 2.

11. NW 12:4 (March 11, 1922), p. 9.

12. On Ferris, see below, chapter 4 and also his lengthy editorial "The World in Which We Live," NW 9:12

(November 6, 1920), p. 2. For Garvey on the
theme of the "survival of the fittest," see for example NW 9:12 (November 6, 1920), p. 8; NW 12:6
(March 25, 1922), p. 11; and NW 13:13 (November
11, 1922), p. 1.

13. "Emancipation Day Speech," NW 11:22 (January 14,
1922), p. 3; partially reprinted, though without reference to the "elect of God," in P&O, I, 79-82.
Emphasis added.

14. NW 13:15 (November 25, 1922), p. 2.

15. Lesson 6, Christ, "Intelligence," p. 1. Emphasis
added.

16. Ibid.

17. NW 17:4 (September 6, 1924), p. 2. The event is
described in detail in Amy Jacques Garvey, Garvey
and Garveyism, pp. 139-142 and in Edmund David
Cronon, Black Moses, pp. 179 ff.

18. Lesson 1, "Intelligence," p. 11.

19. NW 11:2 (August 27, 1921), p. 3.

20. P&O, I, 87-88. Emphasis added.

21. NW 11:25 (February 4, 1922), p. 9.

22. Garvey's Christmas eve sermon entitled "Christ the
Greatest Reformer," P&O, II, 28, 29 and 30.

23. One of the conclusions to be drawn from this fact, Garvey continued, was that man owed no obedience to his
fellow man. "God, when creating man, never set one
race over another; let's behave as men, cringe before
none." NW 10:2 (February 26, 1921), p. 5.

24. NW 12:11 (April 29, 1922), p. 1. The text is also
printed in P&O, I, 24-25, though with numerous editorial changes. I have here used the text printed in
the Negro World.

25. See above, p. 48.

26. Lesson 11, Man, "Intelligence," pp. 1-3.

27. "Speech of Hon. Marcus Garvey ... Delivered at the 71st Regiment Armory Tuesday Night, August 1st," pamphlet, n. d., pp. 8-9. The text of the speech is also reprinted in NW 12:25 (August 5, 1922), pp. 3, 4. For other public explications of the theme of man's sinfulness, see NW 11:6 (September 24, 1921), p. 1 and NW 13:10 (October 21, 1922), p. 2.

28. NW 10:1 (February 19, 1921), p. 1, cited in its full context above.

29. NW 12:10 (April 22, 1922), p. 9; also printed in slightly different form in P&O, I, 87-92. Several of Garvey's poems written while in prison in Atlanta, take up the argument against fatalism. See, for example, the poems "Why Disconsolate?"; "Have Faith in Self"; and "Find Yourself" in Selections from the Poetic Meditations of Marcus Garvey, ed. Amy Jacques Garvey (New York, c. 1927), pp. 7, 8, and 17.

30. NW 12:16 (June 3, 1922), p. 1. Italics in original.

31. "Speech of Marcus Garvey ... August 1st" (1922), p. 16.

32. NW 14:2 (February 24, 1923), p. 2.

33. NW 13:22 (January 13, 1923), p. 1.

34. Marcus Garvey, The Tragedy of White Injustice, ed. Amy Jacques Garvey (New York, 1927), Cantos 65 and 66.

35. St. Clair Drake, The Redemption of Africa, p. 11.

36. NW 12:3 (March 4, 1922), p. 1; also printed in P&O, I, 77-78.

37. NW 10:2 (February 26, 1921), p. 4.

38. P&O, I, 10.

39. NW 14:25 (August 4, 1923), p. 2. Emphasis added.

CHAPTER 3

SECT OR CIVIL RELIGION: THE DEBATE
WITH GEORGE ALEXANDER MCGUIRE

The rituals and beliefs which constituted Garveyism
as a religious movement have been described in some detail
in the preceding chapters. It remains to be shown how these
rituals and beliefs were finally given acceptable organizational expression. The problem was a difficult one, given
the importance of the Black churches to the work of the
UNIA, and a workable solution emerged only after considerable controversy among the UNIA leadership. Principals in
the debate were Garvey and his foremost colleague in the
Association, the Reverend George Alexander McGuire.

McGuire was preeminent among the theologians whom
Garvey had at work rewriting theology for the UNIA, and although there has been confusion and misunderstanding as to
the precise relationship between his African Orthodox Church
and the UNIA, McGuire has been generally recognized as a
central figure in UNIA leadership. In order to appreciate
his contribution to the rituals and beliefs of the UNIA, we
will look carefully at two remarkable documents which Mc-
Guire produced in his first year as Chaplain-General, the
Universal Negro Ritual and the Universal Negro Catechism.
Implicit in these two works, however, were the seeds for
serious conflict between the UNIA and the Black churches.
It has not been widely known that between late 1921 and mid-
1923 Garvey and McGuire were in open conflict with one another, to the point that the latter was read out of the Association and denounced as a traitor. It will here be argued
that an important cause for this episode was the differing
perceptions which each man had concerning the proper organizational form which religion could and should take within
the UNIA. Once these differences were resolved and Mc-
Guire acknowledged the wisdom of making his African Orthodox Church a distinct denomination in no way organically

related to the UNIA, he was welcomed back into the movement and served for several years as honorary Chaplain-General.

Background in the Protestant Episcopal Church

Like Garvey, George Alexander McGuire was a West Indian by origin, born in Sweets, Antigua, in 1866. He received his early theological training in a small seminary sponsored by the Moravians (the church to which his mother belonged) in Nisky, St. Thomas, graduating probably in 1888. For several years thereafter he pastored a Moravian congregation at Frederiksted, St. Croix, but when he came to the United States in 1894 he chose to be confirmed in the Protestant Episcopal Church. His father had belonged to the Anglican Church in Antigua, and he had his son baptized in that denomination.[1]

For four years McGuire served as assistant to Dr. Henry L. Phillips, prominent pastor of the Church of the Crucifixion in Philadelphia, Pennsylvania. Ordained deacon on June 29, 1896 and priest in the following year, he was sent to his first parish assignment, St. Andrews Church of Cincinnati, Ohio, in 1898.[2] From Cincinnati he returned to Philadelphia and there served for five years as rector of St. Thomas Church, the oldest Black Episcopal church in the United States.

The next four years, from 1905 to 1908, constitute an important interlude in McGuire's career, especially with respect to the development of his ideas concerning an interracial ministry. For it was during these years, while serving as Archdeacon of Colored Work in the diocese of Arkansas, that McGuire came into contact with the infamous "Bad" Bishop William Montgomery Brown (1855-1937), who was then presiding over the diocese. The orphaned child of an impoverished Ohio farmer, Brown married the adopted daughter of a wealthy Cleveland philanthropist (who happened to be an energetic Episcopalian) and was sent off to theological school, after which "he wrote a book on why everyone should be Episcopalian, and thus became Bishop of Arkansas."[3] Significantly, it was precisely Brown's thinking on this very point that first got him into trouble with the church. It occurred to him that "everyone" must include Negroes as well as whites; yet the Protestant Episcopal Church had a notoriously bad reputation in terms of work among its Black brethren. To remedy this problem Brown proposed that (another) racial branch of the Episcopal Church be established, this one to be run by Negro clergymen and bishops.[4]

At Brown's request, McGuire wrote, as an addendum to his annual report to the Arkansas Diocese, a statement strongly supporting Brown's "Arkansas Plan" providing for Negro bishops and jurisdictions. This document, included in an appendix to the bishop's book, The Crucial Race Question OR Where and How Shall the Color Line Be Drawn?,[5] reveals both McGuire's eloquent and learned style and the pride of race that characterized his life and thought. Stating from the outset that Brown's proposal "was wise and timely," and would "prove to be an advantage to the growth of the Church ... among both races," he made it clear that the church's record with respect to work among Negroes was nothing in which to take pride. In fact, "that she has been lethargic, penurious, lacking in enthusiastic and united action, and in the thorough arousing of her conscience in this matter, cannot be gainsaid," and indeed, matters are in so bad an estate that "Negro Methodists and Baptists point contemptuously at us as 'a black body with a white head.'"[6]

But it was not the church's neglect that grated most, nor was it simply the sneers of his fellow Christians in all-Black denominations that made the Brown proposal attractive. Rather, he said, it is "my manly dignity, my self-respect, my whole nature--intellectual, social and spiritual--[which] yearns for a Bishop of my own race, who, besides giving me godly admonitions, will enter into my life as he alone can, and who is not prohibited from intermingling in every way, with me and the congregation committed to our charge." Simply put, "We have race pride; and it is that which prompts us to ask for Negro Bishops."[7]

McGuire insisted that there were no circumstances, regardless of the decision made by the hierarchy, which would induce him to leave the Anglican Communion. Nevertheless, the specter was raised of a separatist movement that might result if no affirmative action were taken. He wrote:

> The crucial hour is upon us. Ten million Afro-Americans await anxiously the result of the test. The Church cannot afford to treat us in beautiful generalizations any longer.... Will she rise supremely to the opportunity and the duty of the

> hour, and considering racial differences, prejudices
> and peculiarities, relieve her Negro clergy and
> people of much embarrassment and supply them
> with the entire machinery for doing successful work
> among their own race <u>without becoming schismatics,</u>
> <u>or asking for an autonomous "ecclesiola in eccle-</u>
> <u>sia?"</u>[8]

In spite of his eloquent appeal, the church failed to
respond. In a little over a decade McGuire himself was
cast in the role of the schismatic and was the prime mover
in the founding of the African Orthodox Church. This is to
get somewhat ahead of our story, however, for he remained
at his post in Arkansas for another two years, leaving only
in mid-summer of 1908. The impact of his four-year association with the perhaps well-intentioned and yet obviously
prejudiced Brown, as well as with other more blatantly biased
white Episcopalians in Arkansas, cannot but have sharpened
the edge of McGuire's sensitivity to the potency of racial
prejudice within the United States and particularly within the
churches of the United States. He departed as the result of
a growing awareness that the "Arkansas Plan" for an independent Negro episcopacy was finally unworkable, [9] though
with the firm conviction that the underlying problem it had
addressed must be dealt with if the Episcopal Church were
to prosper among Negroes.

McGuire's reputation as a fiery and articulate spokesman for independent Black Episcopalian churchmen had by
this time reached as far as Boston, where he was called as
the first rector of a Black congregation that had just separated
itself from the white-controlled congregation of St. Peter's.
He remained with the newly formed St. Bartholomew's parish,
Cambridge, from 1909 to 1911, at which time he moved to
New York City to serve as Field Secretary for the American
Church Institute for Negroes. He served at this post for
another two years, returning to his native Antigua in 1913.[10]

There is little evidence as to why McGuire returned
to the West Indies in that year, although one writer suggests
it was the sight of the dilapidated condition of the Church of
St. Paul's (where he had been baptized) while on furlough to
visit his mother in Sweets, Antigua, that had moved him to
return to the Islands and rebuild the parish.[11] In any case,
he did serve at St. Paul's for the next six years, and his
presence there undoubtedly gave him an early opportunity to
become aware of an organization created on the neighboring

island of Jamaica in the summer of 1914, devoted to the
ideals of race pride and race advancement which he himself
cherished. This was, of course, Marcus Garvey's Universal Negro Improvement and Conservation Association.

Election as Chaplain-General

Just when McGuire joined forces with Garvey cannot
be stated with certainty, though within a year of his return
to the United States in July 1919 he was actively participating
in UNIA activities. It is not until August 1920 that his name
appears in the pages of the Negro World, as an energetic
delegate at the spectacular International Convention of the
Negro Peoples of the World, which held its first annual
meeting in Liberty Hall from the first to the thirty-first of
that month. McGuire seems to have taken the delegates by
storm with his eloquent speeches and prayers. His popularity at the convention was assured by the boldness of his
demands for militant action, by his insistent call for a new
style of leadership, and by his verbal blasts at whites. The
Baltimore Afro-American reported that McGuire, "who occu-
pied the Chair in the opening prayer invoked the aid of a God
of Battles. He closed with the last stanzas of Longfellow's
'Psalm of Life' transposing the last line to 'Learn to labor
and fight.' At the substitution of the word 'fight' for that of
'wait' the crowd of 2,000 voiced loud approval."[12]

The New York World, a white newspaper which provided extensive coverage of the annual International Conventions, similarly gave prominence to McGuire's forceful presence. "Excitement among negro delegates to the Universal
Negro Improvement Association in Liberty Hall reached its
highest point yet last night," the paper reported, "when about
1,800 gathered to hear the Rev. Dr. McGuire of Antigua
British West Indies."

> "The Uncle Tom nigger has got to go," he cried,
> "and his place must be taken by the new leader of
> the negro race. That man will not be a white man
> with a black heart, nor a black man with a white
> heart, but a black man with a black heart."
> At that the assembly jumped to its feet crying,
> "Yes sir, yes sir."[13]

Elsewhere the same newspaper quoted McGuire as
having characterized the white race as an avaricious people

which continued to oppress the Negro while claiming to be
bearing, in the name of universal brotherhood, the "white
man's burden":

> The white race is the most avaricious of races.
> Not content with Europe, they took part of Asia
> and Africa. Then they came over here and took
> America from the red man, and because they
> would not work for them, they brought members
> of our race from Africa. They call us the white
> man's burden, and I hope that the burden will keep
> him down until we get back to our homeland. We
> don't want anything from the white man except
> what is ours by divine right. The white people
> say they want humility from the Negro, but what
> they really seek is servility. We must go as
> missionaries among the whites and teach them the
> everlasting brotherhood of man.[14]

At the convention McGuire was elected to the post of
Chaplain-General of the UNIA, replacing the Reverend James
W. H. Eason, an AME Zion clergyman who had been elevated to the post of "Leader of American Negroes." Mc-
Guire showed himself to be more than a good speaker: he
was instrumental in effecting several changes in the UNIA
constitution pertinent to religious issues within the organization. These changes, concerning the role of chaplains at
the local chapter levels and the creation of juvenile branches
in each UNIA division, have earlier been described in some
detail.[15] Their net result was to strengthen the authority of
local chaplains, who were directly responsible to McGuire as
Chaplain-General; and more importantly, to move religion
ever closer to the center of UNIA activities. To appreciate
fully the spiritual, moral, and racial values which McGuire
hoped the UNIA would inculcate, it is important to examine
two documents which he produced shortly after his election
as Chaplain-General, the Universal Negro Ritual and the Universal Negro Catechism.

Universal Negro Ritual

The full title of the one hundred and twenty-eight-page
Ritual is The Universal Negro Ritual containing Forms,
Prayers, and Offices for use in the Universal Negro Improvement Association together with a Collection of Hymns Authorized by the High Executive Council Compiled by His Grace,

Rev. Dr. George Alexander McGuire, Chaplain General Approved by His Excellency, Marcus Garvey, President General and Provisional President of Africa. With this imprimatur of both Garvey and the High Executive Council (the ruling body of the UNIA), it may be assumed that at the time of its publication the Ritual was fully endorsed by the organization's leadership. Adapted from the Book of Common Prayer, the services were not, by Episcopalian standards, especially High Church in tone, though to the predominantly Baptist and Methodist UNIA membership in the United States it may well have appeared exceedingly formal.

The most commonly used of the services found in the Ritual would have been the Order for Sunday Mass Meetings. It began with the processional hymn, "Shine On, Eternal Light," one of the numerous tunes written by the Music Director of the UNIA, Rabbi Arnold J. Ford.[16] The processional was followed by recitation of the most frequently intoned Biblical refrain heard in the halls of the UNIA: Psalms 68, the 31st verse: "Princes shall come out of Egypt; Ethiopia shall soon stretch out her hands unto God."

Next came the official opening hymn of the UNIA, which was none other than the aggressive missionary hymn, "From Greenland's Icy Mountains." It is not without interest that this particular hymn (composed by the well-known English divine and hymnwriter, Sir Reginald Heber) was so honored by the Garveyites, for it was a widely used and popular hymn among white missionary churches of the day.[17] Evidently neither the fact that the author was white, nor the fact that the hymn contains several seemingly condescending references (e.g., to the "benighted" natives of Africa and India, whose lands must be delivered "from error's chain") diminished its popularity. Garveyites did draw the line at singing of "the heathen in his blindness" who "Bows down to wood and stone," and invariably omitted the second stanza from all program notes and hymnals.[18]

The larger significance of the official use of this hymn undoubtedly lies in the self-image of the Garvey movement which is thereby implied: namely, as an avowedly Christian missionary group dedicated to bringing the truth of the Messiah to unredeemed Africa. This explicitly Christian missionary image was not, to be sure, a late addition to the UNIA ideology. As we have previously noted, Garvey himself had included it in his first draft of the "aims and objects" of the Association by inserting as one of its goals, "to promote

a conscientious Christian worship among the native tribes of
Africa."[19] Indeed, for many of the Black churchmen who
were associated with the UNIA, this missionary aspect of
the movement was one of their primary reasons for joining
the Garvey ranks.

The hymn was followed by recitation of the official
motto of the Association, "One God, One Aim, One Destiny,"
and the Lord's Prayer. Then came a remarkable series of
prayers by the chaplain which reveal just how closely Mc-
Guire's conception of the goals of the UNIA was intermeshed
with his reading of God's larger design for the redemption
of the race. The first prayer sought divine guidance in all
UNIA undertakings, dedicating whatever was done to the
greater glory of God:

> Direct us, O Lord, in all our doings, with thy
> most gracious favour, and further us with thy con-
> tinued help; that in all our works begun, continued,
> and ended in thee, we may glorify thy Holy Name,
> and finally, by thy mercy obtain everlasting life;
> through Jesus Christ our Lord. Amen.[20]

The second, adapted from a prayer for missions in
the Book of Common Prayer, made explicit the goal of universal brotherhood, which was a persistent theme in all the
UNIA literature:

> O God, who has made of one blood all nations of
> men for to dwell on the face of the whole earth,
> and didst send thy blessed Son to preach peace and
> good will among all mankind: Grant that men every-
> where may seek after Thee and find Thee. Bring
> all nations into one fold and hasten the day of Uni-
> versal brotherhood; through Jesus Christ our Lord.
> Amen.

The third prayer sought God's blessing on the Association, and especially upon its leadership, whose highest
responsibility (with no apparent sense of dissonance with
respect to the aforesaid goal of universal brotherhood) was
conceived in terms of loyalty to the race.

> Almighty God, whose Kingdom is everlasting and
> power infinite; be gracious unto the Universal Negro
> Improvement Association, and so rule the hearts of
> thy servants, the Provisional President, the

Potentate and Members of the High Executive Council and all others in authority, that they, knowing the great responsibilities of their office, may above all things seek the honor and welfare of this race, and grant that all our people, considering the authority they bear, may faithfully and obediently honor them in accordance with our laws; through Jesus Christ our Lord, with the Holy Ghost liveth and reigneth ever, one God, world without end. Amen.

The next prayer was for the redemption of Africa, envisioning the great day when foreign exploiters would be expelled and Black men would once again rule their own destinies.

O blessed Lord Jesus, persecuted in thine infancy, and thy life threatened by wicked men, remember in thy love and mercy the land of our forefathers in which thou didst find refuge. Redeem Africa from the hands of those who exploit and ravish her. Renew her ancient glory, and grant that her oppressed and down-trodden children at home and in foreign climes may shortly be restored to their divine inheritance, so that under our own vine and figtree we may gather to worship thee, who art with the Father and the Holy Ghost one God, world without end. Amen.

The fifth prayer recalled the faithfulness of Simon of Cyrenia, one of the sons of Ham, who bore Christ's cross up the hill of Calvary and whose descendents have been forced to bear the cross of slavery and oppression at the hands of the sons of Shem and Japheth, the crucifiers of the Lord. One should note here the appeal for strength in overthrowing the enemy, who clearly is the white oppressor.

Almighty Savior, whose heavy Cross was laid upon the stalwart shoulders of Simon the Cyrenian, a son of Ham, in that sad hour of thine agony and mortal weakness, when the sons of Shem delivered thee into the hands of the sons of Japheth to be crucified, regard with thy favour this race still struggling beneath the cross of injustice, oppression and wrong laid upon us by our persecutors. Strengthen us in our determination to free ourselves from the hands of our enemy; put down the mighty

> from their seat, and exalt thou the humble and
> meek, through thy mercies and merits who livest
> and reignest with the Father and the Holy Ghost,
> world without end. Amen.

The final prayer again asked for God's guidance in
all the workings of the UNIA, with a special request that it
be saved from "the great danger of unhappy divisions, " an
indication that even at this early date one of the major problems of the movement was internal dissension among competing factions in the organization. The same problem was
alluded to in the earlier prayer for officers of the Association where the congregation was gently reminded that "considering the authority they bear, " the leadership should be
"faithfully and obediently" honored. [21]

> Almighty God, we beseech thee to assist us with
> thy heavenly grace, and to prosper the godly aims
> and endeavors of this Association in bringing peace,
> justice, liberty, and happiness to our race. Grant
> us wisdom and discretion in all our undertakings,
> patience under our difficulties, triumph over our
> enemies, and a happy issue out of all our struggles.
> Save us, we pray thee, from the great danger of
> unhappy divisions. Take from us envy, hatred,
> malice and whatsoever may hinder us from union
> and concord, that as there is but one Body and one
> Spirit, and one hope of our calling, one God, one
> Aim, one Destiny, so we may be all of one heart
> and of one soul, united in one body of truth and
> peace, of faith and charity, and may with one mind
> and mouth glorify thee; through Jesus Christ our
> Lord. Amen.

Following this series of prayers came the reading of
the Scripture lesson and the singing of the "Hymn of Prayer, "
which was a poem written for the UNIA by John Edward
Bruce, the noted journalist and active AME Zion layman who
was also an ardent Garveyite. [22] Then came the musical and
literary program, receiving of the offering, addresses, and
announcements. The service was concluded with the National
Anthem of the UNIA, [23] a benediction, and the recessional
hymn, "Onward Christian Soldiers. "

Among the eleven "Special Prayers" and "Special
Thanksgivings" included in the Ritual, seven were either
wholly or in only slightly modified form taken from the Book

of Common Prayer. The remaining four included a prayer for use on the anniversary of a division, a prayer for the restoration of peace in a division, a prayer for the ships of the Black Star Line (the most spectacular business venture undertaken by the UNIA), and a prayer to be used at the opening of the annual International Conventions. The latter is notable for invoking God's guidance in all the deliberations of the Association, and in acknowledging God as the one in whose "Name and Presence" the convention had been assembled. The goals of the Association were made evident as the Chaplain-General asked that "the principles for which we stand may be truly proclaimed, truly received, and truly followed by the vast millions of our African fellow citizens; till at length the whole of this dispersed race, being gathered into one great nation in the land of their fathers, shall become partakers of true liberty, peace and happiness."[24]

The last two orders of service contained in the Universal Negro Ritual were the "Baptism and Dedication of Infants" and "The Order for the Burial Service." The latter is without special interest, as it is based directly on the burial service contained in the Book of Common Prayer. The former is significant, however, in that according to its usage, infants were not only baptized as Christians but also dedicated to the principles of the Universal Negro Improvement Association and formally inducted into membership in the organization! This practice was in keeping with the spirit of the UNIA constitution. According to Article Ten, Section One of the constitution, "All persons of Negro blood and African descent are regarded as ordinary members of the Universal Negro Improvement Association and African Communities' League and are entitled to consideration of the organization."[25] Persons were therefore "born" into membership in the Association by virtue of their racial origin, and this fact was made explicit via the baptismal ceremony.

In the baptismal service itself, the traditional Episcopal pattern was followed up to the point where the priest asked of the godparents,

> Dearly beloved, ye have brought this child here to be baptised and to be dedicated to the aims and principles of the Universal Negro Improvement Association.... Do you solemnly believe all the Articles of the Christian Faith, as contained in the Apostles' Creed and do ye acknowledge the obligation,

> as far as in you lies, to provide that this child
> be brought up in the nurture and admonition of the
> Lord, that he be diligently instructed in the Holy
> Scriptures, and that he be taught the Creed, the
> Lord's Prayer, the Ten Commandments, and the
> Catechism of the Universal Negro Improvement As-
> sociation?[26]

When an affirmative reply was received, the priest offered
the appropriate prayers, after which the infant was baptized.
Then the colors of the Association were laid upon the child,
and the priest stated:

> We receive this child into the general membership
> of the Universal Negro Improvement Association,
> and lay upon him these colors, the red, the black,
> and the green, in token that hereafter he may fight
> manfully under this banner, for the freedom of his
> race, and the redemption of Africa unto his life's
> end. Amen. [27]

The service was closed by reminding the parents and
godparents of their responsibility to instruct the child "in
all things that a Christian ought to know and believe," as
well as the importance of inculcating "the aims and principles of this Association, as set forth in our Catechism, so
that when he shall come to riper years, he may be ready
to perform the duties of membership."[28]

The remainder of the Ritual contained some one hundred and thirty-six hymns which McGuire had selected for
use by the UNIA. A majority of the titles he included are
to be found in the Hymnal According to the Use of the Protestant Episcopal Church in the United States of America,[29]
published in 1872, or in the hymns which were published together with the Book of Common Prayer in the 1865 edition.[30]
All but ten of the remaining hymns are listed in Julien's Dictionary of Hymnology, and six of these are taken from A. J.
Ford's Universal Ethiopian Hymnal.[31]

Universal Negro Catechism

McGuire regarded the Universal Negro Catechism as
an important instrument by which the history, purpose, and
theology of the Universal Negro Improvement Association
could be disseminated both among children who were tutored

in it, and among parents who would become familiar with it
in the process of teaching their youngsters its contents. The
Catechism, unlike the Ritual, was not based on the catechism
used by the Protestant Episcopal Church. Designed by Mc-
Guire to meet the specific needs and norms of the UNIA, it
was divided into four approximately equal sections devoted to
religious knowledge, historical knowledge, Constitution and
Laws of the UNIA, and the Declaration of Independence of the
UNIA.

The first section, on religious knowledge, opened with
an inquiry concerning the nature and the attributes of God.
Having established that God is a spirit; that He is One, ever-
lasting, omnipotent, omniscient and omnipresent; and that He
is addressed as "Father" by virtue of having created all human beings "after His own image," the catechist inquired
whether it was part of God's plan of creation to make some
races of men superior to others, and if it was not, to what
could the palpable differences be attributed.

> Q. Did God make any group or race of men su-
> perior to another?
> A. No, He created all races equal, and of one
> blood, to dwell on the face of the earth.
>
> Q. Is it true that the Ethiopian or Black group of
> the human family is the lowest group of all?
> A. It is a base falsehood which is taught in books
> written by white men. All races were created
> equal.
>
> Q. What, then, is the chief reason for the dif-
> ferences observed among the various groups
> of men?
> A. Environment, that is, conditions connected with
> climate, opportunity, necessity, and associa-
> tion with others. [32]

Having established in principle the equality of God's
act of creation, while ascribing to environment the observable
differences among races, the catechist turned to the question
of God's color. (There had been considerable discussion
among both fringe and main-line Black denominational churchmen on this question. Probably the most prominent among
the latter group was the outspoken senior bishop of the African Methodist Episcopal Church, Henry McNeal Turner, who,
in a widely quoted article for the Voice of Missions written

in the year 1898, declared that "God is a Negro."[33]) With
a degree of theological sophistication not always present
among some earlier advocates of a Black or Negro God,
McGuire sought to make clear the context in which he felt
such a concept made sense.

> Q. What's the color of God?
> A. A spirit has neither color, nor other natural
> parts, nor qualities.
>
> Q. But do we not speak of His hands, His eyes,
> His arms, and other parts?
> A. Yes, it is because we are able to think and
> speak of Him only in human and figurative
> terms.
>
> Q. If, then, you had to think or speak of the
> color of God, how would you describe it?
> A. As black since we are created in His image
> and likeness.
>
> Q. On what would you base your assumption that
> God is black?
> A. On the same basis as that taken by white
> people when they assume that God is of their
> color.[34]

Explicitly acknowledging that anthropomorphism in
theology is but a concession to the limited capacity of man
to conceptualize the deity, McGuire only insisted on the right
of the Black man to make the man/God analogy out of his
own existential framework. (Marcus Garvey expressed a
similar sentiment somewhat more vividly when he declared,
"God is not white or black; angels have no color, and they
are not white peaches from Georgia. But if they [whites]
say that God is white, this organization says that God is
black; if they are going to make the angels beautiful white
peaches from Georgia, we are going to make them beautiful
black peaches from Africa."[35])

Turning to the doctrine of Jesus Christ, the Catechism
was mainly concerned to emphasize Jesus' historic ties to
Africa. Mention is made of Balthazar, one of the magi, who
"it is generally believed" was a Black man; of Jesus' escape
to Egypt to elude Herod; and of Simon the Cyrenian, the African who carried the cross up to Calvary. Although Christ is
not explicitly described as a Black man, he was a Hebrew of

the Semitic race with an "admixture" of the blood of other races, as evident by his ancester Pharez, whose mother was a descendent of Ham. [36]

According to the Catechism, the core of Jesus' ethical teaching is embodied in the Sermon on the Mount, while the essential principle of all true religion is "the universal brotherhood of man," stemming from "the universal Fatherhood of God." The vision of the multitude of the faithful from all nations gathered on judgment day (Revelation 7:9) was taken as evidence that there would be no racial separation in heaven. [37]

The place of the Black man in the Old Testament was discussed at some length, beginning with a repudiation of the "curse of Ham," as it has been applied to the Negro. A frank and witty acknowledgment of the presence of race prejudice "even [among] religious teachers" was made in the following exchange, concerning Moses' marriage to a Black woman, Zipporah:

Q. Was Moses' marriage pleasing to his relatives?
A. No, Miriam, his sister, who was a prophetess, and Aaron, his brother, who was a priest, both upbraided him for having married an Ethiopian woman. Read Numbers 12:1.

Q. What does this show?
A. That race prejudice is as old as the human family, and that even religious teachers are not free from it.

Q. What punishment came to Miriam for speaking against the Ethipian woman?
A. She became afflicted with leprosy, and was placed in quarantine for seven days until Moses prayed for her restoration.

Q. What appears then, to be the most effective cure for race prejudice?
A. Leprosy. [38]

After enumerating the Black men and women who are mentioned in the Bible, the first section of the Catechism concluded by asking what prediction is made in Psalms 68:31, which "is now being fulfilled." Having recited the passage the catechumen was asked its significance, to which he should reply, "that Negroes will set up their own government in Africa, with rulers of their own race."[39]

The second section of the Catechism, dealing with historical knowledge, devoted considerable attention to the achievements of the ancient Ethiopian and Egyptian kingdoms. Both of these were "African nations [which] contributed to a high civilization when Europe was still a continent of barbarians."[40] The contributions of the powerful African kingdoms of the Middle Ages were also discussed. McGuire's loyalty to his place of birth was evidenced by the question, "What great event occurred in 1492?"--to which the appropriate response was, "Christopher Columbus made his first visit to the West Indies."[41]

The panoply of African, West Indian, and Afro-American heroes to which McGuire called attention in the Catechism included Edward Wilmot Blyden, the outstanding educator and Liberian politician/diplomat (d. 1912); James Africanus Horton, a West African medical authority and noted African nationalist (d. 1880); Sir Samuel Lewis, a jurist of Sierra Leone (d. 1903); Rev. Samuel D. Ferguson, first African bishop of Liberia (d. 1916); Sir Conrad Reeves, Barbadian Chief Justice (d. 1901); Toussaint L'Ouverture, Haitian liberator (d. 1803); Crispus Attucks (d. 1770); Frederick Douglass (d. 1895); Booker T. Washington (d. 1915); Prince Hall, founder of the Negro Masons (d. 1807); and Alexander Crummell, a prominent Protestant Episcopal clergyman (d. 1898).

The third section of the Catechism dealt with the history of the Universal Negro Improvement Association and consisted mainly of selections from the Constitution and Book of Laws of the UNIA. The rules for organizing a UNIA chapter or division were set forth as follows: "Seven or more citizens of intelligence, having the respect of the educated and cultured people of their community, on application, may be given a charter; provided that there is no chartered Division existing in such community."[42] This was reminiscent of the pattern of organization utilized by Black Baptist churches, in which the cooperation of seven individuals had to be secured, in order to form a new congregation.[43]

The list of officers required by the charter, their qualifications and duties, were included in this section, as were the specific taxes which were to be assessed, the emblem which was to be worn by members, and the various auxiliary organizations and businesses which UNIA members might wish to support. The Catechism explicitly stated that divisions "shall admit none to achieve membership who is not of African blood."[44] It was also stated that infants were "required to be brought by their parents to be dedicated by the Chaplain of the Division not later than three months after birth, at which time they enter the general membership of the Organization."[45]

The final section of the Catechism dealt with the famous "Declaration of Rights of the Negro Peoples of the World" which was adopted on August 13, 1920 during the First International Convention of Negro Peoples of the World. McGuire put the resolutions contained in that Declaration into question and answer form. At the conclusion of this section the catechumen was asked whether Negro people intended to support this Declaration of Rights, to which he was to reply, "They pledge to maintain it as the Magna Charta of their race and solemnly swear to defend it with their lives, their fortunes, and their sacred honor."[46]

Just how wide the distribution and use of the Ritual and Catechism were cannot be ascertained with certainty. On several occasions reports from local UNIA divisions appearing in the Negro World indicated that the new rituals were being utilized. After the visit of the Chaplain-General to Preston, Cuba, for instance, the local Garvey officials sent in the following report:

> The great features that will keep the visit of His Grace fresh in our memories for some time took place on Sunday afternoon the 16th instant, at Liberty Hall, the first being the baptizing and receiving in the Fatherhood of God and brotherhood of the U.N.I.A., a little two months old infant, whose parents and sponsors are all members of the association. The ceremony was so impressive and soul stirring that everybody who witnessed it left as if they could suffer themselves to be baptized again. The other event was the marriage of a Black Cross Nurse; this was the first to be held in Liberty Hall, Preston, under the banner of the red, black and green and by such a dignitary.[47]

Such references in the Negro World are relatively infrequent, however, and on the basis of this datum alone it seems likely that the Ritual and the Catechism were not used extensively.[48] Certainly McGuire's original intent, that a copy of each be owned by every member of the UNIA, was never realized. Several factors undoubtedly inhibited their use, most important of which was resistance among clergy-men of the various denominations, who may have perceived the increasingly explicit religious ethos of the UNIA to be a threat to their own power bases and a direct challenge to the Black denominations. McGuire's temporary fall from grace within the UNIA hierarchy by the end of 1921, and the subsequent "anti-church" phase of the Garvey movement, es-pecially during 1922, meant that much less emphasis would be placed on the Ritual and Catechism. Additional light may be shed upon this question by a careful examination of Mc-Guire's peregrination from Protestant Episcopal clergyman to African Orthodox Church bishop. It is only when the factors which led up to the AOC's creation are clarified that one can understand the divergent conceptions of the place of religion within the UNIA held by George Alexander McGuire and Marcus Garvey.

McGuire and the African Orthodox Church

A great deal of confusion has surrounded discussions concerning the relationship of the African Orthodox Church to the Universal Negro Improvement Association. In particu-lar there has been the persistent but erroneous assumption that Marcus Garvey himself founded or "called upon"[49] Mc-Guire to found the AOC. At the very least, McGuire's church is regarded as an auxiliary[50] of the UNIA, comparable, say, to the Black Cross Nurses or the Universal African Motor Corps, thereby having claim to the title of "official" church for the Garvey movement. As recent scholarship has made clear,[51] Garvey was not the founder of the AOC, nor was he ever a member of that organization. Indeed, there is evidence that he actually opposed its creation, forced Mc-Guire's resignation as Chaplain-General when the latter took on the title of bishop, and read him out of the UNIA (though only temporarily) within three months of the founding of the African Orthodox Church. However, recent scholarship is incorrect in concluding that the only tie between the UNIA and the AOC "was in the person of McGuire himself."[52]

The confusion stems from an imperfect knowledge of the events which transpired at the time of McGuire's move from Episcopal priest to African Orthodox bishop, that is, between August 1919 and September 1921. Although we are

Archbishop McGuire (third from left, front row) and other dignitaries of the African Orthodox Church (from God and the Negro, by A. P. Holly).

still not in possession of all relevant facts, the rough out-
line of events now seems to be clear. The earliest account
of McGuire's activities following his return to the United
States from the West Indies in July 1919 is found in an
article appearing in the Negro World for November 6, 1920.
Entitled "Caustic Reply to Bishop Burch," it was written in
response to a letter from the bishop of the Diocese of New
York, Dr. Charles S. Burch, to the vicar of St. Chrysostom's Protestant Episcopal Church, one C. Nelson Moller.[53]
In his "Caustic Reply" McGuire revealed that on his return
to the United States he had secured from Bishop Burch a
temporary license to preach in the Protestant Episcopal
Church. Within two months, however, he had decided to
affiliate with the Reformed Episcopal Church, a predominantly
white institution which had always retained a substantial Negro membership.[54]

The congregation of the Church of the Good Shepherd,
which McGuire founded on November 9, 1919, was thus
originally conceived as being in communion with the Reformed Episcopal Church. Shortly thereafter even this move
was not sufficient for McGuire's purposes. The reason for
this change of plans was directly related to a new vision of
Black control over Black institutions. This vision he readily
attributes to his association with Marcus Garvey and the
UNIA. He wrote:

> But, among other reasons, the connection of Dr.
> McGuire with The Universal Negro Improvement
> Association, of which he is now the honored Chap-
> lain-General, was the compelling factor in the de-
> cision reached by him and his numbers not to af-
> filiate with any existing body of white Episcopalians,
> but to organize an independent or African Episcopal
> Church to include Negroes everywhere, and of
> which the "Good Shepherd" would be the mother
> church or congregation. In April, 1920, the first
> Independent Episcopal Church was incorporated
> under the statutes of New York. Since the racial
> vision has been caught, and racial independence
> emphasized, the work has grown marvelously.[55]

Thus, by early 1920 at the latest, McGuire was both
identifying himself as a Garveyite and crediting the inspiration for his separatist "Independent or African Episcopal"
organization to Marcus Garvey. On the eve of the first anniversary of the Church of the Good Shepherd (November

1920), he was able to report an active congregation of fifty communicants, a clergy roll of eight, and prospect of further development in foreign fields (presumably in the Caribbean). "The Independent Episcopal Church, " he optimistically concluded, "is the answer of an awakened Negro consciousness to the humiliating racial barriers existing in White Episcopal churches. It is the harbinger of 'The African Episcopal Church, ' for which the New Negro everywhere earnestly waits. "[56]

McGuire's plan at this time appears to have been to do for Negro Episcopalians what had been done long ago by Negro Methodists, namely to establish a parallel racial institution along denominational lines. Within six months, however, he had moved beyond the notion of forming a racial branch of the Protestant Episcopal Church, and was thinking in terms of a much more inclusive structure, operating presumably within the UNIA. This is evident from a front page Negro World article reporting "An Epoch-Making Event in Harlem, " the ordination of Richard Hilton Tobitt as presbyter in the Independent Episcopal Church:

> On Tuesday, in Holy Week, March 22, 1921, the Rev. Richard Hilton Tobitt, B.A., formerly a deacon in the A.M.E. Church, and recently elected leader of the West Indies, was ordained a presbyter of the Church of God, in the Chapel of the Good Shepherd, Independent Episcopal, of the city of New York, by "His Grace, " the Most Reverend George Alexander McGuire.... His Excellency, Rev. Mr. Tobitt, left next day by steamer for his field in the West Indies and bears in addition to his commission from the High Executive Council an appointment from His Grace as General Missionary for religious awakening among our people in the islands who desire to have their own religious teachers. Mr. Tobitt will recommend to his Grace suitable persons on the field who are able to undertake laymen's duties, or who may desire to prepare for Holy Orders. [57]

Circumstances related to Tobitt's ordination indicate that a new relationship was being forged between the Independent Episcopal Church and the UNIA. In the first place Tobitt held a substantial position in the UNIA, and from the description of his appointment as "General Missionary for religious awakening" it appears that his UNIA and his churchly duties were hardly perceived as being exclusive of one another. In the second place, the news article also reported that the UNIA had purchased the episcopal robes worn by McGuire at Tobitt's installation service. Certainly Garvey was not in the habit of purchasing ecclesiastical vestments for Black clergymen, and the fact that the UNIA did so on this occasion suggests that the Association and the newly founded denomination were developing a special relationship.[58] It is in another paragraph of the Negro World article, however, that the outlines of McGuire's latest plans were suggested:

> Archbishop McGuire feels himself fully equipped and authorized for the large work entrusted to his care and supervision, and hopes to prove himself truly an Episcopus, or overseer, of the Church for which Negroes everywhere are looking. When Dr. McGuire left the Church of England in 1919, he left behind him the fragile theory and doctrine of "Apostolic Succession." He believes in the validity of non-episcopal ordinations; he believes that the time has come for church unity among Negroes; he believes that unity does not necessarily mean uniformity in worship, and that the coming African or Ethiopian Church will be big enough for all Negroes to enter, retaining their own worship as Methodists, Baptists, Episcopalians, etc.... We are not concerned about white Episcopalians, or Negroes still in the Anglican Church. But we are concerned about Ethiopians and the Ethiopian Church. Ethiopia is stretching out her hands to God. Princes shall come out of the land of our fathers.... The Negroes of the world in convention assembled [i.e., the August 1920 Convention of the Negro Peoples of the World] made the Most Rev. Dr. G. A. McGuire the first prince of the Church Ethiopia. We understand that plans are under way for his enthronement at the coming Convention in August next.[59]

Several important points are worth highlighting in this passage. Most salient is the implication that the Independent Episcopal Church was regarded by McGuire as transitional, as a stepping stone to the "coming African or Ethiopian Church," which would be an ecumenical (though, of course, racial) institution capable of allowing for a diversity of specific worship patterns but which it was hoped would reduce some of the destructive competitiveness amongst the various Black denominations. It would at the same time provide a number of shared symbols and beliefs growing out of their common experience as an oppressed people now living in exile, but buoyed by faith in the promise presently being fulfilled concerning Ethiopia's redemption. The additional fact that McGuire was expected to be enthroned at the upcoming UNIA convention indicates that at this point, the "coming ... Ethiopian Church" was understood as being integrally related to the UNIA, if not actually becoming its official church. If this interpretation is correct, then one could understand McGuire's having agreed to give up the "fragile theory" of Apostolic Succession (which was certainly no small concession by this High-Church Anglican), since as prince of an ecumenical "Church Ethiopian" he would presumably be presiding over an institution which acknowledged a variety of ordinational patterns.

For reasons which at the moment must remain speculative, events did not unfold as anticipated at the date of Tobitt's ordination in March of 1921. For one thing, McGuire did not give up the quest for a valid episcopal succession which the official history of the African Orthodox Church insists was "so much desired."[60] On the contrary, McGuire seems to have been negotiating throughout this period with a variety of institutions which conceivably might provide the ordination. The church's historian, Arthur C. Terry-Thompson, specifies that unsuccessful overtures were made to Cardinal Hayes of the Roman Catholic Church and Bishop William T. Manning of the Protestant Episcopal Church. Meanwhile an article critical of McGuire's activities appeared in the Protestant Episcopal periodical Living Church on June 11, 1921, and this brought unsolicited offers of assistance from the hierarchy of both the American Catholic Church and the Russian Orthodox Church,[61] from whom ordination was finally received.

On July 16, 1921 while McGuire was traveling in the West Indies on behalf of the UNIA, a preliminary synod was held at the church of one James N. Bridgeman in Brooklyn. At that meeting, McGuire was elected Bishop, while Bridgeman was chosen as Auxiliary Bishop, presumably of the Independent Episcopal Church.[62] It is surely not a coincidence that on the very same day as the preliminary synod, the following item appeared on the editorial page of the Negro World, with the caption "U.N.I.A. Favors All Churches, But Adopts None as U.N.I.A. Church":

> Dear Sir: --To the divisions of the U.N.I.A.
> throughout the world there is a natural tendency
> on the part of the members of the U.N.I.A.,
> when inducted into the new idealism, to come into
> it with the idea of a church, and there has been
> an effort on the part of many in different parts of
> the country to start a Universal Church.
>
> I want it to be distinctly understood, that the
> U.N.I.A. is not a church, and it does not intend
> to be one. So far as the present signs are, there
> will be no church connected with the U.N.I.A. I
> wish to say if anyone comes around and tells you
> of a church bearing the name of the U.N.I.A., re-
> pudiate it from start to finish, for it is absolutely
> false. There is no such church as authorized.
> We favor all churches, but adopt none as a U.N.I.A.
> Church. Let the presidents and officers of the
> various locals take notice and govern themselves
> accordingly. [63]

This letter was signed by the then Assistant President-
General of the UNIA, John Dawson Gordon, who was himself
a Baptist clergyman. [64] It was clearly aimed at squelching
any notion Bridgeman or McGuire might have had that their
new organization, however named, would be given special
status within the UNIA.

Not surprisingly, in light of these developments, Mc-
Guire was not "enthroned" during the second International
Convention as had been anticipated in March of 1921. The
sparsity of information on that August 1921 Convention makes
it difficult to assess the role McGuire played in it, although
he did retain his position as Chaplain-General throughout the
Convention. One available issue of the Negro World dated
late in August, for instance, indicates that "Chaplain-General
McGuire" appeared alongside Garvey at an athletic event, with
no visible indication of friction between the men. [65] Barely
a month after the convention, however, the Negro World describes McGuire as "once Chaplain-General of the U.N.I.A."[66]
This reference occurs in an article detailing McGuire's activities in the month of September, during which time he had
founded the African Orthodox Church and was consecrated as
its first bishop.

It is unnecessary to rehearse those events here as
they are discussed in detail elsewhere. [67] In brief, a synod

of the Independent Episcopal Churches was convened at Mc-Guire's Church of the Good Shepherd on September 2, 1921 at which time it was agreed to establish the African Orthodox Church. McGuire's nomination as Bishop-elect was confirmed, although Bridgeman's nomination as Auxiliary Bishop was set aside.[68] The consecration took place in Chicago on the 28th of September, 1921, at the hands of Joseph Rene Vilatte, "Exarch and Metropolitan" of the American Catholic Church, with the assistance of Bishop Carl A. Nybladh, of the Swedish Orthodox Church.[69] The following evening, in New York City, McGuire was enthroned as first Bishop of the AOC by Anthony R. F. Hill of the Russian Orthodox Church, with William Ernest Robertson (who appears to have emerged as the number two man in the newly formed denomination) officiating.[70]

To be sure, the Negro World article, in reporting these events, was at pains to congratulate McGuire on his new position and to wish him well in his new undertaking. It was even more concerned, however, to make clear to its readers that the AOC had no formal connection with the UNIA:

> The Universal Negro Improvement Association indorsed at its recent convention all churches under Negro leadership. It does not ally itself with any particular church, but as heretofore it has indorsed Methodists and Baptists of the Negro race, so now it indorses this new movement among Negro Episcopalians, which has resulted in the formation of the African Orthodox Church. Bishop McGuire resigned as Chaplain-General of the Universal Negro Improvement Association after his election to the episcopate.[71]

And if these were not sufficiently plain words, the point was made even more explicit in an item appearing in the newspaper some three weeks later:

> NOTICE! NOTICE! This Association has no connection with any other Organization Church or Movement, and any one who claims that their particular Organization, Church or Movement is the same [as] the Universal Negro Improvement Association is endeavoring to deceive.... We are in sympathy with all Negro Churches, but we have no particular Church to support. Any information to the contrary is deceptive![72]

The next time McGuire's name appeared in the Negro World, so far as I am now able to determine, was in an article for the December 31, 1921 issue, entitled "[John Dawson] Gordon, [George Alexander] McGuire and [Cyril] Crichlow, Former Officers of Association, and Now Discredited, Reported Actively Cooperating with Soviets To Bring About Revolution Here."[73] Alas, only the fragment of this issue containing the title has been preserved, so that the details of charges against McGuire are not available. Evidently all three men had been ousted from the UNIA prior to their latest act of "treachery," which may have involved providing UNIA membership lists to Cyril Briggs, a one-time Garveyite who had become a bitter opponent of the Garvey movement.[74] One week later, another jibe at McGuire was taken by Ulysses S. Poston, one of the editors of the Negro World, with the following rather cryptic note in the editorial section:

> I trust that Bishop Alexander McGuire in whom the Universal Negro Improvement Association placed implicit trust, and who in turn betrayed that trust by disregarding the sacred oath he took to serve the association and joining the ranks of the enemy in battle against the association, will read the "Handwriting on the wall" and interpret it to read that "My fate may be the common fate of all traitors." But he is not as perverse as Judas Iscariot, Alcibiades and Benedict Arnold.[75]

From neither of these articles are we able to tell what was the precipitating factor of the McGuire/Garvey alienation, though certainly the roots of the controversy stemmed from Garvey's refusal to adopt the African Orthodox Church as the official religious institution of the UNIA. Behind this was Garvey's rejection of the logic of institutionalization which was already implicit in McGuire's Universal Negro Ritual, and in the direction in which he sought to force UNIA chaplains immediately following his election as Chaplain-General. Much as McGuire endeavored to convince his chaplains to the contrary, pedobaptist formularies drawn from the Book of Common Prayer, intonation of the Jubilate Deo, and singing of the Te Deum and the Venite Exultemus Domino, were hardly nonsectarian rituals likely to draw ready acceptance and appreciation among the heterogeneous group of religious believers and non-believers comprising the Universal Negro Improvement Association. It was one thing when the Chaplain-General talked of becoming the "first prince of the Church

Ethiopia, " a non-episcopal, ecumenical religious supra-organization that would seek no "uniformity of worship. " However, when he in fact had himself ordained head of an African Orthodox Church, and was invested with crosier and miter, it was clear that he had gone too far and would have to be removed from office. Like his old mentor from Arkansas, Bishop Brown, McGuire's problem was in failing to see that not everyone wanted to become an Episcopalian.[76]

At the Third International Convention (1922), which of course McGuire did not attend, one of the featured items on the call to meeting was "The Future Religious Faith and Belief of the Negro. " When the question came up for debate at the convention, Garvey sought to clarify the UNIA's position with the following remarks:

> It was not the desire, he explained, of the Universal Negro Improvement Association to dictate any one's religious faith or religious belief; that was to say, we were not assuming to tell any one to become a Catholic or Baptist or Episcopalian or Seventh Day Adventist or Holy Roller or anything else. The idea was to bring the [sic] to the Negro a scientific understanding of religion. What was desired was one great Christian confraternity without regard to any particular denomination, believing ourselves to be religious Christians.[77]

Such a "great Christian confraternity" could not have the explicit institutional form which McGuire had adopted for the AOC; to the extent that this "confraternity" had institutional parameters at all, they would have to be identical with the Universal Negro Improvement Association itself.

It is possible at this point to make a few general observations concerning the African Orthodox Church and its relation to the Universal Negro Improvement Association. In the first place, recent assessments of the AOC are correct in pointing out that Garvey was not the founder of this church, nor was he ever a member of it, nor was it in any way formally associated with the UNIA. As we have seen, there are strong indications that Garvey was actively opposed to its being established, at least in so far as it was conceived as being integrally related to the UNIA.

However, it is not correct to move to the extreme and opposite conclusion that "The link [between the AOC and the UNIA] was in the person of McGuire himself, "[78] as if McGuire were the only tie between the two organizations. It has already been demonstrated that for McGuire himself, there was no question but that the initial impulse for creating the Independent Episcopal Church came as a direct result of his encounter with the vision of Black men controlling their own institutions, a vision which he found embodied in the person of Marcus Garvey. Furthermore, at least two men, Tobitt and Bridgeman, among the small number of clergymen who joined the embryonic Independent Episcopal Church, were active supporters of the UNIA and evidently saw the two organizations as, at the very least, complementing one another in their ultimate goals.

It remains to be pointed out that while neither of these two men evidently continued in McGuire's African Orthodox Church after it was reorganized in September 1921, there were numerous clergymen, either present as members of the founding synod or joining the AOC shortly thereafter, who were also active members of the UNIA. Among these were Frederick A. Toote, head of the Philadelphia Division, UNIA, and one of the founders of the AOC;[79] David E. Ewart, executive secretary of the Florida, Cuba, UNIA and on the AOC clergy list for 1927;[80] George S. Brookes, an AME pastor in New Haven, Connecticut, who took part in the founding synod of the AOC and who had previously written in the Negro World concerning UNIA activities in Connecticut;[81] and John C. Simons, one of the signatories of the 1920 Declaration of Rights, listed on the 1927 AOC clergy list and still active in the UNIA as late as 1934, when he was elected Chaplain-General.[82] And the list could be extended.

There were, in a word, numerous links between the AOC and the UNIA, both in terms of individuals and ideals that were shared by the two organizations. That it was not theology, but ecclesiology, which separated Garvey and Mc-Guire is further evidenced by the fact that a little more than a year after McGuire had established the African Orthodox Church, he resumed activities on behalf of the UNIA, and by the 1924 International Convention was heralded as Honorary Chaplain-General. His brilliant speech at the opening session of that convention, setting the stage for the canonization of Jesus as the Black Man of Sorrows, also pointed to the centrality of religion and of Black religious institutions in the work of the Universal Negro Improvement Association:

Let it be understood, once and for all, that no

constructive program for the Negro can be effective
which underestimates the hold his religious institutions have upon him.   The material without the
spiritual is as bad as, nay, worse than the spiritual without the material.   We must have the anchor
of religion, but we must make certain that it is
what we consider conscientious for us as Negroes.
That is what is meant by that object in our constitution, which reads, --"to promote a conscientious
spiritual worship among the native tribes of Africa,"
implying, of course, that we shall first promote it
among ourselves.   That is what is meant when in
our Declaration of Rights we demand "freedom of
religious worship."   This means freedom in our
theology, freedom in our ritual and freedom in the
control of our ecclesiastical organizations.   We demand the exercise of a conscientious, spiritual freedom for the reason that spiritual freedom is the
basis of all other freedoms.   "Ye shall know the
truth and the truth shall make you free."   And in
the exercise of this freedom we claim the right to
set forth theology as we understand it. [83]

NOTES

1.   McGuire was rescued from obscurity by the article of
      Gavin White, "Patriarch McGuire and the Episcopal
      Church," Historical Magazine of the Protestant Epis-
      copal Church 38 (1969), 109-141.   Writing out of the
      framework of the Protestant Episcopal Church himself,
      White focuses attention on the vicissitudes of McGuire's
      relationship to that tradition, culminating in the break
      which eventuated in the creation of the African Ortho-
      dox Church.   From the present writer's point of view
      the major defect in White's presentation is his under-
      estimation of the extent and importance of McGuire's
      participation in the UNIA from 1920 to 1925.   The
      most comprehensive and reliable account of McGuire's
      life is found in Richard Newman's "Introduction" to
      the reprint edition of the official magazine of the AOC,
      The Negro Churchman (Millwood, N. J., 1977).

2.   George F. Bragg, Jr., History of the Afro-American
      Group of the Episcopal Church (Baltimore, 1922), pp.
      115 f., 176 f., 273.   Cf. White, "Patriarch McGuire,"
      p. 111.   In the same year he moved to Cincinnati,

McGuire became a naturalized citizen of the United States. See also G. A. McGuire, "Caustic Reply to Bishop Burch," NW 9:12 (November 6, 1920), p. 5.

3. White, "Patriarch McGuire," p. 112. The book White referred to was entitled The Church for Americans (New York, 1895).

4. White is undoubtedly correct in observing that Brown's views on race were "way out" (White, "Patriarch Mc- Guire," p. 112), i.e., he was operating out of a barely concealed conviction of the racial superiority of white over Black. In fairness to Brown, however, one ought at least to point out that Brown himself later came to this same realization and sought to make amends for it. In his autobiography, written some two decades after the so-called "Arkansas Plan" for a segregated Episcopal Church was first advanced, Brown recalled how "nettled" he was by northern Negro criticism of his proposal as an effort to jim crow religion: "The reason they nettled me, as I see it now, is that my own position was so unsound. After all, I did believe in Jim Crowism. I was certain in my heart that I had no prejudice against the Negro: but I had accepted the current assumption as to the racial differences; and from this assumption nothing but misunderstanding could result." My Heresy: the Autobiography of an Idea (New York, 1926), p. 45. On the basis of the observation just cited, as well as others like it in the autobiography, one has the suspi- cion that Brown was a far more complex and interesting character than White would allow.

5. Little Rock, 1907, pp. 276-282.

6. Ibid., pp. 274, 276, and 279.

7. Ibid., pp. 280 and 282.

8. Ibid., pp. 276-77. Emphasis added.

9. White, "Patriarch McGuire," p. 115.

10. Ibid., pp. 116-118. Bragg, Afro-American Group, pp. 226-27, notes McGuire's arrival at St. Bartholomew's and comments on the circumstances of that congrega- tion's origin. The American Church Institute for

Negroes was established by the Board of Missions of
the Protestant Episcopal Church in 1906, to assist
the denomination's educational work among Negroes.
Its first officers included Bishop David Hummell
Greer, president; George Foster Peabody, treasurer;
and Rev. S. H. Bishop, field secretary. Southern
Workman 35 (1906), p. 470.

11. Arthur Cornelius Terry-Thompson, The History of the
African Orthodox Church (New York, 1956), p. 50.

12. Baltimore Afro-American, August 27, 1920, p. 1.

13. New York World, August 7, 1920, p. 10.

14. New York World, August 27, 1920, also quoted in Vincent, Black Power, p. 121.

15. Because I have not seen issues of the Negro World for
August 1920, which would contain the day by day reports of debates over the constitutional revisions, I
cannot state with certainty that the revisions were
authorized by McGuire. They were singled out for
emphasis by him, however, in an article he wrote
for the Negro World, April 2, 1921, and they fit in
well with his overall purpose of heightening the religious self-consciousness of the UNIA. Both revisions are discussed above in chapter 1.

16. Ford published for the UNIA a collection of his hymns
in a booklet, The Universal Ethiopian Hymnal (New
York, n.d.).

17. Heber (1783-1826), who is perhaps best known for another of his hymns, "Holy, Holy, Holy," wrote
"From Greenland's Icy Mountains" on special com-
mission from The Society for the Propagation of The
Gospel, in 1819. John Julian, ed., A Dictionary of
Hymnology (London, 1907, 2nd revised edition), pp.
399 and 503. The hymn was evidently popular among
Black churchmen of the day as well as among whites;
it was, for instance, given first place among mis-
sionary hymns in the Hymn and Tune Book of the
African Methodist Episcopal Church, published by the
AME Book Concern, Philadelphia, in 1902.

18. The text of the first stanza is as follows:

From Greenland's icy mountains,
  From India's coral strand;
Where Africa's sunny fountains
  Roll down their golden sand;
From many an ancient river,
  From many a palmy plain,
They call us to deliver
  Their land from error's chain.

It is very possible that the words of the official
opening hymn as sung by Garveyites were suffused
with meanings and interpretations that were never
dreamt of by their original composer. Thus the
"error's chain" from which India and Africa were
to be delivered, according to the hymn's first stanza,
might be understood as the manacles of oppression
by imperialist foreign powers as much as it was
bondage to the pagan gods. Similarly, the "Messiah's name" which was to be shared by those "whose
souls are lighted with wisdom from on high," according to the third stanza, could either be that of
Jesus or of Garvey, for both men had brought a new
vision of salvation to the world.

19. See above, Introduction, especially n. 17.

20. This and the following five prayers are taken from Mc-
     Guire's Universal Negro Ritual (n. p., 1921), pp. 10-
     14.

21. So great was the problem, indeed, that elsewhere in the
     Ritual, under the section of prayers for Special Thanks-
     giving, McGuire included the following prayer "For the
     Restoration of Peace in a Division": "O Eternal God,
     our heavenly Father, who alone makest men to be of
     one mind in a house, and stillest those that are vio-
     lent, unruly, and disloyal; we bless thy holy name,
     that it hath pleased thee to appease the disorderly
     tumults which have been lately raised up amongst us,
     most humbly beseeching thee to grant to all of us
     grace, that we may henceforth obediently govern our-
     selves according to the laws and rules of this Asso-
     ciation; and leading a quiet and peaceable life in unity,
     godliness, and honesty, may continually offer thee
     praise and thanksgiving, through Jesus Christ our
     Lord. Amen." Ibid., p. 21.

22. The "Hymn of Prayer" reads as follows:

> God of the right our battles fight
> Be with us as of yore
> Break down the barriers of might
> We rev'rently implore.
>
> Stand with us in our struggles for
> The triumph of the right
> And spread confusion ever o'er
> The advocates of might.
>
> And let them know that righteousness
> Is mightier than sin
> That might is only selfishness
> And cannot, ought not win.
>
> Endow us, Lord, with faith and grace
> And courage to endure
> The wrongs we suffer here apace
> And bless us evermore.   Amen

The Universal Negro Ritual, pp. 14-15.   On Bruce, see below, chapter 5.

23. The score for the National Anthem was written by Ben Burrell, while the poem was that of Arnold J. Ford, and the hymn was adopted as the official anthem of the Association at the first International Convention of Negro Peoples of the World in August 1920.   Vincent, Black Power, pp. 78, 85 n., 263-264.   For the text and circumstances of its writing, see above, chapter one.

24. McGuire, Universal Negro Ritual, p. 19.

25. Adelaide Cromwell Hill, and Martin Kilson, eds., Apropos of Africa: Sentiments of Negro American Leaders on Africa from the 1800s to the 1950s (London, 1969), p. 202.   Emphasis added.   The full text of the constitution of the Universal Negro Improvement Association is printed there, pp. 184-206.   The constitution distinguishes these "ordinary" members from the "active" members, who paid dues to the organization, attended meetings, and so on.

26. McGuire, Universal Negro Ritual, p. 23.   Original emphasis omitted, emphasis added.

27. Ibid., pp. 24-25. Emphasis omitted.

28. Ibid., p. 25.

29. Boston, A. Wilson and Company.

30. New York, D. Appleton and Company.

31. I have been unable to locate a source for the remaining four hymns. The first lines of the four are: "O God Creator of our race"; "O perfect love all human thoughts transcending"; "Safe upon the billowy deep"; and "Savior, lead me lest I stray."

32. George Alexander McGuire, comp., Universal Negro Catechism (n.p., 1921), pp. 2-3.

33. Henry M. Turner, "God Is A Negro," Voice of Missions, February 1, 1898, reprinted in John H. Bracey, Jr., August Meier, and Elliott Rudwick, eds., Black Nationalism in America (Indianapolis, 1970), pp. 154-55.

34. McGuire, Catechism, p. 3.

35. Marcus Garvey, in a speech delivered in Cincinnati and reprinted in NW 10:2 (February 26, 1921), p. 6.

36. McGuire, Catechism, p. 5. It was not until the Fourth International Convention in August 1924 that Jesus Christ was canonized by Garveyites as the "Black Man of Sorrows."

37. Ibid., p. 507.

38. McGuire, Catechism, p. 8.

39. Ibid., p. 11.

40. Ibid., p. 12.

41. Ibid., p. 16.

42. Ibid., p. 21.

43. Benjamin E. Mays and Joseph W. Nicholson, The Negro's Church (New York, 1969), p. 10, state that

"Four laymen and three ordained ministers can start a Baptist Church."

44. McGuire, Catechism, p. 24.

45. Ibid., p. 25. Emphasis added.

46. Ibid., p. 34.

47. NW 10:1 (February 19, 1921), p. 10.

48. The fact that neither the Universal Negro Catechism nor the Universal Negro Ritual is mentioned in either Vincent's book, Black Power, or in Cronon's book Black Moses is further indication of their lack of penetration to the movement at large.

49. Cronon, Black Moses, p. 78.

50. E. U. Essien-Udom, Black Nationalism; A Search for an Identity in America (New York, 1964), p. 51.

51. Cf. Gavin White, "Patriarch McGuire," p. 132, passim, and also Byron Rushing, "A Note on the Origin of the African Orthodox Church," Journal of Negro History 57 (1972), 37-39.

52. As Rushing argues, ibid.

53. NW 9:12 (November 6, 1920), p. 5. It appears from the text of McGuire's "Reply" to Bishop Burch, that Rev. Moller had been jim crowing his services at St. Chrysostom's, requiring Black parishioners to attend an early service or else to remain in segregated sections of the church during the regular service. According to McGuire, Moller had been losing his Black parishioners to McGuire's recently established "Independent" Church of the Good Shepherd (see below), and it was a desire to stem the exodus from St. Chrysostom's which had prompted Moller to request the letter from Bishop Burch.

54. The Reformed Episcopal Church was established as an off-shoot of the Protestant Episcopal Church in 1873, and according to Gavin White, "Patriarch McGuire," p. 124 n., has to this day a large proportion of Blacks among its membership. White does not

mention, however, that McGuire originally intended
to affiliate with the Reformed body.   Note also that
White places McGuire's resignation from St. Paul's
Church, Antigua, in the year 1918 (p. 117).   Mc-
Guire states, however, that he served in the diocese
of Antigua until July 1919.   (McGuire, "Caustic Reply," p. 5).   On the Reformed Episcopalian Church,
see Frank S. Mead, Handbook of Denominations in
the United States (New York, 1970), fifth edition,
pp. 188-89.

55.   McGuire, "Caustic Reply," p. 5.   Gavin White places
the founding of the Independent Episcopal Church
more than a year later, in June 1921.   "Patriarch
McGuire," p. 127.

56.   McGuire, "Caustic Reply," p. 5.   Vincent, Black Power,
suggests, on the basis of a personal conversation with
ex-Garveyite James B. Yearwood, that McGuire returned to the United States in 1919 in the expectation
of being appointed by the Protestant Episcopal Church
as bishop to Liberia, and that when a white man was
appointed instead, "McGuire turned to Garveyism."
(p. 135).   A biographical article on McGuire appearing in the New York World, August 3, 1924, which
Vincent also cites, alludes to the event as follows:
"When he [McGuire] went to Arkansas in 1903 [?] as
an archdeacon he ran into Jim Crowism and it left
scars on his spirit.   In 1919, when the white Bishop
Overs was consecrated as successor to the Black
Bishop Ferguson in Liberia, a Negroes' country, it
opened the wounds." (p. 3).   There is no indication
in this article, however, that McGuire himself expected to be selected for the post.

57.   NW 10:7 (April 2, 1921), pp. 1, 5.   Tobitt had been one
of the original signatories of the Declaration of Rights.
His conversion to the UNIA is discussed in chapter 1.

58.   Ibid.   Garvey was traveling in the West Indies from
February to July 1921, and it is very possible that he
was unaware of or did not approve of events trans-
piring at UNIA headquarters during this period.

59.   Ibid.

60.   Terry-Thompson, History of the African Orthodox Church,
p. 51.

61. Ibid., pp. 51-56 and White, "Patriarch McGuire," pp. 127-130.

62. The name of the organization was not settled until the September 1921 synod. Little is known about Bridgeman's background. White speculates that he was "A Moravian pastor from Barbados," (White, "Patriarch McGuire," p. 129) although he gives no source for this information. There is a reference in the New York Age to a Rev. J. N. Bridgeman "of the M.E. Church, Brooklyn" which may be the same individual. See the issue for January 4, 1919, p. 8. Bridgeman was active in the UNIA as well as being an early member of the Independent Episcopal Church. According to a Negro World article appearing April 9, 1921 he delivered the Easter sermon at the Brooklyn Division meeting, and is quoted as having remarked that "in this present era the sons and daughters of Ethiopia have risen through the inspiration of Marcus Garvey,--their noble leader, [and] having their trust placed in God, their cry is 'One God, One Aim, One Destiny.'" NW 10:8 (April 9, 1921), p. 8.

63. NW 10:22 (July 16, 1921), p. 4.

64. Gordon was a graduate of Atlanta Baptist College, Atlanta, Georgia, and was pastor of Tabernacle Baptist Church in Los Angeles, California in the years just preceding and following his involvement in the Garvey movement. Delilah Beasley, The Negro Trail Blazers of California (Los Angeles, 1919), p. 161.

65. NW 11:2 (August 27, 1921), p. 12.

66. NW 11:8 (October 8, 1921), p. 3.

67. Terry-Thompson, History of the African Orthodox Church, passim, and White, "Patriarch McGuire," pp. 127-132.

68. Although from Terry-Thompson's account it is not altogether clear why Bridgeman was not confirmed in this post, he does indicate that Bridgeman argued vigorously in the synod debates over the title of the new organization. Evidently the entire convention was out of sympathy for his point of view, as he was able to muster only a single vote for his proposal that the title "African Episcopal" be adopted instead of "African

Orthodox." Terry-Thompson, History of the African
Orthodox Church, pp. 54 and 55. Bridgeman's name
does not subsequently appear on any of the clergy
lists for the African Orthodox Church, in spite of
the fact that by special vote, all members of any
Independent Episcopal Church who had participated
in the first general synod were made "Life members"
of the AOC's governing body. Ibid., p. 53.

69. The Swedish Orthodox Church was in communion with
the American Catholic Church, and was formed in
1920 to minister to its Swedish speaking constituency.
E. O. Watson, ed., Yearbook of the Churches,
1924-5 (Baltimore, 1934), p. 15.

70. NW 11:8 (October 8, 1921), p. 3. Robertson, an Anglican by training, had been rector of St. Philip's
Church in Sydney, Nova Scotia. After joining the
AOC he evidently took a church in Boston, and was
himself made Auxiliary Bishop in the AOC on November 18, 1923, and eventually succeeded McGuire
as Archbishop shortly before the latter's death in
1934. Watson, Yearbook ... 1924-5, p. 14. See
also The Orthodox Messenger 2:10 (October 1942),
p. 12.

71. NW 11:8 (October 8, 1921), p. 3.

72. NW 11:11 (October 29, 1921), p. 6.

73. NW 11:20 (December 31, 1921), p. 2. Emphasis added.

74. This hypothesis is suggested by the following comment
from the Negro World: "Cyril Briggs, august chief
of the African Blood Brotherhood, is getting it good
and hot from those U.N.I.A. members whose names
and addresses he got hold of through his exquisite
association with that disgraced official of the U.N.I.A.,
'Bishop' Alex. McGuire." NW 11:22 (January 14,
1922), p. 8. No further information is provided, and
I have been unable to find any indication that McGuire
was ever actively involved with the A.B.B. Briggs,
who had come to the United States from the British
West Indies in 1905, shared with McGuire an Episcopalian heritage, but he was not to my knowledge attracted to the African Orthodox Church. On Briggs,
see Frank Lincoln Mather, ed., Who's Who of the

Colored Race (Chicago, 1915), p. 38 and Vincent,
Black Power, esp. pp. 77-84.

75.　NW 11:21 (January 7, 1922), p. 4.

76.　A much different explanation for the Garvey/McGuire
　　　split is offered in a letter sent to the Office of the
　　　British Consul in New York City, dated September
　　　24, 1924. The letter was sent by Rev. Edwin Ur-
　　　ban Lewis, a one-time member of the African Ortho-
　　　dox Church who had recently been expelled from the
　　　organization at its Fourth General Synod. Lewis
　　　was still smarting from the rebuff of having been
　　　found "guilty of laxity of duty" and receiving a six-
　　　month suspension from the body, and the over-all
　　　intent of his letter seems to have been an attempt at
　　　retaliation against the AOC by discrediting it in the
　　　eyes of British authorities. In particular, he charged
　　　that the recent appointment of an AOC Bishop for
　　　Nova Scotia was made in the hopes of confusing colo-
　　　nial officials in the West Indies so that they would not
　　　suspect church work emanating from Canada as being
　　　associated with that of the radical McGuire.
　　　　　It was in setting the stage for this charge that
　　　Lewis made the following comment concerning Mc-
　　　Guire's disaffection from Garvey: "This McGuire
　　　held a very prominent position in the capacity of Hon.
　　　Chaplin [sic] General, and resigned after his return
　　　from Cuba where he visited under the auspices of the
　　　Universal Negro Improvement Association, collected
　　　large sums of money from the poor illiterate people
　　　who unfortunately took stocks in the Black Star Line
　　　swindle and the said McGuire did not account for the
　　　greater portion of the amount which was given by
　　　these people and so like that, himself and Garvey
　　　fell out, and so McGuire resigned." E. Urban Lewis
　　　to British Consulate, New York, November 24, 1924,
　　　in Great Britain, Public Record Office, CO 318/380.
　　　　　Lewis offers no concrete evidence that McGuire
　　　was guilty of malfeasance of funds. It is possible
　　　that a rumor about McGuire's misuse of funds was
　　　circulated by Garvey's allies after the two had split
　　　on ideological grounds. I am grateful to William F.
　　　Elkins for bringing the Lewis letter to my attention.

77.　NW 13:3 (August 25, 1922), p. 12. Emphasis added.

78. White, "Patriarch McGuire," p. 120; also cited approvingly in Rushing, "A Note," p. 38.

79. Vincent, Black Power, p. 270, and Terry-Thompson, History of the African Orthodox Church, p. 54.

80. NW 17:22 (January 10, 1925), p. 10, and The Negro Churchman 4:11 (December 1926).

81. Terry-Thompson, History of the African Orthodox Church, p. 55, and NW 8:17 (June 12, 1920).

82. The Negro Churchman 4:11 (December 1926). His election as Chaplain-General was reported in the Journal and Guide, September 1, 1934.

83. NW 16:26 (August 9, 1924).

CHAPTER 4

CLERGY IN THE UNIA: I

George McGuire had said it well in his opening address at the Fourth International Convention: "No constructive program for the Negro can be effective which underestimates the hold his religious institutions have upon him."[1]
The critical factor in determining the viability of what has
here been characterized as Garvey's "Black civil religion"
was the perception and the reception it would receive among
the powerful and the not-so-powerful in Black religious institutions. A barrier to accurate assessment of the complex
relationships between the UNIA and the Black churches has
been the false assumption that there was a pervasive and
mutually held hostility on both sides of the equation: by Garvey and the UNIA as a whole toward the Black churches, and
by the churches vis-à-vis the UNIA. Any comments by Garvey that would indicate an openness toward or an appreciation
for the Black churches are understood at best as but a prag-
matic recognition on his part of the power which the churches
wielded in the Black community. The African Orthodox
Church, in this view, is understood either as a concession
to those who desperately wanted some kind of "official"
church, or as a cynical attempt to minimize the influence
of existing Black churches by drawing individuals out of their
loyalties to the traditional Black denominations and realigning
them within the UNIA. As for clergy attitudes, it is generally agreed that "Except for an insignificant handful ... the
regular Negro clergy firmly rejected the new black religion"
which Garvey had promulgated.[2]

It is certainly the case, as was made clear in chapter
2, that Garvey did not hesitate to chastise the Black churches
for their too-ready acceptance of a white God and their per-
sistence in espousing an otherworldly theology that fostered
acquiescence to injustice in the present world. Yet there
was no doubt in his mind that clergymen who were genuinely

interested in their race and who were faithful to the "right idea of God"[3] would support the UNIA. Such was the implication of advice which Garvey gave to prospective UNIA leaders in his confidential lesson guides for the School of African Philosophy. He there counseled,

> In approaching ministers of the gospel, be always diplomatic enough to convince them of the Christian policy of the organization. The willingness of the organization to support the cause of the Christian religion. [sic] If the preacher is won over and himself contributes, you may get further assistance from him by seeking permission to speak to his congregation.... No preacher should be left until he has consented to help in some way, as there is no greater way of the Church showing its willingness to expand the functions of the Church than by helping a cause like that of the U.N.I.A. If a preacher refuses it is evident that he has not been in touch with the proper argument or that he is positively selfish. [4]

A substantial number of ministers were indeed convinced of "the Christian policy" of the UNIA. It is striking to note, for instance, that of the one hundred twenty-two men and women who on August 20, 1920 signed the "Declaration of Rights" which was the charter document of the Universal Negro Improvement Association and African Communities League, fully one-sixth were men or women of the cloth.[5] In fact, if one subtracts the seventeen women signatories (only one of whom was a professional church worker) it becomes evident that more than one in five of the men who signed this "Magna Charta of the Negro Race" either had been before, were at the time, or were later to become religious professionals.

Furthermore, it is far from true that none of the religious leaders who supported Garvey were prominent, either nationally or within the ranks of their own denominations. [6] To the contrary, there are a significant number of leading Black clergymen who at one time or another identified themselves with the Garvey movement, and they were by no means restricted to membership in the newly formed African Orthodox Church. It has already been demonstrated in the previous chapter that the relationship between the AOC and the UNIA has been imperfectly understood, and that the key to the distinctiveness of the two institutions hinged on the fundamentally different conceptions held by McGuire and Garvey concerning the form that religion ought to take within the UNIA. As will become evident in the following pages, it was virtually imperative to Garvey--given the number of clergymen from nearly every spectrum of Black religious life who were associated with the UNIA--that a manifest distinction between the two organizations be made, so that no pastor would have to defend himself from the charge of having abandoned his denomination by supporting the UNIA.

Black Churchmen in the UNIA

There has been a tendency in the Garvey studies presently available to underestimate both the number of clergymen who supported Garvey and their prominence within the ranks of the Black churches. This may in part be due to the appalling lack of information available about Black church leaders in the early twentieth century. Biographical information is scattered and painstakingly difficult to uncover. Church historians have only recently begun to give attention to the histories of Black denominations, so that even for the period only fifty years distant, little is known about the institutions which sociologists and historians of the Black experience alike agree have "left [their] imprint upon practically every aspect of Negro life."[7] For this reason, an effort has been made to provide as much biographical information as possible concerning clergy discussed here, in the hope that it will both contribute to the development of the history of the Black church in this period and demonstrate the range and depth of church support for the UNIA.

On the basis of careful scrutiny of the earliest consecutive collection of the Negro World presently available, I have compiled a directory of more than two hundred and fifty clergymen (plus a few prominent laymen) who were reported as active on behalf of the UNIA. This chapter will examine clergy in the two most powerful Black denominations, the National Baptists and the AMEs. The following chapter will look at clergy participation in the UNIA from the AME Zion and CME Churches, the Protestant Episcopal Church, Black Jews, and the relatively few UNIA supporters from predominantly white denominations such as the Christian, Congregational and Presbyterian Churches, and some Holiness and Pentecostal Churches. It will conclude with an analysis of patterns of association, similarity of background, and identity of interests, either religious or political, which

might account for the surprisingly large number of clergymen who at one time or another were either active on behalf
of, or sympathetic to, the UNIA.

Baptists in the UNIA

The most amorphous, though certainly the largest, of
the Black religious bodies in the 1920s were the Baptists,
who were for the most part affiliated under the National Baptist Conventions, USA, founded as late as 1896. Like their
white counterparts, the Black Baptists placed a high premium
on local autonomy and individual conscience, so that the national organization was very slow to achieve the cohesiveness
and ability to mandate policies that was possible in other denominations. The independence thereby afforded individual
clergymen, however, meant with respect to participation in
the UNIA that greater weight would be given to local con-
siderations and to the particular preferences of each pastor.

Of the two hundred and fifty clergymen in our survey
associated with the UNIA, more than one-third are identified
by denominational affiliation, and, as would be expected, by
far the largest number are Baptists. The thirty-eight Baptists for whom the hometown is given represent eighteen different states, including ten in the Midwest and East, five in
the South, and three states in the West.[8] We will examine
in some detail the biographies of three of these men, and
look more cursorily at a half dozen others.

Junius Caesar Austin (1887-1968)

Junius C. Austin,[9] the minister who was selected to
speak at the opening session of the Third International Convention (1922) "Representing the Negro Ministry," was one
of several nationally prominent Baptist clergymen who were
Garvey enthusiasts. Born and raised in Virginia, Austin received the call to the ministry at the early age of eleven.
He was educated at Lynchburg (Virginia) Theological Seminary
and College between 1901 and 1910, and then for five years
held parishes first in Clifton Forge and later in Staunton,
Virginia. In 1915 he was called north to Pittsburgh, Pennsylvania, where for eleven years h e pastored a t the
Ebenezer Baptist Church.

Evidence of Austin's prominence in Baptist circles is

Junius C. Austin (center, elbow on piano), with evangelization team in Pittsburgh.

found in the fact that he was selected to preach the Introductory Sermon at the annual National Baptist Convention
which met in Chicago, Illinois, in 1921.[10] He was elected
president in June 1924 of the Pennsylvania State Baptist
Convention, and was reported the following year, in William
H. Moses's Colored Baptists' Family Tree, as being chairman of his denomination's Foreign Mission Board.[11] His
selection for inclusion in the first volume of Who's Who in
Colored America, published in 1927, provides further documentation of his stature as a leading Baptist clergyman.
From Pittsburgh he would go in the mid-1920s to Chicago
to accept the pastorate of the enormous Pilgrim Baptist
Church, which reportedly had a membership of upwards of
five thousand persons.[12]

Austin was, in a word, one of the coming young
clergymen in his denomination, and it was doubtless for
this reason that Garvey invited the handsome Baptist preacher
to deliver a ten-minute address at the opening of the 1922
International Convention on behalf of the Negro Ministry.
The date, August 1, 1922, happened to coincide with Austin's
thirty-fifth birthday, and when he was introduced to the crowd
of some ten thousand persons as "America's Greatest Pulpit
Orator," Austin rose to the occasion with a stirring defense
of the Universal Negro Improvement Association and culmi-
nated his speech with a ringing endorsement of Marcus Garvey.

> We have a just cause and we have faith in the
> justice of God [Austin declared].... Most of all
> we have among our assets a Moses whom we can
> trust. He is not a spy; he comes not as a traitor
> nor a hired servant for foes, but is appointed by
> God and is recognized and accepted among the
> leaders of the race and is going to lead us on to
> victory.[13]

Although there is no indication on the basis of issues
of the Negro World presently available as to the length of
time Austin was active in behalf of the UNIA, it is known
that for a year or more his church served as a forum for
the discussion and advancement of Garvey's program. An
announcement in the March 17, 1923 issue of the paper, for
instance, indicated that the prominent Garveyite Arnold H.
Maloney would speak the following day at Austin's Ebenezer
Baptist Church in Pittsburgh on the subject, "Philosophy of
Garveyism." Maloney and Austin were evidently close
personal friends, and the ex-Episcopal clergyman spoke on
several occasions from Austin's pulpit.[14]

The continuing influence of Garvey on Austin's thought is suggested by a Pittsburgh Courier article announcing one of Austin's militant sermon topics for the coming week: "Slavery! Slavery! Slavery! Political Slavery, Social Slavery, Economic Slavery, Peonage, and race injustice in general must go. This is the thing which will be emphasized by Dr. J. C. Austin in his address Sunday afternoon Nov. 23."[15] The style and subject matter of this sermon are reminiscent of those preached weekly at Liberty Hall, and it is reasonable to conclude that Garvey's influence was still being felt. The announcement also noted that the pastor was seeking "to form a Negro [political] Party," a proposal which Garvey had advocated some years earlier.[16]

William Henry Moses (1872-1940)

A second nationally known Baptist clergyman who surpassed even Austin in terms of his militancy and outspoken criticism of white racism, and who also for a period of time was an active Garvey supporter, is the Reverend William H. Moses. Born in 1872, Moses, like Austin, was raised in Virginia and moved north to Pennsylvania to begin his ministry. With Philadelphia serving as his base of operation, Moses early evidenced the dual interest in the politics of protest and religion that eventually led him to support of the UNIA. An illustration of this dual interest was his co-founding, with Richard R. Wright, Jr. (later a Bishop in the AME Church, and also a Garveyite) and other Philadelphia clergymen, of the Colored Protective Association. Established in 1918, the purpose of the CPA was "Carrying on propaganda, and securing legal defense for Negro-Americans who were unjustly arrested, or attacked, in trying to lawfully occupy their homes, and to help adjust themselves."[17] The Association was one of many which sprang up in the wake of violence perpetrated upon Black Americans throughout the United States in the latter part of the second decade of this century.

Moses, at this time, was pastor of the Zion Baptist Church in Philadelphia, and was also corresponding secretary of the National Baptist Church of the USA. A remarkable book published in 1919 through his denominational press indicates even more vividly than membership in the CPA the radical danger to which he saw his people exposed in the post-war period. The book was entitled The White Peril, and, as he bluntly stated in the preface, "The Peril is, that the darker races in general, and the black race in particular is in danger of political, industrial, social and economic slavery or extermination by the white Christian nations of the world. "[18]

Despite the numerous parallels which Moses's <u>The White Peril</u> offers to Garvey's general critique, both of

"The White Peril"

What is it? How does it work? What is it doing to the Negro and to Civilization today?

HEAR DR. W. H. MOSES
PASTOR ZION BAPTIST CHURCH

In His Sensational Address "The White Peril"

ALLEN A. M. E. CHURCH, 17th and Bainbridge Sts.

THURSDAY EVE., DEC. 11th, '19

DR. MOSES will make you think, think, and then think some more. Without doubt the Greatest, most Original and most Instructive address being delivered today on the American platform. It is worth coming a hundred miles to hear. You will never forget it, and never regret it.

REV W. H. MOSES, D D
Editor The Baptist World Aso
then of The White Peril Member Board of Managers C P A

Black and white Christianity and of the importance of Africa, there is no evidence that either Moses or Garvey was then aware of the other's program. It was not, in fact, until mid-1923 that Moses began to speak on behalf of Marcus Garvey and the Universal Negro Improvement Association. Moses's name had first appeared in the pages of the <u>Negro World</u> some six months earlier, in November 1922, when the paper reported that he was to be one of five candidates seeking the position of president of the National Baptist Convention of the U.S.A., Inc. The lengthy news article contained Moses's seven-point platform for the office.[19] A week later, Moses's name appeared in two different places in the pages of the <u>Negro World</u>. In one of his chatty editorials, literary editor William Ferris reported that he had had lunch that week with Moses and Prof. James E. K. Aggrey of Livingston College.[20] Elsewhere in the paper an article appeared endorsing, on behalf of the Negro World, Moses's candidacy for presidency of the NBC. [21] Presumably these two news items were not unrelated.

Although the Negro World endorsement did not suffice to insure Moses's election (Lacey K. Williams was chosen as NBC president), it doubtless left him favorably disposed to the UNIA. When Garvey found himself in grave legal troubles, having been convicted and imprisoned for using the mails to defraud in the matter of selling stock for the Black Star Line, Moses led the roster of prominent New York City clergymen who spoke out in Garvey's behalf. He did this first in a sermon preached on July 8, 1923 at his own National Baptist Church, 125th and Madison Avenue, New York City. The following week he was invited to speak on the platform at Liberty Hall, and the full text of his speech was published in the UNIA newspaper. [22]

The banner headline in the Negro World, describing the "Rousing" and "Eloquent" quality of "Dr. Moses' Masterly Oration," paid just tribute to the speech which was delivered that Sunday. Moses characterized himself as "one of that large group of sympathizers with this organization who has not become an active member."[23] Having just returned from a two-month speaking tour of the United States, however, he could report that he had encountered virtually no opposition to Garvey wherever he went. To the contrary, the sentiment he detected uniformly supported Garvey's immediate release. "Whether we are members or not, we want Marcus Garvey out. Because as long as Mr. Garvey is in, you and I are on the way in. He must come out."

The Biblical texts for his speech were taken from I Chronicles 12:32 and Joel 2:28, 29 and these Old Testament passages were exegeted so as to apply directly to Marcus Garvey. The first text spoke of the men of Issachar, who "had understandings of the times to know what Israel ought to do." This passage, Moses explained, offered a practical definition of prophecy, namely, "understanding a time to know what to do" as well as "the telling forth what God is doing in your day and generation." And who is the one who understands his time? He is the man "upon whom God has poured out his spirit," the young man who, according to Joel, will see visions, while the old men dream dreams, "[A]nd, brothers," declared Moses,

if the Spirit of God is not on Marcus Garvey, it is

not on anybody else. (Loud Applause.) Mr. Garvey can truly say: "The Spirit of the Lord is upon
me. He hath annointed me to open the eyes of the
blind and preach the acceptable word of the Lord."
Today is this Scripture fulfilled. Right here today
I want to say this, that God's spirit is poured out
in a simple way on the world. . . .

There comes a time when the Spirit of God
takes the form of protest, and anything besides
protest is a mockery of God and a mockery of
justice. What are you going to say Glory Hallelu-
jah for, when somebody is beating your boy? That
is the spirit of the devil. Somebody has taken
your homeland and is dominating the whole earth,
and is not associating with you and do not want you
to associate with yourself. And you stand grinning.
Any spirit that makes you submit to that is the
spirit of cowardice and the spirit of the Devil.
(Applause.) . . . There is a spirit of protest, and
the man who stands for that, the Spirit of God is
upon him, and he has proclaimed the era of opportunity. . . . You need not think that the smart Negroes and the smart white folks are the only real
reformers in this world. Those folks down in
Mississippi and the people in every corner of the
world know it is not running right, and under God
the people of the earth are beginning to see what's
wrong and are going to fix it. There is more religion than you think. I mean, there are more
forces at work for God than you have folks baptized.[24]

Prophets, Moses insisted, do not come from the ranks
of the educated, the "smart Negroes" or "smart white folks."
Nor do they come from the priestly class, and indeed, one
of the hopeful signs of the times was that "folks are cursing
preachers," for the preachers have abandoned the principles
of Jesus Christ--they are preaching lies. The stark fact is
that "the whole world wakes up to hear more what Marcus
Garvey has to say than all the Negro preachers in the world."

You may talk about you come from Harvard
and "I come from Yale" and "I am from Cornell"
but the man that speaks to the multitude must come
from Heaven. He is not born in a day. No man
can make him. He comes out of the groaning and
travail of ages. Mr. Garvey is the pent-up feeling

of the race that has been in the region of the shadow of death for ages. [25]

Garvey has even taught us how to pray, Moses continued. The problem in the past has been that Negroes have
not been asking for anything worthwhile; but Garvey has taught
us to pray for stores, mills, factories, railroads, and ships.
He has taught us to seek our salvation here and now, rather
than in the far off tomorrow. He has begun to force the
preachers to wake up to the fact that the Negro wants to
know not where he is going to spend eternity, but where he
is going to spend the night and the day that follows, and "not
only where I am going to spend the day, but where my race
is going to spend it."

In the course of his speech, Moses managed to touch
on all of the major issues that were at stake in the general
debate over Garvey's program. No, Garvey does not himself expect to live in Africa, nor does he expect all Negroes
to leave the United States for Africa. Rather, "God has
chosen this America of ours to lay the keel for the ship that
shall bring success to the black peoples of the world," and
Garvey's program is to use his American-based organization
to effect change in Africa. Yes, Garvey's program for the
creation of our own "Shoe stores, grocery stores, hardware
stores, drug stores, all sorts of manufacturing concerns,"
is correct, for without them we stand at the economic, and
hence the political mercy of the white man. No, the Black
Star Line was not a mistake or a misadventure, whether it
is profitable or not. It is not a waste of the people's money
to create visible signs of the power which we seek. And
yes, we are willing to fight for our rights, if need be, just
as we did in the World War. If we fought so gallantly in
that war, which in reality was a white man's war, then "Do
you think we are going to let them divide Africa now?" Don't
stand between us and the promised land, he challenged the
white man, and no one would get hurt! His speech concluded
with an eloquent description of the vision which he had
glimpsed from the podium in Liberty Hall:

> I see a time when black people everywhere
> are going to rise and shine, for the lie is given
> and the Light of God is shining on the books. I
> see a larger day. I see a city of schools and
> churches. I see cities everywhere, extending from
> the Cape of Good Hope to Cairo in Egypt. I see a
> crowd yonder extending from the Zambesi to the

> Niger River. I see this race of mine waking up,
> hand in hand, American and what not, pressing on
> together, having a home together. Let nobody de-
> ceive you. It may take a year. It may take ten
> thousand years. But under God the hour will come
> when Ethiopia shall stretch forth her hand unto God
> and black men shall hold their heads high, and the
> name of Marcus Garvey shall be embalmed in our
> memories and our children's memories. [26]

With Moses, as with Austin, it is difficult to deter-
mine how long, or to what extent he remained an active supporter of Marcus Garvey. A leaflet advertising a Madison
Square Garden UNIA meeting for March 16, 1924 listed William H. Moses as giving a sermonette on the perennial theme,
"Ethiopia Shall Soon Stretch Forth Her Hands Unto God. "[27]
Some months later, a Moses sermon topic published in the
Pittsburgh Courier was taken from a stock UNIA theme, "The
Power of Righteous Propaganda. "[28] Thus, for at least a
year this influential and popular Baptist leader was actively
identified with the UNIA.

James Robert Lincoln Diggs (1866-1923)

Although both Austin and Moses spoke actively in behalf of Marcus Garvey and the UNIA, there is no evidence
that either of them ever became dues-paying members of the
Association. There were many Baptist clergymen who did
so, however, and among these none was more prominent in
Baptist circles than James R. L. Diggs, pastor of Trinity
Baptist Church in Baltimore. Remarkably little has been
written about Diggs, who was among the first Black men to
earn a Ph.D. in the United States, and who was active in a
variety of radical protest organizations during his lifetime.
He was born in Upper Marlboro, Maryland, on November 7,
1866, and was raised in Washington, D.C., where he attended
the prestigious Nineteenth Street Baptist Church. [29] Pastor of
that church was the influential Walter H. Brooks, who baptized and later ordained Diggs, and who remained a friend
and spiritual guide throughout Diggs's lifetime.

Diggs was extremely well educated, receiving both the
A.B. and M.S. degrees from Bucknell. After post-graduate
work at Cornell, he taught Latin and French at Virginia Union
University in Richmond, Virginia, and then enrolled at Illinois
Wesleyan University, where he earned a Ph.D. in 1906.

J. R. L. Diggs (center) and faculty of Virginia Seminary and College (from *An Era of Progress and Promise*, by W. N. Hartshorn).

According to Harry W. Greene, Diggs was the first Negro to be awarded a doctorate in the field of Sociology, and at the time was only the ninth Black man to have earned the Ph. D. at a university in the United States. [30]

Diggs taught at a variety of Black Baptist colleges around the country. He served for a time as president of State University in Louisville; was dean of the English and Languages departments of Selma (Alabama) University; and was later head of Virginia Theological Seminary in Lynchburg. [31] As historians George Shepperson and Thomas Price have remarked, "many of these Negro schools and colleges taught doctrines and inculcated attitudes which some call politely 'racial radicalism,' and others, more bluntly, 'sedition.'"[32] Whether Diggs imbibed his radicalism from colleagues while teaching at these institutions or already held these ideals from an earlier period is difficult to determine. His obituary noted that he had proposed to then Maryland Governor Emerson C. Harrington the idea of a "colored Council of Defense during the war," and that he had for many years fought "for better pay for school teachers in rural schools."[33] He was, then, actively working on behalf of his race throughout his lifetime.

In October 1920 the Thirteenth Annual Convention of William Monroe Trotter's National Equal Rights League was held in Diggs's Trinity Baptist Church. Diggs was elected vice-president of this early civil rights organization. Less than a year later the Daily Star reported that a "master pulpit orator" from Baltimore, Maryland preached a "most scholarly sermon" to the closing sessions of the UNIA's Second International Convention, 1921. [35] Diggs's star within the UNIA rose just as that of George Alexander McGuire was waning. McGuire, who had been elected Chaplain-General of the UNIA at the 1920 Convention, resigned his post under a cloud following the Second International Convention. [36] Shortly thereafter Diggs was being referred to in the Negro World as "Acting Chaplain-General," and it was as such that he preached the Convention sermon at the opening of the Third International Convention in August 1922.

His sermon text was from Isaiah 42:4, "He will not fail or be discouraged till he has established justice in the earth." The topic he chose to discuss with seven thousand assembled delegates was the Biblical warrant for the UNIA program and the error committed by some Garveyites who were inclined to turn their backs upon the Black church in their struggle for social justice. He began the sermon by drawing the familiar analogy between the people of Israel as a chosen people and the people of Africa and of African descent who were also uniquely chosen by God for a special destiny. It is not only the Jews who have a special prophecy, he declared:

> There is one other class of people who have a special prophecy in regard to their future and sudden development. It is declared that the black-faced people of the earth, commonly called the Ethiopian shall suddenly or shall soon stretch forth their hands to God. The Messiah is the Eternal agent for the accomplishment of this high purpose. The nations are at the service of Jehovah, the Messiah is to lead them unto a larger liberty and until judgment shall be set upon the earth he will not manifest in his fullness the plan for the ages.[37]

Those who are discouraged should take heart and those who are doubtful should believe, for God is a just God, and the very success of the UNIA is proof that His promises to His Black people are even now being fulfilled. Diggs advised his audience to

> Hear the voice of Jehovah when He says that "He shall not fall nor be discouraged until He shall set judgment upon the earth." Judgment and justice are the habitation of His throne. Truth and peace shall come before His face and Ethiopia shall enjoy her right as a world power and shall receive what He has intended for her, and the Red, the Black and the Green are not inconsistent institutions in their proclamation of the great truth for which they stand.
> One finds warrant in Revelation for hopefulness and assurance. Let no black man doubt that he will come into his own, for God has led us during the last hundred years so wonderfully toward a true and real freedom....
> Why be discouraged, oh men clothed in black, hold up your heads and look into the face of God who calls you to a nobler service.
> DARKNESS IS NOT ASSOCIATED WITH EVIL.[38]

There is some indication that certain aspects of Diggs's message encountered hostility among the Garveyites assembled,

and that this hostility was at least in part shared by Marcus
Garvey himself. "I hope that the distinguished president will
excuse me," he said on the convention floor some days after
his sermon. "He may not see this in the text, but it is in
there. We must stand for the defense of the gospel when
you are doing a great work that God has called you to do."[39]
Whatever may have been the full ramifications of this dis-
agreement between Garvey and Diggs, the two men were in
basic agreement on most matters before the convention. Garvey, for instance, led the fight on the convention floor against
accepting the offer of a "well known Bible Society" which
sought permission to give each delegate present a copy of the
Bible. After the meeting Diggs supported the convention's
decision in a statement to a reporter for the New York World:

> I am a Christian and a pastor, but I agree
> with the action of this organization in refusing to
> accept any Bibles from the Bible Society. We are
> not atheists by any means, and we are not rejecting
> the Bible. What we are doing to-day is registering
> an emphatic protest against Christianity as it is in-
> terpreted in this country.[40]

Despite the criticism of some delegates that he was
too prone to compromise, Diggs was unanimously elected to
the office of Chaplain-General in the closing days of the Convention. Alas, whether or not the criticism raised against
him was deserved cannot be judged on the basis of his per-
formance in office, for barely two months after his election
an item in the Negro World reported that the Chaplain-General
had been hospitalized for a serious operation.[41] Within six
months Diggs was dead of cancer, at the age of 56. His
death, along with that of John E. Bruce a year later, would
deprive the UNIA of two of its most influential and nationally
respected leaders, and was a severe blow to the organization
which was already reeling from the trial of Marcus Garvey
then under way in the federal courts.

There are numerous other Baptist clergymen who were
at least as active in the UNIA as the three men whose biographies have just been chronicled. The following vignettes are
illustrative of the range of their backgrounds and activities.

James David Brooks and John Dawson Gordon

Two Baptist ministers were among the signatories of

the famed "Declaration of Rights of the Negro Peoples of the World," adopted at the First International Convention, 1920. J. D. Brooks was listed as Foreign Mission Secretary of the National Baptist Convention of America when he first spoke in Liberty Hall in June 1920, declaring that his faith in God had been renewed by what he had seen and experienced there, and that the white man had for too long been allowed to fix his own interpretation of the Bible.[42] Brooks was elected in August 1920 to the post of Secretary General of the UNIA, responsible for organizing local conventions and raising funds for the Association.[43] Much of his time was spent traveling to UNIA divisions around the country, and monthly reports from Okmulgee, Oklahoma, to Belhaven, North Carolina, chronicled Brooks's visits to their meetings.[44] A sample of the success he achieved is the report of the Raleigh, North Carolina, UNIA Division, which stated that the ministers' union which he addressed there "went on record as endorsing 'Garveyism' and tendering Dr. Brooks a vote of thanks for his message."[45] (Equally interesting in that report is the list of those attending a meeting held on the campus of Shaw University who "pledged their loyalty to the UNIA." Among them were Prof. L. M. Cheek, listed as treasurer of the local UNIA Division and editor of the Raleigh Independent; Prof. W. H. Thomas, ."returned missionary from Liberia and teaching at Shaw University"; the Reverend Dr. C. E. Askew, pastor of First Baptist Church; and Prof. Ligon, superintendent of the Raleigh public schools).

We have earlier encountered another Baptist pastor who signed the Declaration of Rights, namely, John Dawson Gordon of Los Angeles. Gordon had graduated from Atlanta Baptist College and moved with his brother around the turn of the century to Los Angeles, where he was pastor at the flourishing Tabernacle Baptist Church. He had long been interested in a variety of colonization efforts (including a fascinating land project in Arizona, in which he had funds invested as late as 1921 and in which he endeavored to secure UNIA support)[46] and he was one of the leading figures in the very active UNIA Division in Los Angeles. By virtue of his leadership in Los Angeles and his skill as an orator he was elected at the 1920 Convention to the post of Assistant President General of the UNIA, second only in authority to Garvey himself. Although he resigned his position at the 1921 Convention, he is reported as late as June 1926 speaking at the Los Angeles Division meeting on the subject of the principles of the UNIA.[47]

W. W. Brown, pastor of Metropolitan Baptist Church.

Willis W. Brown (1858?-1930)

The Reverend W. W. Brown, pastor of Metropolitan
Baptist Church, New York City, was frequently characterized
in the pages of the Negro World as "a true friend of the
UNIA."[48] Brown had a long record of support for radical
causes, and at least one aspect of this radical perspective--
his Africa-consciousness--can be traced directly to his introduction to John Chilembwe in 1898. His encounter with the
young African Christian, who was later executed for leading
the 1915 revolt against British colonial authorities, had a
profound effect on Brown. As he remarked in his autobiography, "The coming of that African into my home brought me
face to face, as never before, with my responsibility for the
redemption of all the world and especially Africa."[49] His
exposure to the tragic consequences of the Nyasa Rising
would make Brown well aware of the deadly seriousness of
a program advocating "Africa for the Africans."

It was not only Brown's experience with Chilembwe,
however, which made him a likely candidate as a Garvey supporter. As early as 1904, he was characterized by J. R. L.
Diggs as one who "may well be classed with men like the
Vanderbilts, Goulds, Stewarts, Rockefellers, et al. for clear
sound business sense," and as "the chief organizer for the
new social teaching which was beginning to emerge from the
Negro pulpit."[50] The new social teaching to which Diggs referred was, of course, the social gospel tradition, which demanded attention not just to the needs of the individual, but
to the imperative of a restructured social order. When Walter
Rauschenbusch had declared that "The old religious aims over-
emphasized the other world and undervalued the present world,"
whereas "the faith of the Kingdom puts a new religious value
on this earth of ours and on the present life," he was offering
the theoretical base on which to criticize the main line white
denominations which had inured themselves to the injustices
of the gilded age.[51] But the rejection of an "otherworldly"
emphasis on the salvation of the individual to the neglect of
man's social needs was a theology readily accepted and advocated by men like Willis W. Brown, who sought to use the
Black church as a basis for social protest and social action.[52]
And rejection of an otherworldly religious orientation was, as
we have seen, a hallmark of the Garveyite critique of the
Black churches.

One would hardly be surprised, then, to find W. W.
Brown on the platform at Liberty Hall introducing Junius C.

Austin as speaker of the Third International Convention, 1922. Brown had served as pastor at Ebenezer Baptist Church in Pittsburgh prior to coming to Metropolitan Baptist in New York, and it is possible that Brown was instrumental in securing for Austin the invitation to address the UNIA convention.[53] Though numerous of Brown's own speeches in Liberty Hall could be cited to indicate his support for Garvey, none illustrates the point better than the remarks of <u>Negro World</u> editor William H. Ferris. The occasion of Ferris's remarks was an editorial expressing appreciation to New York clergymen who had participated in "Marcus Garvey day" at the previous Sunday's morning church services. Characterizing the degree of commitment to the UNIA of this man known as the "father of the African Baptist Missionaries," Ferris said:

> The Rev. W. W. Brown of the Metropolitan Baptist Church gave a lengthy address encouraging his members to assist in doing all they possibly can for the cause. Mr. Brown has always been with us, and we believe he is one of Marcus Garvey's best friends and supporters.[54]

Thomas W. Anderson

Many Garveyite clergy had worked for the NAACP prior to joining the UNIA. A case in point is Thomas W. Anderson, a Baptist clergyman from the Midwest who was ordained in Detroit in 1918.[55] Shortly thereafter he assumed the pastorate of the Second Baptist Church in Adrian, Michigan. While in Adrian he organized a NAACP chapter and served for eighteen months as its president. At the time, he was affiliated with the National Baptist Publishing House in Nashville. In December 1921 he became commissioner to the state of Louisiana for the UNIA, and at the 1922 Convention was elected Assistant Secretary General. Anderson defended the UNIA against the perennial charge that it was anti-religious, declaring "We are intensely religious, but the difference between us and the others is that we think."[56] A year later, in a Christmas address at Liberty Hall on the topic "Our Religion," he identified the basic problem of Black religion, and specified the remedy prescribed by the UNIA:

> The black man, if he ever expects to become what the Universal Negro Improvement Association is striving to make him, must learn to fight; he

must believe that God Almighty, the God that he believes in, that he prays to daily, believes also in
fighting. The black man's conception of God, as I
understand it, is a mighty bum conception. He believes in the white man's God. The white man's
God, as I understand Him and as I understand the
white man to understand Him, is a God of jim-
crowism, a God of lynching, of burning at the stake,
that believes in keeping black folks down. How can
you believe in the same God and get up? It cannot
be done.... The white man believes that the highest
conception of God is seen in the face of a white
man. And the black man believes the same thing.
(Laughter.) He sees God in everything except in
himself. That is a thing that we have got to get
away from. I do not believe in the white man's
conception of God. I believe that God wants all
races to be up and no races down. But God will
not raise us up, God will not fight our battles for
us as long as we are not capable of fighting them
ourselves. As the President-General of this organization often says, God will not give us jobs,
for He does not run an employment bureau. He
will not do for us those things that we should do
for ourselves. And at this time it seems to me
the best way for us to celebrate the Birth of Jesus
Christ is for us to set about and get a proper conception of God and what our duty is to ourselves.
If we would do that, then His coming will not have
been in vain.... If you do not have a bit of heaven
here, don't worry, you won't have any hereafter. [57]

J. Francis Robinson

The Reverend J. Francis Robinson, like Anderson,
was connected with the National Baptist Publishing Board,
serving as its field secretary for a number of years. As a
returned missionary to Africa he was an especially popular
speaker in Liberty Hall, and the audience responded with
thunderous applause when he declared in an Easter week
speech that the UNIA was the best organization for racial uplift yet devised. "I would call the founder of this movement
a Moses, " he said of Marcus Garvey, "because he came to
us at a psychological moment in the history of our race in
this country, and tells us to lay our buckets down where we
are and not only to lay our buckets down where we are, but

J. Francis Robinson, Baptist missionary and Garvey supporter.

to work out the redemption of Africa, our fatherland."[58]
Robinson himself was an active member of the Cambridge,
Massachusetts, UNIA branch.

John Gibbs St. Clair Drake

One who came rather late to membership in the UNIA
was the West Indian-born Reverend J. G. St. Clair Drake.
Drake was educated at Virginia Theological Seminary in the
pre-World War I years, and then became active with William
M. Trotter in the National Equal Rights League. It was evidently not until he made a return visit to his native Barbados

Virginia Theological Seminary and College, Lynchburg, Va.
(from An Era of Progress and Promise, by W. N. Hartshorn).

that he became convinced of the "relevance of Garvey's inter-
nationalism," as one recent commentator has remarked, and
decided to join in the work of the UNIA.[59] Drake took an
active role in the leadership of the UNIA from 1924 to 1927.
A UNIA calendar for 1927 includes a picture of Drake, who
is given the title "International Organizer."[60] In the years
from 1924 to 1927 his speeches were frequently published in
the Negro World, and he reportedly took charge of "Liberty
University," a UNIA-sponsored college which eked out a pre-
carious existence for a number of years on the site of the old
Smallwood-Carey Institute in Virginia.[61]

AME's in the UNIA

In a speech delivered to the Bishop's Council of the African Methodist Episcopal Church in February 1920, some months before Garvey had captivated the attention of Black Harlem with the spectacular success of his First International Convention, the president of Wilberforce College, the Reverend John A. Gregg, addressed his distinguished audience on a subject dear to the hearts of all present: the redemption of Africa, and the AME Church's responsibility in that work. His speech places in perspective both the interest and the caution with which the AME's would approach the UNIA. Gregg began with the iteration of a fundamental theme in the self-understanding of the AME Church, namely, its special destiny and unique role as a chosen instrument of God for the Christianization first of Negro America, and then all of Africa.

> Conceived in a spirit of manhood and born of necessity, this churchh [sic] as always stood out as an exponent for the noblest and best for the black man, both at home and abroad.... [A]fter all, it has been God's hand which has guided the destinies of this great church, and I believe that adown [sic] the years He will continue to lead us, until our motto shall be accepted by all men, "God our Father, Christ our Redeemer, and man our Brother." ...
> AFRICA! AFRICA! How that word has always thrilled me, since as a boy of six in my father's home, I first heard it on the lips of a returned missionary! And to him who really has vision, what wonderful possibilities it opens up to the African Methodist Church! What an opportunity for consecrated, albeit sacrificial service! [62]

Having made the case for the AME Church's special calling and its missionary role in Africa, Gregg turned to the specific situation of the Church in South Africa, where the majority of its missionary effort was focused. The imperative need and the primary emphasis of AME work there had been in the area of education, from the earliest days of the work of Bishop Henry McNeal Turner to the recent efforts of Bishops Coppin and Johnson. However, a major stumbling block to the denomination's work had emerged as a consequence of the much discussed "Ethiopian Movement," the

tendency of Black Africans to form their own religious organizations which coincidently also served as bases for political agitation in opposition to white colonial rule. Gregg
cited the words of an otherwise unidentified "Miss Markham"
(evidently well known to all present), who had summed up
British hostility and fear of this movement:

> A strange leaven is at present working among
> the educated Kaffirs throughout the country, a leaven
> to which the affairs of the Ethiopian church bear
> emphatic testimony.... [I]mpossible, pitiful even
> though it may seem to us, slowly and in the shadow
> of the greater conflict, a new idea is taking pos-
> session of the black man's mind--Africa for the
> Africans. It is a dream, a mad dream, the reali-
> zation of which is impossible; but it is a delusion
> which may bring strange events in its train. [63]

Miss Markham made it clear, Gregg continued, whom
she thought responsible for this lamentable state of affairs,
as she decried the "regrettable circumstance" of the "introduction of the American Negro into this country." In fact,
although the Wilberforce president did not publicly repeat the
charge, Miss Markham had laid the blame for recent diffi-
culties specifically at the feet of the AME missionaries. [64]
Gregg sought to dispel this calumny by insisting that the
church was "exercising nothing more than religious effort":

> It has never been the purpose of our church
> to in any way enter into the political life of South
> Africa other than as religious activity does and
> should. It has only been our intention to go to
> those who are our brothers and lead them to better
> and higher living. We only wish to teach the native
> that he has a soul to save, a mind to develop and
> a life to make. We only wish to teach him that he
> is a man and should bear a man's burdens and be
> fitted for a man's reward. [65]

"Perhaps," Gregg remarked on second thought, Great
Britain "has some grounds for her fears and to question our
motives" after all! What would be the church's response to
the implied threat from spokesmen for colonial rule such as
Miss Markham? Though there might be some who would advise that the AME Church leave to other denominations and
other races the task of Christianizing Africa, this policy, to
Gregg, was inconceivable:

Shall the great African Methodist Episcopal
church turn a deaf ear to the pleadings of that
vast continent, coming from the souls of her teem-
ing millions of blood brothers and allow those of
another race to assume the responsibility that is
justly our own? Let me give you an interpretation
which a native African gave me of that Scripture
which says, "Princes shall come out of Egypt;
Ethiopia shall soon stretch forth her hands unto
God." He said that Egypt means bondage; that
years ago his brothers, sisters and loved ones
were away for the fatherland and placed in bondage
in America, which meant Egypt to them; while here
they learned of God and became His sons. Now
God is a King and His sons must be princes. These
princes--the native brothers--will now come back
out of Egypt and Ethiopia shall soon stretch forth
her hands unto God.

... [I]f the church accepts this man-sized job,
and does a full day's work, Africa promises to
African Methodism one of the brightest gems to
adorn her brow in this the morning of her second
century. [66]

I have quoted at length from this AME educator (soon
himself to be elected bishop) because I think his speech suggests the ambivalence with which many AME clergy would
regard the UNIA. On the one hand, there was the immediate
sense of a shared mission, of common goals, of a mutual
enemy, and a similarity of religious imagery by which the
two institutions articulated their special tasks. On the other
hand, the AME Church was never a very ecumenically-minded
institution. Indeed, it not only repulsed overtures from white
Methodists seeking to break down racial barriers which had
been erected in the house of God, but it was even leery of
offers from the AME Zion and Colored Methodist Episcopal
Churches to unite the various branches of Black Methodism.
The reason for this reluctance to compromise its institutional
identity was not simply a case of obstinate denominational
narrow-mindedness, but rather a deep-seated belief that the
AME Church had been called into being by God for a special
purpose, namely, to bring the message of Christ to His down-
trodden Black people, first in America and then in Africa. [67]
Understandably, then, the AME Church would be especially
cautious about entering into alliance with an organization such
as the UNIA, where the danger would loom of being swallowed
up by a much larger social and political movement.

Richard Robert Wright, Sr. (1855-1947) and
Richard Robert Wright, Jr. (1878-1967)

This is not to suggest, of course, that there were no
AME's who would join the UNIA. One of the most influential men to do so was a layman, Richard R. Wright, Sr.,
the so-called "Black Boy of Atlanta," whose aphorism "Tell
'em we're rising" supposedly galvanized a generation of white
philanthropists in the late 1860s to great acts of generosity.[68]
A half-century later Wright was putting new meaning into that
phrase by dint of his support of the Universal Negro Improvement Association. The immediate impetus to his conversion
to the UNIA is perhaps suggested in his son's autobiography.
Wright there describes the combination of rage and anguish
experienced by his father, who, after having served for some
thirty years as president of State College in Savannah, Georgia,
discovered that his own daughter could be insulted by an in-
consequential bank teller in that city and that none of his
white "friends," including the bank president and the chairman of the human relations committee of the city, would so
much as raise a word of protest in his behalf. The result
was that the senior Wright quit his post as college president
and moved to Philadelphia where, in the year 1921, he founded
with his son the Citizens and Southern Bank and Trust Company.[69] These factors may help to explain the following item
in the Negro World describing a March 28, 1921 meeting, in
which "Philadelphia Division celebrates Easter Sunday":

> The next speaker was Dr. R. R. Wright, [Sr.]
> president of the Citizen's and Southern National
> Bank, who said, in part, that he was glad to be
> with the members of the U.N.I.A. on this beautiful
> Easter afternoon, and that it seemed that God Al-
> mighty had made that afternoon for them. This
> afternoon, when the whole Christian world is cele-
> brating the risen Christ, we are here celebrating
> the rising race. (Cheers.) ...
> There have been only two great Negro move-
> ments in the history of America ... [one] was
> started in Philadelphia in the year 1787 and is
> known as the African Methodist Episcopal Church,
> and the other movement is the Universal Negro Im-
> provement Association, both organizations being
> owned and controlled by Negroes. (Cheers.) The
> U.N.I.A. is educating the Negro and inspiring him
> with the sense of racial consciousness, that God
> Almighty made him as good as anybody else, and

Richard R. Wright, Sr. (from Progress of a Race, by Nichols and Crogman).

when that is done, nothing is going to stand in his
way, but he will be going out into the world to occupy. When he does that he will be emancipating
himself, and I will congratulate you because you
will be doing part of your duty. (Applause.)[70]

Evidently the Wrights' support for the program of
Marcus Garvey did not have a deleterious effect on their
newly founded business enterprise. In a Negro World editorial some months later R. R. Wright, Jr. reported that
following a UNIA meeting in Philadelphia the bankers "found
it easy to get bank deposits there."[71] The younger Wright,
who had earned a Ph. D. at the University of Pennsylvania in
1911, and who later became a bishop in the AME Church,
was also a Garveyite. He was frequently reported as appearing on the stage of Philadelphia UNIA meetings, staging debates in his congregation between DuBois and Garvey factions
or sympathetically editorializing in the Christian Recorder
(the AME Church's official weekly newspaper which Wright
edited from 1909 to 1936) concerning the UNIA.[72] In fact,
he was sufficiently enamored of the UNIA to accept, at its
Second Annual Court Reception of the Potentate of the UNIA,
the honorary title of Knight Commander, Order of the Nile,
for "Faithful and distinguished service to the Negro Race."[73]

William Henry Heard (1850-1937)

The highest award of distinction made by the UNIA at
the Potentate's Reception in August 1922 went to another AME
clergyman, seventy-two year old Bishop William H. Heard.
The awarding designation read: "Right Hon. Bishop William
H. Heard, D. D., of the A. M. E. Church of Philadelphia, on
whom was bestowed the title of His Grace the Duke of Niger,
because of the great work done by him in Africa among the
native people there."[74] Heard, who had been a pioneer in
the AME missionary effort in West Africa, was by coincidence
a member of the original Board of Trustees of Citizens and
Southern Bank and Trust Company of Philadelphia.[75]

William Henry Ferris (1874-1941)

An AME churchman who devoted a number of years to
full-time work on behalf of the UNIA and who wielded considerable influence in the organization as editor of the Negro
World from 1919 to 1923 was William H. Ferris, M. A.,

author, lecturer, philosopher, preacher and bon vivant.[76]
Ferris was born in New Haven, Connecticut, in 1874 and attended Yale University, where he received both a B.A. and
an M.A., the latter being awarded in 1897. From Yale he
went to Harvard, where he attended Harvard Divinity School
from 1897 to 1899, and then was awarded an M.A. from
Harvard in 1900. In spite of, or perhaps because of, his
considerable education Ferris never seemed to find his niche
in life, and he seems to have gone from job to job, serving
as journalist, free lance writer, lecturer and friend of the
great and the near great in radical and religious circles without ever seeming to have the decisive influence in any field
that he expected of himself or that others expected of him.
Indeed, one suspects that the closest he ever came to achieving the power and influence which he so much desired was in
the years while working on behalf of the UNIA.

His only major item of publication was a verbose and
somewhat meandering two-volume work, The African Abroad:
or, His Evolution in Western Civilization; Tracing His Development Under Caucasian Milieux, which was published in
1913.[77] The subtitle of his book is significant, for it points
to the cornerstone of his philosophy of history, namely the
social Darwinist conception of evolution and the associated
ideas of conflict and the never-ending struggle for the survival of the fittest. These ideas were combined with Ferris's
understanding of the German theologians whom he had read
(especially Hegel, Lotze, and Rudolf Eucken, as well as the
American John Fiske), all of whom he interpreted as speaking
in terms of an all-pervading world spirit which was guiding
history inexorably toward the accomplishment of its seemingly
opaque but ultimately rational purposes. "The result," as
recent commentator S. P. Fullinwider has observed, "is a
scheme of history ... in which the world spirit (freedom and/
or love) is working through the bloody struggles of peoples to
the purpose of finally manifesting itself in the living reality
of human intercourse."[78] In this struggle, according to Ferris, each race has its own contribution to make, so that to
the theology of the Jews, the philosophy of the Greeks, the
organizational ability of the Romans, and the "spirit of freedom of the Anglo-Saxons," will be finally added "those spiritual and emotional qualities which can soften human nature
and spiritualize religion and music."[79] The latter would be
the contribution of the Negro race.

In The African Abroad Ferris was loud with praise for
the white man, for his political acumen, his power and

aggressiveness; in fact, Ferris goes so far as to demand
that the Negro become a "Negro-Saxon, " a "black-white man"
if he would desire to "share in the political inheritance of
the Anglo-Saxon. " As a social Darwinist, convinced that
Western civilization was the most advanced culture in existence, Ferris could do little else but hold the white man
up as a model. Yet he would not have the Black man suc-
cumb to the gross materialism which characterizes the white
race, and indeed this was his own people's special mission:
"to spiritualize Western civilization, " by purging its materialism with Christian love as that love was uniquely embodied
in the Negro race. [80]

Fullinwider has correctly identified the key elements
in Ferris's philosophy of history, although I think he misses
a crucial point by portraying Ferris simply as an anti-Bookerite and an unqualified supporter of W. E. B. DuBois. While
it is true that Ferris was hardly reverent of Booker T. Washington, he did express admiration for his self-reliant program
of boot-strap economics, for such a program would prove that
the Negro race had the ability and determination to secure its
own destiny. His primary criticism of Washington lay elsewhere: "Dr. Washington was unable, " he declared, "in his
palmiest days, when the star of his greatness was at its
zenith, when the sun of his glory was shining at its maximum, to secure a grip upon the hearts of his race. "[81] As
a national race leader he was compared unfavorably in this
respect to Henry McNeal Turner, to Alexander Crummell,
and to Frederick Douglass. Washington simply did not have
the capacity "to stir the soul. "

Interestingly enough, after a generally more favorable
assessment of W. E. B. DuBois, Ferris concluded with an
evaluation quite similar to the one he had given for Washington:

> So we may conclude our discussion of Dr.
> DuBois by saying that while his personality, [sic] in
> fact one of the most remarkable personalities thus
> far evolved by the colored race, it is not such a
> powerful personality that it holds the destiny of the
> colored race in its hands. [82]

Ferris was, in short, already when writing his book, looking
for a powerful and dynamic, soul-stirring and prophetic individual who could capture the imagination of the masses of his
race and lead them out of their slumber and into self-

consciousness. This he found in the person of Marcus Garvey, a man who coincidentally shared both Ferris's rejection of materialism and his espousal of a social Darwinian conception of the necessity for individual and racial struggle for survival.

It was barely four years after the publication of his magnum opus, in January 1917, that Ferris first met the "Moses" for whom he had been searching, when Marcus Garvey came to speak in the city of Chicago. [83] At the time Ferris was on the editorial staff of the A.M.E. Church Review, which was then edited by the fiery social gospeler Reverdy C. Ransom. Later that same year he went to work in the offices of the AME Book Concern, the publishing house of the AME Church located in Philadelphia. The head of the publishing house, who was also editor of the Christian Recorder (the oldest continuously published Black weekly), was none other than R. R. Wright, Jr. [84] Ferris continued with the Book Concern until 1919, when he moved to Harlem to become editor of Garvey's paper, the Negro World.

One cannot help but gain the impression, on reading issues of the Negro World during the years Ferris served as literary editor, that he immensely enjoyed his work as peripatetic evangelizer for the Universal Negro Improvement Association. Long excerpts from the speeches he delivered at Harlem's Liberty Hall were frequently reprinted; reports of his travel to address a local UNIA chapter in Elms, Connecticut, or New Bedford, Massachusetts, or Oberlin, Ohio, were regular features of the "News and Views of UNIA Divisions" section (also edited by Ferris); book reviews and feature articles also appeared carrying his by-line. And every week there were the editorials--sometimes turgid and prolix, sometimes thoughtful and provocative, invariably chatty and informative. Clearly, Ferris saw himself as one of the chief philosophers of the UNIA, and he regularly expounded for the benefit of his readers on such weighty issues as the conflict between science and religion, the meaning of religion, the Black Man's philosophy, or the deeper meaning of Christmas. [85] One of his early editorials, entitled "The World in Which We Live," illustrates well how Ferris integrated his Darwinian social philosophy with a conception of God as benign disciplinarian, who has given man the opportunity to create his own destiny. The result is that the race is thrown back on its own resources, and can make of its future what it will:

[M]an not only fights and battles for bread, in
the effort to preserve his physical organism and
rear his offspring, but he strives and struggles for
recognition, for power and place and fame and for
political and religious freedom. And he does it because he is a man, because there is that something
in him which is not satisfied when he has fed,
clothed and sheltered his body. That is why,
there is so much unrest in the world. That is
why the darker races are restless, they have soul
needs which demand satisfaction.

It looks as if the Maker has said to His children "I have given you a brain, five senses, two
arms and hands and two legs. I have placed you
in a world, which can easily support three billions
of peoples. I have given you a sun to shine upon
you by day and moon and stars by night. I have
given you a garden, which will respond to the touch
of man. I have placed wealth in the ground under
the surface of the earth. Now it is up to you to
do the rest." Now this is the sort of world we
live in.... It looks to us as if the Being who pre-
sides over the destinies of the universe is a disciplinarian moving calmly on towards the realization
of His majestic purpose and vast designs, beneficent
if we work in harmony with His physical and moral
laws and somewhat stern if we violate ... the law
of our own being.

And, it seems that the Negro must work out
his own salvation like the rest of mankind. "He
who would be free must strike the blow himself."
Since the Negro's brawn and muscle and toil and labor
has [sic] played a part in building up the material
prosperity of the Caucasian in America, Central
America, the West Indies and Africa, somehow or
other in the dispensation of Divine Providence he
ought to get some of the fruits of the tree of civilization, whose roots he helped to water. 86

Although in this passage it would seem that Ferris's God was
but a deistic Divine Clockmaker, other passages make it evident that He was more than this. Ferris's primary concern,
however, was to make it clear to his fellow Negroes that they
could not simply rest on the assumption that God would rescue
them from their present condition; that would have to be accomplished by their own effort.

There is no question that Ferris was important to the UNIA for his prolific discussions of Garveyite theology and religion. He was perhaps even more important to the work of the UNIA, however, as a man of letters with ready access to the Black intellectual and religious leaders of his day. His ties to the Black intellectual elite dated as far back as 1898, when he had presented a paper to the Bethel Literary and Historical Association in Washington, D. C. Ferris was evidently an active member of both this organization and its successor, the American Negro Academy, and Ferris letters contained in the published work of Francis Grimké illustrate how Ferris used his editorials in the Negro World as a conduit for the dissemination and furtherance of ideas being advanced by his friends. [87] And certainly his work with the A. M. E. Church Review and the Book Concern would have put him in close contact with national church leaders not only in the AME Church but also in most of the other Black denominations. These contacts he used to good advantage as Negro World editor.

A typical example of Ferris's value as an advocate for the UNIA is found in his report to a Liberty Hall audience on his recent visit to the 70th Bishop's Council, AME Church, which met at Bethel Church in New York City in 1922. The Council, which W. E. B. DuBois once characterized as "the most prestigious and influential group of men in the Black community,"[88] had invited Marcus Garvey to address them in convention, and Ferris had been selected to go in his place, along with the Reverend J. W. H. Eason. "As we moved among the brethren," Ferris reported, "we heard Rev. Dr. M.[ilton] H. Mickens of Huntington, West Virginia, a candidate for Missionary Secretary; Rev. S. H. V. Grumbs of Brooklyn, N.Y., Rev. T. J. Linton and Dr. [C. A.] Wingfield of Atlanta, Georgia, speaking favorably of the U.N.I.A. It is worthy of note that Bishop [William O.] Fountain of Atlanta, Georgia, spoke kindly of the U.N.I.A. at the Thursday night banquet."[89] Ferris was always careful to note favorable remarks of AME leaders concerning the UNIA. Bishop Fountain, for instance, had declared at the New York convention that "the U.N.I.A. has a tidal wave of Negro aspiration behind it and its aims were high." Bishop Archibald J. Carey of Chicago was reported a few weeks earlier at an AME convention in New Bedford, Massachusetts, as having paid a glowing tribute to Marcus Garvey. And two months later, the redoubtable Reverdy C. Ransom was reported as having spoken with at least qualified support of the UNIA program when he said,

> Some men criticize Marcus Garvey because
> of his vision of a redeemed Africa, but when we
> reflect that there are almost three times as many
> black people in Africa as there are people of all
> races in the United States of America, Marcus
> Garvey is right when he says that Africa should
> be a land of sovereign black people. [90]

Whether it was an AME Bishop's Conference, then,
or a National Baptist convention selecting a new president,
or editorials such as the one in an AME Zion journal critical of the Garvey program, Ferris was busy ferreting out
supporters for the UNIA, making comments and even en-
dorsements in important elections, or defending the Association from attack. [91] By knowing personally most of the
leaders of the various denominations, he was of considerable
strategic value to the UNIA either in eliciting a favorable
statement from those whom he knew would be most likely to
support its program, or in blunting criticism by hostile denominational officials. He was also, of course, an able defender of the UNIA among Black intellectual elite, many of
whom were opposed to the Association.

While it is true that Ferris's many editorials, articles, and speeches, give the impression of a man very much
convinced of his own importance and intellectual accomplishment, it is important as a corrective that his abilities
and his basically humanistic perspective not be underesti-
mated or minimized. There was a remarkable sense of fairness and open-mindedness to be found in the pages of the
Negro World during the years he served as literary editor.
Ferris never hesitated to report critical comments that were
made about the UNIA, though of course he always took care
to rebut the criticism reported. Sometimes full-length articles opposing the UNIA were published, along with appropriate
replies.

Ferris was especially sensitive to attacks on religion,
or to correspondents who suggested that the UNIA was or
should be opposed to religion, and he invariably set out fully
the criticism being made before answering such writers. He
was also a moderating influence on the extremely anti-white
tendencies of some Garveyites. A good case in point was
his editorial on "The Passing of Lyman Abbott," written
shortly after the latter's death in October 1922. True, as
Ferris's good friend John E. Bruce had remarked just a few
months earlier in a Negro World column, Abbott was hardly

a paragon of enlightenment on the race question; and yet, Ferris insisted, "we must not criticize Dr. Abbott too severely. We must judge men not from the light that we have, but from the light that they had, remembering that they, too, were the product of their environment and were influenced by the Zeitgeist."[92] And on another occasion he cautioned against the categorical assumption that every white person shared the racist presuppositions which were so wide-spread in American society as a whole.

> Just as there are good, bad and indifferent black men, so there are good, bad and indifferent white men. And the fact that there are many bad white men should not blind us to the fact that there are some good white men. It always pays to be just and fair.[93]

"A. M. E. Church Review": George Washington Forbes (1864-1927) and Reverdy Cassius Ransom (1861-1959)

In the denomination's influential and highly regarded quarterly periodical, the A.M.E. Church Review, there were at least five different editorials concerning Garvey which were published between 1920 and 1923. Two of these were signed by George W. Forbes, an AME layman and Amherst graduate who worked as West End Branch Public Librarian in Boston, Massachusetts, and who served as literary editor of the Review for a number of years. Forbes had been one of the co-editors with William Monroe Trotter of the Boston Guardian, but his ardor for radical politics had mellowed over the years. Consequently, both of his editorials concerning Garvey were extremely hostile to the UNIA. In the first of these Forbes queried rhetorically where in Africa it was that Garvey planned to put all the American Negroes whom he presumably was intending to transport there; and he praised the wisdom of the majority of Negroes who, according to Forbes, rejected these "vagaries and obsession of an alien who neither from a knowledge of our past history is able to understand our present status nor with the orderly reflection of a logical mind is able to sketch a plan for our future that would win credence anywhere outside of a mad house."[94] Forbes's second article shed crocodile tears over Garvey's recent conviction on mail fraud charges, noting however that "We never saw in his scheme anything other than arrant charlatanism."[95]

The remaining three Review editorials concerning Garvey were unsigned, and were written by the journal's editor-in-chief, Reverdy C. Ransom. Ransom was one of the most able, articulate, and outspoken of the AME leaders in the first half of the twentieth century. A product of Wilberforce, he first came to national prominence as a minister in Chicago, where he counted among his friends such free-thinking individualists as Jane Addams, Robert Ingersoll, and Clarence Darrow. His national reputation as a radical spokesman for racial justice was enhanced during his tenure as pastor in Boston and then in New York between the years 1905 and 1912, during which time he joined forces with William Monroe Trotter and W. E. B. DuBois in opposing the program of Booker T. Washington. Ransom was one of the charter members of the Niagara Movement, the militant all-Black organization which preceded the establishment of the NAACP. One of his most memorable speeches was a commemorative address delivered to Niagarites on the occasion of the anniversary of John Brown's death, in which Brown was portrayed as acting with divine approbation in striking the first blow for elimination of slavery. A recent historian has summarized Ransom's social thought, along with that of his good friend R. R. Wright, Jr., as having "transformed Christianity from a God-centered religion to a race-centered one," and under the influence of Social Gospel theology, of having had the signal effect for a generation of Black students of transforming "the old slave religion into a religion of militancy."[96]

The most effective forum for propagating his radical ideas was the Review, edited by Ransom from 1912 to 1924, at which time he was elected a bishop in the AME Church. His first editorial concerning Garvey was published in October 1920, and reported at length on the contents of the UNIA's recently promulgated Declaration of Rights. Ransom characterized it as a welcome document, calculated to rouse Black people around the world "to preserve their national and territorial inheritance in Africa, and take a place of racial respect and independence among the free and liberty-loving people of the world." Declaring that its contents would have made Bishop Henry McNeal Turner's pronouncements appear mildly conservative, he concluded that "nothing quite so militant as this 'Bill of Rights' has ever issued from a body composed of the rank and file of Negroes."[97] Coming from Ransom, who held great respect for Turner, this was high praise indeed.

Ransom's second editorial appeared the following year,

and offered excerpts from remarks by DuBois, Ferris, Garvey, Kelley Miller and others on the merits of the recent Pan-African Congress held in Paris. Considerably more space was given to the UNIA spokesmen (who, of course, were bitterly opposed to the DuBois-sponsored Paris meeting), though Ransom himself took no editorial position on the debate between the opposed factions.[98] His last editorial concerning Garvey appeared in the same issue with Forbes's second editorial on Garvey, and was entitled "The Golden Dream of Negro Nationality." In it he accepted the Negro World's analogy comparing Garvey favorably to Denmark Vesey, and observed that "It is not often that a prophet appears among the people of any race." While acknowledging that the UNIA was beset with certain internal problems (whether of its own making or not was left unclear), Ransom concluded with a basic affirmation of the dream of "Negro nationality" which Garvey had inspired:

> Shall black men in Africa and elsewhere cease to dream of reclaiming a part of Africa and administering a government of their own? So long as race and color stand a bar to freedom and equality in all the varied relations of life, black men who have not lost pride in the manhood of the race will continue to aspire to control some part of this earth in which they may exercise and enjoy manhood and freedom.[99]

Some four years later, after himself having been elected to the episcopacy of the AME Church, Ransom again commented publicly on the career and the program of Marcus Garvey. The occasion for his comment was Garvey's recent deportation from the United States, after he served nearly three years' imprisonment on a mail fraud conviction. The twin notions of prophet and martyr were uppermost in his mind as he declared concerning Garvey,

> He proclaims for the unity and solidarity of the black people throughout the world. He pleads that we put into commission and organization the intellectual, financial, professional and industrial resources of the entire race and use this power to participate in the redemption and development of the continent of Africa....
> As a prophet, Mr. Garvey has run true to form by meeting the age-long rewards of the

prophet--he has been stoned, he has been imprisoned
and now he has been banished. But truth, aspira-
tions and ideals can neither be imprisoned nor deported.[100]

While thus never actively identified as a "Garveyite," Ransom
was obviously impressed by Garvey and defended his program
on numerous occasions. His sympathetic editorials over the
years could not help but increase respect for the UNIA among
the numerous clergymen who regularly read the A.M.E.
Church Review.

There were many other AME religious leaders who
were active Garveyites. Mrs. Emily Christmas Kinch, for
instance, an AME missionary in Africa, had been one of the
signers of the 1920 Declaration of Rights, and she spoke on
occasion from the Liberty Hall podium.[101] We have already
encountered the Reverend Richard H. Tobitt, AME pastor in
Bermuda, whose congregation took the (evidently unique) action
of ejecting him from his parish for his work on behalf of the
UNIA. Both Milton H. Mickens and C. A. Wingfield
were active Garveyites, the former serving for a time as
secretary for the UNIA. The list could be considerably extended.[102]

NOTES

1. NW 16:26 (August 9, 1924), cited above in chapter 3, in
    full context.

2. Cronon, Black Moses, p. 182, citing numerous authori-
    ties.

3. Garveyite official Adrian Johnson, in a speech delivered
    in New Orleans during February 1921, offered the fol-
    lowing clarification of the UNIA's understanding of the
    "right" idea of God: "Some tremble before the blue-
    eyed God, here and elsewhere, believing that the God
    of Isaac and of Jacob trembled also before this Son
    of Belial. (Deafening cheers.) We want the preachers
    to understand that the U.N.I.A. is solidly behind the
    preachers and the churches who have the right idea of
    God. What do I mean by the right idea of God? I
    mean that God created man to enjoy the earth, with
    unlimited possibilities. He desires man to so unfold
    the Godlike spark in him that when he has accomplished

so many wonderful things that will amaze even himself he will, when baffled by the ways of nature, conclude that his Creator is the evident Superior and will
by intuitive conviction worship Him as he should in
spirit and truth. But the preacher who teaches to
Negroes that they must not desire silver or gold, but
desire only to enter the fold, 'take all this world and
give me Jesus, ' must go as being spiritually and
morally unfit to live as a man created after God's
own image. Much less are they fitted to lead folks
of the most downtrodden and abused race. Be aware!
be aware! the ways of God are different. Awake to
righteousness and sin not against Him as being responsible for the race's condition." NW 10:7 (April
2, 1921), p. 8.

4. Garvey, "Intelligence," Lesson 21, Five Year Plan of
the U.N.I.A., pp. 4-5.

5. From the list of one hundred and twenty-two signers I
have thus far been able to identify the following clergy-
men: James D. Brooks, James W. H. Eason, Rudolph Ethelbert Brissaac Smith, Richard Hilton Tobitt,
George Alexander McGuire, Peter Edward Batson,
Reynold R. Felix, Gabriel E. Stewart, Arnold Josiah
Ford, Francis Wilcome Ellegor, J. Frederick Selk-
ridge, O. C. Kelly, James D. Williams, Emily Christmas Kinch, John C. Simons, Frederick Augustus Toote,
E. J. Jones, Joseph Josiah Cranston, J[ohn Dawson]
Gordon, Ira Joseph Touissant Wright, Richard C.
Noble, and Ratford E. M. Jack. Of the seventeen
signers who were women, so far as I know only one,
Emily Christmas Kinch, missionary, was a professional
church worker. The complete list of signers is found
in P&O II, pp. 142-43.

6. On this point I must demur from the position taken by
Theodore G. Vincent in his provocative study Black
Power and the Garvey Movement. In a personal conversation, Vincent himself in fact readily acknowledged
that a too-hasty and erroneous judgment was made in
his sweeping observation that "the Garvey movement
did not attract a single prominent Negro minister."
p. 18.

7. E. Franklin Frazier, The Negro Church in America
(New York, 1966), p. 85, is typical in his characteri-

zation of the church's importance with respect to Black culture.

8. The following individuals, arranged by state, have been identified as associated with the UNIA. This is by no means, of course, a comprehensive listing of Baptist clergymen active in the UNIA, but rather includes those who by virtue of their national prominence or explicit statements of support for the Association have come to the attention of the writer.

Arizona:	Rev. M. Boyd, Mesa
California:	L. B. Brown, Los Angeles
	Rev. J. D. Gordon, Los Angeles
	Dr. William A. Venerable, Los Angeles
Colorado:	Rev. Dr. Over, Denver
Florida:	Rev. J. M. Royster, Jacksonville
	Rev. P. M. Scoot, Odessa
	Rev. Selmore, Key West
	James I. Truesdell, Tampa
Illinois:	Rev. Barnett, Chicago
	Rev. Dr. D. W. Boyd, Chicago
	Dr. O. M. Locus, Chicago
	Dr. Tittle, Chicago
	Rev. Tyson, Chicago
Kansas:	Rev. F. K. Leath, Winfield
Maryland:	Rev. Dr. J. R. L. Diggs, Baltimore
Massachusetts:	Rev. S. Y. DuPree, Springfield
	Rev. Dr. J. Francis Robinson, Cambridge
Michigan:	Rev. T. W. Anderson, Adrian
Missouri:	Rev. Broden, Poplar Bluff
	Rev. Daniels, Kansas City
New Jersey:	Ref. Rufus Montague, Woodbridge
New York:	Rev. W. W. Brown, New York City
	Rev. J. Morris Lawson, Syracuse
	Rev. William H. Moses, New York City
North Carolina:	Rev. C. E. Askew, Raleigh

Ohio:	Rev. D. W. Bowen, Columbus
	Rev. Harris, Toledo
	Rev. R. A. Jones, Akron
	Rev. James W. Pace, Oberlin
	Rev. S. P. Phillips, Youngstown
Oregon:	Rev. E. C. Dyer, Portland
Pennsylvania:	Rev. Junius C. Austin, Pittsburgh
	Dr. Delaney, Warren
	J. G. St. Clair Drake, Pittsburgh
	Rev. Dr. P. P. Samuel, Philadelphia
South Carolina:	Rev. J. D. Dinkeris, Charleston
Virginia:	Rev. Dr. Johnson, Richmond

9. A brief biographical sketch of Austin is provided in Who's Who in Colored America (1927), pp. 7-8.

10. Lewis G. Jordan, Negro Baptist History, U.S.A. 1750-1930 (Nashville, n.d.), p. 336.

11. Pittsburgh Courier (June 14, 1924), p. 3; William H. Moses, The Colored Baptists' Family Tree (Nashville, 1925), p. 71.

12. Jordan, Negro Baptist History, informs us that Austin's Chicago congregation had the third largest membership of any of the churches in the denomination, and that as a substantial contributor to the work of the Baptist Foreign Mission Board it was "regarded as a real bee-hive in Christian service." p. 80.

13. NW 12:26 (August 8, 1922), p. 7.

14. NW 14:5 (March 17, 1923), p. 9. Maloney recalls in his autobiography one of the speeches delivered in the church of "my friend Rev. Austin," the title of which was "Elements Making for Survival in Negro Psychology." Amber Gold: An Adventure in Autobiography (Boston, 1946), p. 377. On Maloney, see below, chapter 5.

15. Pittsburgh Courier (November 22, 1924), p. 5.

16. A tantalizing aside offered by Carter G. Woodson, in his History of the Negro Church, 2nd. ed. (Washington, D.C., 1945) illustrates the coalescence of ideas which had drawn Garvey and Austin together during the years 1922 and 1923. Describing the active sense of social responsibility which was shared by many Black churches, Woodson observes, "In Negro churches, moreover, as with Dr. J. C. Austin, once in Pittsburgh but now in Chicago, there were once organized banks, housing corporations, insurance companies, and even steamship projects in keeping with the ideas of Dr. L. G. Jordan," p. 258, emphasis added. Although Woodson attributes to Dr. Jordan sole responsibility for Austin's attraction to such business ventures as steamship lines and banks, it seems clear that Austin's affiliation with Marcus Garvey was a significant factor in shaping the economic and political programs Austin espoused as part of his church's social responsibility. Furthermore, Lewis G. Jordan himself spoke at least once in Liberty Hall, as reported in NW 8:12 (May 8, 1920), p. 3.

17. Richard R. Wright, Jr., Eighty-Seven Years Behind the Black Curtain (Philadelphia, 1965), p. 202. In his address to the National Conference on Social Work in 1919, Wright characterized the Colored Protective Association as "the largest local civic organization in America." R. R. Wright, Jr., "What Does the Negro Want in Our Democracy?" reprinted in Herbert Aptheker, ed., A Documentary History of the Negro People in the United States, 1910-1932 (Secaucus, N.J., 1973), pp. 285-293, at p. 286. Information on the CPA may be found in Vincent P. Franklin, "The Philadelphia Race Riot of 1918," Philadelphia Magazine of History and Biography 99 (1975), 336-350.

18. It is intriguing that at least four themes in Marcus Garvey's political and religious critique were also advanced by Moses in his book The White Peril. First, white Americans were perceived as having violated both the spirit and the letter of Christian teachings-- the former evidenced by the way whites treated Blacks and the latter evidenced by the form of Christianity which they proffered to Blacks. Moses baldly stated that his aim in writing the book was "To realize the need for haste in spreading unperverted Christianity, in view of white domination of the world with unjust

economic, political, industrial and social discrimination against the darker races and the awful amount
of corruption and filth introduced among them by
Western civilization." (p. xxii).

Second, Moses took the Black churches to task
for their otherworldliness, which he saw as resulting
in neglect of the day-to-day needs of his people. On
this point he quoted approvingly a remark of fellow
Baptist minister, Dr. Lacey K. Williams: "Hitherto
the most pronounced tendency of church life among
Negroes has been to promote individual subjective
feelings and Godward relations, but now the call is
for that and for the gospel that recognizes and is adjusted to existing human needs and conditions, and
emphasizes the importance of correct manward relations. The efficient church must help to solve the
daily problems of its members and followers." (p.
xix.)

A third concern of Moses's book which was
shared by Marcus Garvey, was the imperative need
to counteract the subversive influence of white missionaries in Africa. Indeed, the book as a whole
was intended to be a mission study guide for local
churches, and was published by the denomination's
Foreign Mission Board, of which Moses was a member. Although at this point he was still open at least
in principle to the possibility of white Christians
working effectively and out of sincere motives in the
mission field, Moses made it clear that the overall
impact of white missionaries had been deleterious in
the extreme. Speaking of the need for Black Baptists
to act decisively in this area he remarked, "The time
has come for this independent colored American group
to join the unprejudiced white Christians of the world
in helping to change the spirit of many missionaries
who have carried a perverted gospel of humiliation to
the darker races. (Emphasis added.) We must have
missionaries who will insist that black people of
Africa and the whole world be given what is given to
others, to make them fit for citizenship in the kingdom of God anywhere on the face of this earth; and
that they be allowed to live like free men on the
streets of the world, as well as the streets in heaven."
(pp. xix, xx.)

Fourth, Moses was concerned for the emergence
of strong independent nation states in Africa. In the
final chapter of his mission guide, entitled "Hope of

Africa in the New World Order," he insisted, "The
new world order makes no provision for great black
African States: like China and Japan or even like
the proposed Jewish state in Palestine, but great
black African states are inevitable." (p. 233.) Such
a statement is strongly reminiscent of Garvey's frequent demand for an independent and autonomous
Black African nation which would protect the rights
of Black men throughout the world.

There is no direct evidence that Moses was
aware of Garvey's program prior to the former's
arrival in New York. It is possible, however, that
his association in Philadelphia with R. R. Wright,
Jr., who was an early Garvey supporter, may have
provided him with the opportunity for an early and
favorable introduction to the UNIA.

19. NW 13:13 (November 11, 1922), p. 12.

20. NW 13:14 (November 18, 1922), p. 2.

21. Ibid., p. 5.

22. NW 14:23 (July 21, 1923), pp. 2, 10.

23. Ibid., p. 2. Emphasis added.

24. Ibid., p. 10.

25. Ibid.

26. Ibid.

27. This leaflet is included in the Alexander Gumby Scrap-
    book collection on Negro life in America, vol. 32,
    located in the Columbia University Manuscripts De-
    partment.

28. Pittsburgh Courier (May 24, 1924), p. 15.

29. John W. Cromwell, "First Negro Churches in the Dis-
    trict of Columbia," Journal of Negro History 7
    (1922), p. 79.

30. Harry W. Greene, Holders of Doctorates Among Ne-
    groes (Boston, 1946), pp. 26, 46-47, 56. Diggs's
    dissertation, entitled "The Dynamics of Social

Progress," has evidently been lost in a fire of archives at Illinois Wesleyan University.

31. "Obituary," Baltimore Afro-American, April 20, 1923, p. 3. Vincent, Black Power, p. 160, incorrectly states that Diggs was president of Morgan State College.

32. Independent African: John Chilembwe and the Origins, Setting and Significance of the Nyasaland Native Rising of 1915 (Edinburgh, 1958). Indeed the African Baptist revolutionary John Chilembwe had attended Virginia Theological Seminary between 1898 and 1900. Cf. Ibid., pp. 112-123. J. C. Austin, W. H. Moses, and J. G. St. Clair Drake were also alumni of the school.

33. "Obituary," Baltimore Afro-American, April 20, 1923, p. 3.

34. Baltimore Afro-American, October 29, 1920, p. 5. The NERL had been founded by Trotter in 1908 (then called the Negro-American Political League) to oppose the accommodationist philosophy of Booker T. Washington, and Trotter had refused to merge with the equally anti-Bookerite NAACP because of what he regarded as the undue influence of whites in that organization. On Trotter and the NERL, see generally Stephen R. Fox, The Guardian of Boston: William Monroe Trotter (New York, 1970).

35. Cited in Vincent, Black Power, p. 204.

36. On McGuire, see chapter 3.

37. NW 12:25 (August 5, 1922), p. 2.

38. Ibid.

39. Ibid., p. 8.

40. New York The World, August 15, 1922, p. 3. According to Amy Jacques Garvey it was suggested that instead the Bibles should be sent to the South, to be "circulated among those obsessed with race and religious prejudice." Garvey and Garveyism, p. 104.

41. Criticism of Diggs was leveled on the convention floor by Ulysses S. Poston, then Minister of Industries for the UNIA. NW 13:4 (September 9, 1922), p. 3. The item concerning Diggs's operation appeared in NW 13:13 (November 11, 1922). The funeral oration was delivered by his long time friend and mentor from Washington, the Reverend Walter H. Brooks. Baltimore Afro-American, April 20, 1923.

42. NW 8:18 (June 19, 1920), p. 2.

43. Reported in Vincent, Black Power, p. 120.

44. NW 10:8 (April 9, 1921), p. 5; NW 10:20 (July 2, 1921), p. 9.

45. Ibid.

46. See above, chapter 1.

47. NW 20:21 (July 3, 1926), p. 6.

48. NW 12:26 (August 12, 1922), p. 6; NW 14:23 (July 21, 1923), p. 4.

49. Quoted in Shepperson and Price, Independent African, p. 113, who cite Porter W. Phillips, W. W. Brown, Host (New York, 1941), p. 58 as quoted in L. G. Jordan, Negro Baptist History, p. 241.

50. J. R. L. Diggs, "Negro Church Life," p. 49. Emphasis added.

51. Walter Rauschenbusch, Christianizing the Social Order (New York, 1912), pp. 76, 97.

52. James Weldon Johnson, "Harlem: The Culture Capital" in Alain L. Locke, ed., The New Negro: An Interpretation (New York, 1968), pp. 301-311, describes Brown as one "who repeatedly makes 'Buy Property' the text of his sermons," p. 306; while Carter G. Woodson characterizes him flatly as a "preacher of the social gospel" in History of the Negro Church, p. 278.

53. Evidence of their friendship is found in Austin's tribute to Brown, as reported in the memorial volume written

by Porter Phillips: "I regard Dr. Brown as the
most unique and powerful preacher of his day and
generation. Out of his fertile mind were born institutions and out of his great character standards and
ideals were lifted by which youth might be inspired.
He is a signpost of nobility, with a decisive finger
ever pointing toward the highway of righteousness."
W. W. Brown, Host, p. 11.

54. NW 14:23 (July 21, 1923), p. 4.

55. A biographical sketch is found in NW 15:20 (December
    29, 1923), p. 5.

56. NW 13:9 (October 14, 1922), p. 2.

57. NW 15:28 (December 29, 1923), p. 3.

58. NW 10:7 (April 2, 1921), p. 3.

59. Vincent, Black Power, pp. 160-61.

60. A copy of the calendar is to be found in the Archives
    collection of the UCLA Library.

61. Vincent, Black Power, p. 160 and NW 20:24 (July 24,
    1926), p. 3. For a sampling of Drake's speeches
    on behalf of the UNIA, see NW 20:21 (July 3, 1926),
    p. 6; NW 20:26 (August 7, 1926), p. 10 and NW 21:2
    (August 21, 1926), pp. 5, 6.

62. John A. Gregg, "Africa and A Way Out," A.M.E.
    Church Review 37 (1921), pp. 205-206. The speech
    was delivered in Baltimore, Maryland, on February
    13, 1920. Bishop John Hurst stated the case for the
    special responsibility of the AME Church in even
    more forceful terms in the Quadrennial Sermon de-
    livered at the Twenty-seventh Conference of the AME
    Church: "Have you ever thought what it would mean
    to the Negro Race were the African Methodist Epis-
    copal Church to fall down on its mission? As a race,
    we have lost out almost completely in the government.
    Not one member of this race in the Congress of the
    Nation. Our status as citizens is not up to the stan-
    dard of the years past. In the face of our helpless
    condition we can't but conclude that the hope of this
    race is in the Church, and this old Church that has

come up through the prayers and tears of our fathers must not be allowed to be pulled down. Palsied the hand that would smite her!" Journal of the Twenty-Seventh Quadrennial Session of the General Conference of the A.M.E. Church (Philadelphia, 1924), p. 56.

63. Gregg, "Africa," p. 212. Emphasis mine. The quote may be found in its original context in Violet R. Markham, The New Era in South Africa (London, 1904), p. 178. See especially chapter 12, "Natives and the Native Church Movement," passim.

64. Ibid., p. 184. Miss Markham observed, "The assumption of the African Methodist Episcopal Church and the aims which the negro [sic] evangelists set before themselves in South Africa are not a little startling. They are explained in the American organ of the denomination, the 'Voice of Mission,' with a point and fullness which leave no doubts as to the self-confidence of this body as regards the task they set before themselves. They approach the subject, in fact, in a spirit marked by any characteristic save that of modesty." p. 184.
    By the mid 1920s, the problems created by contentious Black American missionaries led to severe restrictions on their activity from white authorities. Dr. J. E. East, corresponding secretary of the National Baptist Convention Foreign Mission Board, in his 1925 Report, notes that missionaries from all-Negro denominations had been refused entry to South Africa when it became clear that there were no white officials in the United States overseeing the missionary effort. Wilbur C. Harr, who quoted East's report in his dissertation "The Negro as an American Protestant Missionary in Africa" (Ph.D. dissertation, University of Chicago Divinity School, 1945), commented, "The reason for such treatment ... was that American Negro missionaries were not practical, and ... they had tendencies which led toward political agitation, stirring up Africans to a spirit of rebellion against European masters." In a footnote he went on to observe, "The writer will personally validate this point of view taken by the National Baptist Convention. Repeatedly government men and commercial agents have stressed this argument, using as illustrations the Garvey movement which was not a missionary movement at all ... and the movement of Kimbangu

in the Congo which seemed to be stirred more by racism practiced by the whites than encouraged by the Negroes." (Emphasis added.) All quotes from Harr may be found at p. 40.

65. Gregg, "Africa," p. 212.

66. Ibid., p. 213.

67. For an amplification of this theme with specific reference to the AME Church, see "The Black Church: Manhood and Mission," Journal of the American Academy of Religion 40 (1972), 316-333.

68. See, for example, Wright's obituary in Journal of Negro History 32 (1947), 29-30; and also the biography of Wright by Elizabeth Ross Haynes, The Black Boy of Atlanta (Boston, 1952).

69. R. R. Wright, Jr., Eighty-Seven Years, pp. 189-196. August Meier, who evidently followed the elder Wright's career only up to 1905, concludes that he typified those Black leaders who were by "the pressures of the times" reshaped from "an ambitious youth into a conservative educator with an affinity for politics." Thus Meier cites as representative of his political thinking Wright's statement near the turn of the century that it is "not wise to give any heed to those who advocate that we ought to fight for our rights." Meier, Negro Thought, pp. 210-211.

70. NW 10:8 (April 9, 1921), p. 3.

71. NW 13:1 (August 19, 1922), p. 4.

72. NW 12:25 (August 5, 1922), p. 11; NW 10:8 (April 9, 1921), p. 2; NW 12:4 (March 11, 1922), p. 4; NW 14:4 (March 10, 1923), p. 6.

73. NW 13:1 (August 19, 1922), p. 5.

74. Ibid.

75. Richard R. Wright, Jr., The Bishops of the African Methodist Episcopal Church([Nashville], 1963), p. 220.

76. Biographical details are provided in Who's Who in Colored America (1927), p. 65.

77. New Haven: The Tuttle, Morehouse and Taylor Press, 1913.

78. S. P. Fullinwider, The Mind and Mood of Black America: 20th Century Thought (Homewood, Illinois, 1969), p. 22.

79. Ibid., p. 23, quoting Ferris.

80. Ibid.

81. Ferris, African Abroad, II, pp. 900 and 909. Emphasis added.

82. Ibid., p. 920. Emphasis added.

83. The event is described in one of Ferris's Liberty Hall speeches, reported in NW 13:16 (December 2, 1922), p. 2.

84. Ferris's move from the A.M.E. Church Review to the AME Book Concern is reported by George W. Forbes, in his column "Within the Sphere of Letters," A.M.E. Church Review 35 (1918), 122-23.

85. See, for example, the following editorials: "Viewpoint of Science and Religion," NW 13:22 (January 13, 1923), p. 4; "What is Religion," NW 14:7 (March 31, 1923), p. 4; "The Black Man's Philosophy," NW 14:3 (March 3, 1923), p. 4; and "A Christmas Reverie off Morningside Park," NW 13:9 (December 23, 1922), p. 4.

86. NW 9:12 (November 6, 1920), p. 2.

87. On Ferris's participation in Bethel Literary and the American Negro Academy see further Fullinwider, Mind and Mood, pp. 21-22. Each of the two Ferris letters addressed to Francis Grimké is acknowledgement of receipt of materials Grimké had sent to him for publication in the Negro World. One of the letters contains a fascinating postscript concerning Ferris's position as literary editor of the paper, in which he disclaims responsibility for certain anti-DuBois editorials published in recent issues of the

paper. "P.S. I did not write the 'Color Line' editorial of last week, the short 'DuBois' editorial of
two weeks ago or the 'Sit at Ease Prophet' of this
week. These were written by other members of the
editorial staff, although I polished up the style of
two of the editorials. As Literary Editor, I am only
a Limited Monarch, regarding the 'matter' that goes
in the Negro World, although I have the authority to
improve the English of anything that goes into the
paper, and to make such additions and subtractions,
as will add to the dignity of the article. Of course
this P.S. matter is confidential. W. H. F." Both
Ferris letters are contained in Carter G. Woodson,
ed., The Works of Francis J. Grimké, Vol. 4:
Letters (Washington, 1942), pp. 247 and 297-98.

88. According to Wilmore, Black Religion, p. 197.

89. NW 12:20 (July 1, 1922), p. 5.

90. NW 12:26 (August 12, 1922), p. 4.

91. See, for example, Ferris's criticism of a Star of Zion
[AMEZ] editorial critical of the UNIA. Ferris insisted that the three authors, J. Francis Lee, R.
Farley Fisher and W. H. Davenport, had conspired
to write the article while the regular editor, William
J. Walls, was in London attending a religious conference. Walls (later a bishop of the AMEZ Church)
was presumably more favorably disposed to the UNIA.
The Star of Zion editorial appeared in September 8,
1921. Ferris's reply is printed in NW 11:7 (October
1, 1921), p. 4.

92. In his regular column, Bruce had taken Abbott severely
to task for having remarked that "There is not room
enough in America for two races alien to each other
to live together in peace and harmony." NW 12:15
(May 27, 1922), p. 5. Ferris's editorial may be
found in NW 13:13 (November 11, 1922), p. 4.

93. NW 14:9 (April 14, 1923), p. 4. We must, on the basis
of this and similar statements, categorically reject
S. P. Fullinwider's conclusion concerning Ferris,
that he "broke out of the morass of conflicting loyalties and passion by turning racist--by joining the
black nationalist Garvey movement of the 1920's....

His earlier humanism was unable to survive the in-
dignities suffered in 20th century America." This
statement is completely unsubstantiated by Fullinwider, as is his gratuitous assertion that Garvey
was a spokesman "for the most virulent racist movement of the time among Negroes." Fullinwider,
Mind and Mood, p. 25.

94. "Marcus Garvey and His League of Nations," A.M.E.
Church Review 37 (1921), 166. On Forbes, see
Fox, Guardian of Boston, pp. 29-30.

95. "Garvey's Plight--The Pity of It All," A.M.E. Church
Review 40 (1923), 50.

96. Fullinwider, Mind and Mood, pp. 36-46, especially at
p. 46. Much useful information on Ransom is provided in David W. Wills's "Reverdy C. Ransom:
The Making of a Black Bishop" published in Burkett
and Newman, eds., Black Apostles.

97. "Back to Africa, a Militant Call," A.M.E. Church Review 37 (1920), 88.

98. "A Quadrilateral View of the Attitude and Outlook for
Negroes Throughout the World," A.M.E. Church
Review 38 (1921), 82-85.

99. "The Golden Dream of Negro Nationality," A.M.E.
Church Review 40 (1923), 44.

100. "Marcus Garvey Mightiest Prophet," Pittsburgh
Courier (December 17, 1927), p. 4, reprinted in
NW 23:20 (December 24, 1927), p. 2.

101. See, for example, NW 8:19 (June 26, 1920), pp. 3, 6.

102. There is no evidence that any church in the U.S. ever
contemplated such an action as that reportedly taken
against Tobitt as a penalty for supporting the UNIA.
Biographies of both Mickens and Wingfield may be
found in Richard R. Wright, Jr., ed., Centennial
Encyclopedia of the African Methodist Episcopal
Church (Philadelphia, 1916). On Mickens, see H.
V. Plummer, "The U.N.I.A. as I See It--Then and
Now," The Spokesman 2 (May-June, 1927), 29 and
NW 10:20 (July 2, 1921), p. 1. Other AME clergy-
men I have discovered whose names appeared in

local or national news reports as actively supporting the UNIA are: ex-Trinidad missionary Peter Edward Batson, New York; Rev. Dr. Cunston, Jersey City, New Jersey; Rev. W. M. Brown, Portsmouth, Virginia; Rev. C. T. McNeill, Fairmont, West Virginia; Rev. T. L. Scott, Gary, Indiana; one Rev. Parks, Oakland, California; Rev. Eugene Thompson, Gary, Indiana; a Rev. Hayes of Poplar Bluff, Missouri; Rev. I. E. C. Steady, New Haven, Connecticut; Rev. S. E. Churchstone Lord, Haiti; Rev. Dr. C. W. Stewart, Wilmington, Delaware; and Rev. D. Ormond Walker, Raleigh, North Carolina. Walker later served as president of Wilberforce University and was elected bishop of the AME church.

CHAPTER 5

CLERGY IN THE UNIA: II

AMEZ's and CME's in the UNIA

The African Methodist Episcopal Zion Church, like the AME Church and the National Baptists, had its strong advocates for the importance of missionary work in Africa. Preeminent among them was Bishop Alexander Walters (1858-1917), co-organizer of the 1900 Pan-African conferences in London, for many years president of the Afro-American Council, and a member of such activist organizations as the Niagara Movement and the Negro-American Political League.[1] In his autobiography he placed the missionary effort at the center of his own and his church's concern:

> The important question with our Church today is, shall we commence a more aggressive work in Africa? This can best be answered by asking another--are we prepared to do aggressive work in Africa? I answer unhesitatingly, yes. Since its origin the Zion Church has been known for its independence--race pride and true patriotism.[2]

Walter's explicit objective was to assist his denomination's efforts to "civilize and Christianize ... Africa." It would have been reasonable to expect, therefore, that he would evince great interest in the work of the Universal Negro Improvement Association, which defined itself, in its "Aims and Objects," as a missionary endeavor. Walter's death in 1917 prevents more than speculation on this point, but the active participation in the UNIA of two of his closest associates, each of them AMEZ churchmen, suggests that had he lived, he too would have been one of Marcus Garvey's most enthusiastic supporters.

165

John Edward Bruce (1856-1924)

One of these associates was the noted newspaper columnist John E. Bruce (Bruce Grit), who was frequently cited by anti-Garvey critics as the "only" Black intellectual to have joined the UNIA.[3] Bruce and Walters were friends of long standing, and Bruce was selected to write the introduction to Walters's autobiography. In this essay, Bruce revealed much about himself and about the ideals which shortly would draw him into the UNIA. He also made clear the basis of his affection for the AMEZ bishop. Bruce evidenced a marked sense of hostility to "white" Methodism, which he insisted had violated the fundamental Biblical tenets of the brotherhood of man and the Fatherhood of God, and which had to bear responsibility for the racial divisions into which Methodism was broken. As a result of their "caste and color prejudices" white Methodists were surely unfit to undertake the crucial work of evangelizing Africa; indeed, such prejudice is "a terrible reflection upon the genuineness of the religion of white men in that church."[4] His opposition to white Methodist missionary activity in Africa was coupled with a strong conviction about the unique religious responsibility for which the African at home and abroad had been specially selected by God. Describing the great enthusiasm for missionary work evidenced by Bishop Walters, Bruce spoke rapturously of the so-called "Dark Continent," from which, in fact, "The light proceedeth which will ultimately fill all the world with the vitalizing, purifying power of the Holy Spirit, which is to revolutionize Christian thought and teach true men what true and undefiled religion is and means."[5] The African, Bruce insisted, would be the vehicle for the genuine Christianization of the entire world, and he believed that task would begin with Black Christians in America taking the gospel message to their homeland.

Bruce was militant with respect to the racial question, and adamantly refused to participate in any organization which was led or controlled by whites. He had served with Walters as a member of the Afro-American Council and in 1911 founded with Arthur A. Schomburg the Negro Society for Historical Research, a "society of Black and Colored men" which would enable the darker races "to get together and to fight for every right with all our might ... and to meet organized wrong with intelligently organized resistance."[6] Especially critical of those of his race who took the values, culture, or religion of the white man as a model to which one should aspire, he declared on one occasion,

> The Negro in America has absorbed the civili-
> zation and adopted customs, religion and character-
> istics of the white man and he will be no better
> qualified to carry the message to Africa than the
> white man until he learns to think black [emphasis
> added]. Until that time comes he can have nothing
> in common with Africa or the Africans. It is to
> nations, races, families, to whom Almighty God
> gives missions. The mission of the Negro race in
> America is to find its true place in the social pro-
> gression and to cease seeking to be other than what
> God intended it to be. Its destiny and that of the
> white man is not coordinate and can never be and
> the sooner we wake up to this fact the better for
> us.[7]

The journalist always thought about Black American
responsibility with respect to Africa within the missionary
frame of reference Walters had provided. As this passage
illustrates, however, his open avowal of the utter irrecon-
cilability of Black and white interests represents a significant
move beyond the Bishop's public statements on the racial
question and places Bruce in the main stream of Garveyite
thinking. It is little wonder that he was the most popular and
widely read Negro World columnist, or that on his death Garveyites would turn out by the thousands to pay their last respects to this articulate defender of the goals of the UNIA.[8]

Lelia Coleman Walters

The second close associate of Bishop Walters who became an officeholder in the UNIA was the Bishop's wife, Lelia
Coleman Walters. An articulate and forceful woman in her
own right, Lelia Walters could be found every Sunday night
for at least a year on the platform of Harlem's Liberty Hall.
At a banquet held in honor of Marcus Garvey on the eve of
one of his tours through the United States, she rose to speak
about the guest of honor.

> Ladies and Gentlemen, it is a pleasure for me
> to be here tonight. Last night I was at a great
> meeting where they discussed the cause of Ghandi
> [sic] and the great nationalist movement in India
> under his leadership. As I sat there and listened
> to this cause expounded and set forth my mind was
> drawing comparisons between the Ghandi movement

and our own great movement, the Universal Negro
Improvement Association, under the leadership of
the Honorable Marcus Garvey. There they spoke
very feelingly of the outstanding leaders of mankind
coming down the line from Hannibal, Napoleon,
George Washington, Toussaint L'Ouverture, and as
no one spoke of our own great leader, Hon. Marcus
Garvey, I thought that a serious omission had been
made. To my mind he has reached the pinnacle of
fame and is the most outstanding figure in the world
of mankind today. To him I say, "Carry on Marcus
Garvey. Thy great work that will lead others to
their goal and thy name shall be sacred in the an-
nals of history. "[9]

Mrs. Walters was not an uncritical supporter of the
UNIA, as evidenced on one occasion when she took the organization to task for not allowing sufficient expression for
women within the movement.[10] At that same meeting, however, she was characterized as an "ardent lover of the
U. N. I. A. ," and she concluded her speech by insisting that
Garveyites stand behind their leaders. Her presence on the
UNIA platform was a symbolic statement attesting to the fact
that everything for which her husband had stood, as foremost
exponent for the missionary consciousness of Zion Methodism,
found logical expression and extension in the work of the
UNIA.

The only editorial comments discernible in AME Zion
journals concerning the UNIA were hostile to its program.
Reference has earlier been made to a critical Star of Zion
column which William H. Ferris sought to parry with an editorial in the Negro World.[11] There was also a vituperative
editorial entitled "The Menace of Garveyism" which appeared
in the December 1923 issue of the A. M. E. Zion Quarterly
Review. Describing the UNIA as "black Ku Kluxism" and
Garvey as a "mistaken, misguided misanthrope, " the editorial
concluded that this movement embodied "the greatest menace
to the race today."[12] To this editorial Bruce replied with a
stinging rebuke to the author, C. C. Alleyne, suggesting that
he "stick to editing his magazine along religious lines and
judge not, that he be not judged, etc."[13]

William Yancy Bell (1887-1962)

In the third major branch of Black Methodism, the

Colored Methodist Episcopal Church, there is one nationally
prominent clergyman, William Yancy Bell, who stands out as
an articulate defender of Marcus Garvey. Bell was a graduate of Northwestern University, where he was awarded the
M. A. and S. T. B., and of Yale University, where he earned
a Ph. D. in Semitic languages. He had served as professor
of Latin and Greek at Lane College (where he received his
B. A.) and then served briefly as Chaplain in the United States
Army during 1818-1919, prior to assuming pastorate of the
prestigious Williams Institutional CME Church in New York
City. [14]

There is no evidence that Bell was ever a dues-paying
member of the UNIA. However, an eloquent speech he delivered in Liberty Hall in August 1923, while Garvey was in-
carcerated in the Tombs Prison, well illustrates both the
brand of militant Christianity to which he subscribed and the
extent to which he saw this social Christianity as being
allied to the ideals and objectives of the UNIA. Bell began
by noting that many critics, especially those in Soviet Russia,
insisted that there could be no alliance between Christianity
and any program for race redemption because the former is
only "an opiate or narcotic, lulling the plain people to a
soothing slumber, when they should be aroused to a holy unrest and stirred to vigorous and determined action for self-
improvement. "[15] This, he observed, was not a difficult line
of argumentation to sustain. In spite of the apparent aptness
of the Marxist critique of Black Christianity, however, Bell
did not find it finally convincing. To the contrary, he retained without reservation his confidence in that faith whose
central principle he characterized as brotherhood. "Genuine
Christianity is essentially brotherhood," he insisted, "and
the conviction was never firmer in my heart than now that
Christianity groans to make itself articulate--through the
medium of a people humane enough to accept, and brave
enough to dare to express the principle of world brotherhood
in terms of life and practice." Indeed, Bell continued, expressing a conception of the Black man's chosenness which
we have seen as endemic to Garveyism, "may it not be that
in the divine scheme of things Ethiopia comes to her awakening for such an end as this?"[16]

Before brotherhood could be achieved among the races,
Bell saw a proximate goal which must first be realized,
namely, brotherhood within the race. Here was a serious
danger, for there were many individuals and groups seeking
to divide the race. And yet, Bell said, "thank God, there

is a hope" that this danger would be averted:

> There is also a hope. And I speak here to-
> night neither as pro or anti anything. I speak first
> of all as a Negro interested in Negroes. This is
> the hope--that in the fullness of time a Negro has
> arisen with faith enough to believe and courage
> enough to attempt to prove that Negroes universally
> could be taught to forget their differences. Inspired
> to hope and nerved to strive for a better and brighter
> day when the world would be compelled to admit
> again that Negroes can function successfully else-
> where than at the woodpile and well. (Applause.)
> It may not require an inspired seer, a Pittsburgh
> lawyer, nor a Wall Street broker to find a flaw in
> the plan or system of the U.N.I.A. but when it
> comes to the matter of Ethiopia's awakening and of
> Ethiopia's organization, you've simply got to hand
> it to Marcus Garvey. (Loud and prolonged ap-
> plause.)[17]

Bell declared that "all our notions to the contrary not-
withstanding," and regardless of the "interpreters with sinis-
ter and selfish designs," who would have you believe otherwise, "Christianity is socially militant." Jesus not only taught
his followers to turn the other cheek, but he also told them
to sell their coats in order to buy swords!

> And herein lies, my friends, what we may call
> the genius of our Christianity as applicable to the
> program of race redemption. Christianity teaches
> us to equip ourselves for heroic racial endeavor
> even at the price of personal comfort. "Sell your
> coat and buy a sword." In other words, "make a
> personal sacrifice in order to bring into realization
> a better day." It is the voice of militant Christianity
> speaking through a militant Christ. And I know, I
> submit to you of no voice nor message more suited
> at this hour to the Negro peoples of the world in
> general, and to the members of the U.N.I.A. in
> particular, than this word of Jesus....
> "Onward Christian soldiers, marching as to
> war, with the cross of Jesus going on before.
> Christ the royal Master, leads against the foe."
> They nailed Him on the cross, but His truth still
> goes marching on. They have incarcerated your
> leader in the Tombs prison. But shame be upon

you if at the cost of personal sacrifice you don't
see to it that the cause he so manfully and hero-
ically and fearlessly espoused, woe be unto you
and shame be upon you, if you do not see to it,
at whatever personal cost, that this cause that your
leader espoused goes marching triumphantly on.
(Loud applause.)

　　"Sell your coat and buy a sword," remembering that while yesterday Ethiopia grinned and endured, while today she smiles and strives, tomorrow, please God, she shall exult in glorious achieve-
ment.   (Prolonged applause.)[18]

This is the only occasion on which Bell spoke in Liberty Hall. Some weeks earlier, however, William Ferris
noted the "stimulating sermon on the injustice of curtailing
the liberty of any man illegally," which this CME minister
preached in his church.[19] Bell was certainly well aware of
Garvey's activities, since his Director of Religious Education
at the Williams Institutional CME Church, the Reverend G.
Emonei Carter, had been writing a weekly sermon published
in the Negro World since at least February 1922. Carter
served for a time as president of the New York Local Division, UNIA, and later held the post of Secretary-General of
the national organization.[20]

Episcopalians in the UNIA

There are more than half a dozen ordained Black
Episcopalians who became active in the UNIA. Foremost
among these, of course, was George Alexander McGuire,
who had been an Anglican priest in Antigua prior to his
coming to the United States in 1893. Because of McGuire's
extraordinary importance for the theology and religious infra-
structure of the UNIA, a separate chapter has been devoted
to his contribution and role, including the founding of the
African Orthodox Church.

It should be pointed out that prior to the First World
War, Black Episcopalians were concentrated primarily in the
South, especially in the states of North and South Carolina,
Tennessee, Kentucky, Texas, Missouri, and Virginia; and it
was only with the influx of West Indian immigration (espe-
cially to New York but also to New Jersey, Connecticut,
Maryland, Pennsylvania, and Illinois) that the balance shifted
to the North as the Anglican-trained West Indians flooded into

the United States.[21] Black Episcopalians who were non-West
Indian were generally regarded as upper class or as aspiring
or newly arrived members of the Black middle class seeking
outward signs of their improved social status. Describing
religious life in Harlem, for instance, novelist Wallace Thurman wrote,

> The better class of Harlemites attends the
> larger churches. Most of the so-called "dictys"
> are registered as "Episcopalians" at St. Phillips,
> [sic] which is the religious sanctum of the socially
> elect and wealthy Negroes of Harlem. The congre-
> gation at St. Phillips [sic] is largely mulatto. This
> church has a Parish House that serves as one of
> the most ambitious and important social centers in
> Harlem.[22]

Regardless of the validity of this stereotype, it does
suggest that Black Episcopalians generally (as was probably
the case with most Blacks during the 1920s in predominantly
white religious denominations) would not be noted for the
militancy of their social protest concerning the racial question. There were exceptions, of course, such as George
Freeman Bragg, Jr. and George Frazier Miller, but they
were clearly in a minority.[23]

Among the clergy with a West Indian background, however, there was less willingness to acquiesce to both ecclesiastical and political domination by whites. G. A. McGuire
may in this respect be seen as typical of a small group of
highly educated, astute and socially conscious northern-based
Black Episcopalian clergymen who were critical of the church
for its irrelevance to contemporary life and who were attracted
to the Garvey movement as a way of vitalizing the social commitment of Black Christians. An ordained Episcopal priest of
remarkable intellectual ability who fits this same mold and
who made a substantial contribution to the UNIA was Trinidad-
born Arnold Hamilton Maloney.

Arnold Hamilton Maloney (1888-1955)

Maloney studied at more than half a dozen institutions
of higher learning during his remarkable academic career,
and earned at least that many degrees, including an M.A. in
philosophy, a B.D., an M.D., and finally a Ph.D. in pharmacology. In between, he studied forestry, served as chairman

of the psychology department at an AME university, and
served as columnist for several newspapers. His B.D. thesis at General Theological Seminary was published in book
form while he was serving as vicar of an Indianapolis church,
St. Philip's. Entitled The Adequate Norm: An Essay on
Christian Ethics, it was an attempt to reconcile Herbert
Spencer's evolutionary ethics with the doctrine of freedom of
the will and the finality of the Christian ethic, which he saw
embodied in the "adequate norm" of "Met-adelphism, or Infinite Brotherhood." The latter was best articulated in its
social as well as its individual dimensions by such men as
Lyman Abbott, Shailer Matthews, and Walter Rauschenbusch.[24]
While he was studying for the B.D., Maloney enrolled in a
joint M.A. program in philosophy offered by Columbia University. This degree was awarded in 1910. On weekends he
regularly traveled around New York City to hear prominent
religious speakers.[25] Among those whom he found to be particularly inspiring were Reverdy C. Ransom, Rabbi Wise,
Felix Adler, and the Swedenborgian, G. G. Daniels.

Maloney was ordained a deacon in the Protestant Episcopal Church in 1911, and was priested in the following year.[26]
His first parish was in Annapolis, Maryland, and he noted in
his autobiography that "The Reverend Dr. Alexander McGuire,
then secretary of the American Church Institute for Negroes,
was my personal sponsor." His friend the Right Reverend
Shirley Heathe Nichols, Bishop of Kyoto, had tried to interest
him in Liberia and a missionary bishopric, but to no avail.
He was equally dissatisfied with the parish ministry, however,
finding that he took religion more seriously than his parishioners and that they, on the other hand, took him too seriously in the praise they lavished upon him. ("It was a species
of anthropomorphism which was too concentrated to be socially
efficacious,"[27] Maloney writes.) He was sufficiently dissatisfied with the church to write, with fellow Episcopalian George
Frazier Miller, a report on the state of the church, in which
the authors reportedly concluded that the Protestant Episcopal
Church was too conservative politically, that its ties to monied
parishioners kept it so, and that it neglected education for
Negroes.[28] By this time Maloney had been elected vicar of
the Indianapolis church, but after a few years he found this
position, also, to be too confining. He thus took the decision
of his bishop, who refused to allow him to hold simultaneously
his pastorate and a job at the YMCA, as an excuse to resign
from the parish.

Maloney had several options before him, having left the

active Episcopal ministry. He was, he writes, offered ordination in the Roman Catholic Church by Cardinal Gibbon,
but he turned this proposal down as he did that of a "close
personal friend, a Methodist Bishop," who tried to get him
to join his church. Another offer appeared, however, which
he thought he could not refuse, when "the Reverend Dr. Mc-
Guire, my mentor and spiritual foster-father during my
younger days in the priesthood, now Archbishop and Metropolitan of the African Orthodox Church, got into communica-
tion with me and induced me to join forces with him."29
Although no date is given in his autobiography, this must
have occurred no earlier than late September or early October 1921, as McGuire was not elevated to the post of Archbishop until early in September. Maloney reports that he
was "duly elected Bishop and the date of my consecration
was set for the Sunday following my last services in Indianapolis," and his posts were to include those of coadjutor
bishop, dean of the pro-cathedral, dean of the divinity school,
and editor of the official journal of the AOC.

Maloney offers a long and rather tortuous explanation
as to why he did not assume these posts. Evidently he
stopped on his way from Indianapolis to New York to visit a
sick friend in Buffalo, and requested a postponement of his
ordination to stay with his friend. The request was denied;
Maloney refused to come directly to New York; and when he
finally arrived he found his mentor, McGuire, "in retreat
till next day."30 Rebuffed, he left the church and took a job
as psychology professor at Wilberforce University. This position he held for two years, from 1922 to 1924.31 What
Maloney fails to mention is that precisely at this time Mc-
Guire had been ousted from the UNIA and was being denounced
in the Negro World as a traitor to the organization. Furthermore, at this same time Maloney was becoming a prominent
and popular Garveyite, speaking frequently in New York's
Liberty Hall and writing articles regularly for the Negro
World. Many of his articles and speeches were published
under the title Some Essentials of Race Leadership by the
Aldine Publishing House of Xenia, Ohio, in 1924. The first
essay, a survey of contemporary "Types of Racial Leadership," characterized as inadequate (1) the accommodating
"politicians of the old school"; (2) the coalition of church/
press/wealthy, who were indifferent to the race issue; and
(3) the "New Negro" literary, educational, and independent
institutional church leaders, whom he saw as holding some
promise, as "diamonds in the rough." The real cutting edge
in racial leadership, however, was to be found elsewhere:

But there is a fourth group representing a reaction from the others which holds to a new racial philosophy. It contends that two races, heterogeneous and divergent, cannot live within identical territory on terms of absolute parity. One group will rule the other, will create and shape the ideals of culture, and will furnish the criteria of social heredity. It believes that the dominant group will respect the rights of the other group only if that other has some seat of power, outside of the given territory, whose sanctions command objective respect....

For this reason, the fourth group is declaring for political and governmental autonomy as against protective mimicry. It feels that its paradise is to be sought not in the course of the centrifugal but of the centripetal direction of its racial energy. It represents the crystallization of the virile element within the race, the pioneering element, the element that is not afraid to stake its fortunes upon the adventure of national house-building and house-keeping on its own account. It is like a youngster grown to maturity who feels the urge of nature to build up and rear a family of his own. It is the spiritual scions of the Pilgrim Fathers. [32]

The method to achieve this grandiose plan, Maloney concludes, is not "wholesale deportation, which would be impossible, but universal racial awakening." Maloney had, of course, been referring throughout to the program of the Universal Negro Improvement Association. Through this and other articles, he echoed in eloquent prose nearly all of the major themes of the UNIA.

Maloney was particularly insistent on the importance of intra-racial unity, which he believed to be of paramount concern. It is evident that he had considerably modified his earlier "Met-adelphic ideal" of infinite brotherhood, when he spoke, in his chapter on "Religion and Prejudice," of two kinds of brotherhood, the spiritual and the biological, and observed that the "bane of Christianity ... is its crushing extravagance," in suggesting that the two types were in reality but one. The fact was, it would be easier to regain an empire in Africa than to drive from the minds of whites their notions of superiority. "This [white] race has never," he concluded, "allowed its conception of the Christian doctrine of brotherhood to extend beyond the bounds of its own group."[33]

Thus, Blacks must place their emphasis on unity within the race.

The starting point for building this unity, Maloney insisted in a Liberty Hall speech, was precisely in the Negro churches. After all, the white church and the Negro church were not the same things; they stand for "two distinct psychological phenomena":

> In the former the people congregate to render
> "service" as Ruskin puts it. They pay God a call
> to offer their help to him in the difficult problem
> of guiding the course of the world. They make
> God their debtor. They bring Him down to them.
> To the latter the Church is a "meeting place." It
> is the centre of the entire higher life of a people.
> It is there that their social instincts and ideals
> find a field for expression. It is there that the
> talent for racial leadership is developed. It is
> there that the musical and dramatic faculties of
> the race have the freedom of range to soar in
> the more refined and enobling regions of art. It
> is there that the problems of the home, and of the
> community are threshed out. It is from this social
> meeting place that the soul of the Negro soars up
> "to meet its God in the skies." ... That will be a
> great day in the life of our race when the Negro
> churches come together and quit wasting time fight-
> ing sham battles about theological "nothings." To
> keep the Negro Churches divided is to keep the
> Negro race divided. [34]

Maloney was notable in his long-standing loyalty to the UNIA. As late as 1929, when most of the once prominent Garveyites had long since abandoned the cause, "the old war horse" A. H. Maloney addressed a local UNIA chapter in Indianapolis. [35] Having recently been awarded an M.D. from Indiana University, he was soon off to new fields of intellectual endeavor, going from there to the University of Wisconsin, where he earned a Ph.D. in pharmacology in 1931. He then moved to Washington, D.C., where he assumed the position of chairman of Howard University's Department of Pharmacology.

With his wide range of acquaintances, both within and without the Episcopal Church, Maloney was a major asset to the UNIA in securing a sympathetic hearing of the Association's program. The Episcopal priest of St. Philip's Church in Buffalo indicated as much when he wrote an encouraging letter to Maloney (published in the Negro World) stating, "I feel that you are doing a much larger work in the U.N.I.A. and one that will be most beneficial to others."[36] Maloney's friend George Frazier Miller, Rector of St. Augustine's Church in Brooklyn, New York, had earlier spoken positively of Garvey as "the most remarkable man of our times," who has "done more to emphasize the restlessness of the black people than any other man."[37]

Francis Wilcom Ellegor

Another Episcopal priest active in the UNIA was Francis Wilcom Ellegor, originally of Guiana. Ellegor was an early Garveyite, having participated as a signatory at the 1920 Declaration of Rights. He was introduced to a Liberty Hall audience in April 1920 as "ex-Professor of Liberia College in Monrovia, Liberia," and held several posts in the UNIA, including that of High Commissioner General. Ellegor was long interested in mission work in Liberia, and was selected as chaplain to the newly consecrated Black bishop, Theophilus Momolu Gardiner, when the latter was installed as Suffragan Bishop of Liberia in 1921.[38] Ellegor was active in the UNIA at least through the Third International Convention (1922), when he participated in opening ceremonies.[39]

Joseph H. Hudson and David Richard Wallace

Two other Episcopal priests are known to have participated in local UNIA Division meetings. The Reverend Joseph H. Hudson, pastor of St. Augustine Episcopal Church in Philadelphia, addressed the UNIA audience there as late as 1931; and the Reverend David Richard Wallace, of St. Augustine Mission in Oakland, California, spoke at an Oakland UNIA rally in 1927.[40] Wallace had earlier been a founder of Oakland's chapter of the NAACP, and had led the protest in that city against the showing of the infamous film "Birth of a Nation," which had been a cause célèbre more than a decade earlier.[41]

Black Jews in the UNIA

Arnold Josiah Ford (d. 1935)

A leader of one of the first Black Jewish groups
formed in the United States, Arnold J. Ford came to this
country from his native Barbados and served as Director
and Band Master of the New Amsterdam Musical Association from 1912 to 1920.[42] He was a very early Garvey
supporter, as evidenced by a letter from John E. Bruce to
Ford, dated September 27, 1917, in which Bruce indicated
his regret at having missed Ford at a recent UNIA meeting.
Ford was present as a signer of the 1920 Declaration of
Rights, and by this time held the post of Choirmaster and
Bandmaster of the UNIA. We have already examined two
of his major contributions to the Association: the Universal
Ethiopian Hymnal, official hymnbook of the UNIA which contained several of his own compositions; and the National
Anthem of the UNIA, "Ethiopia, Land of Our Fathers," for
which Ford composed the music and assisted in writing the
text.[43]

There is much apocryphal and often contradictory
speculation concerning Ford, so that it is difficult to reconstruct with any confidence his background and career. His
father was evidently an itinerant preacher in Barbados ("a
fanatical evangelist," according to one source[44]) whose exu-
berant preachments presumably helped shape his thinking.
Another writer observed concerning Ford that according to
"the testimony of those who know him personally ... he was
a man of unusual intelligence," and furthermore, "It is certain that he studied Hebrew with some immigrant teacher and
was a key link in transmitting whatever approximations there
are to Talmudic Judaism in the practices of these sects."[45]

A recent study has suggested that Ford was first a
Black Jew, and that he later joined the UNIA, bringing with
him into the Garvey movement a very large membership from
his congregation.

> A sizable minority of New York Garveyites
> were black Jews--some six hundred marched in a
> special contingent of the 1922 convention parade,
> and Rabbi J. Arnold [sic] Ford, the Association's
> musical director, had adopted Judaism long before
> he joined the Garvey movement, bringing most of
> his Beth B'nai congregation with him.[46]

Rabbi Arnold J. Ford (from Universal Ethiopian Hymnal).

Another writer, however, whose work was based on original research conducted in Harlem during 1929-1931, insisted that Ford was first a Garveyite, "until personal clashes with Garvey led to his expulsion in 1923," and that he then established his congregation, Beth B'nai Abraham. She further indicated that Ford never had more than thirty-five followers.[47]

Both writers seem to be incorrect in at least certain respects. A biographical sketch of Ford in the 1930-32 Who's Who in Colored America substantiates the claim that Ford was not called to the head of the congregation until after he had joined the UNIA.

> The Congregation Beth B'nai Abraham purports to be a congregation of men and women from the West Indies, Arabia, Abyssinia, and other European countries of the Jewish faith. They now reside in this country and term themselves Aethiopian Jews of America. He was called to the Rabbinate by this congregation in 1924.[48]

However, there is hard evidence that Ford continued as an active Garveyite long after this time. For instance, the following remarks to the 1924 UNIA Convention were reported in the Negro World:

> Hon. Arnold Ford, New York, said he was not a Christian though he believed in a Superior Being. Jesus was depicted as a black man, he said, until the time of the Renaissance in Europe, when a German, the burgomaster [sic] of Dresden, conceived the idea of having a white man substituted, and gave Europe and the white world a picture of himself, which it readily accepted to further its superiority propaganda. He warned the convention that it should be remembered that the majority of black men dwelt in Africa, and they were not Christians, but Mohammedans. The great need of the moment for the black man is education.[49]

Two years later, Ford was active at the abbreviated UNIA Convention of 1926, where, according to a Pittsburgh Courier article, he officiated at religious ceremonies, and tried to reconcile two conflicting factions fighting for control of the UNIA.[50]

It is reasonable to assume that Ford did advocate the

adoption of Black Judaism as the official religion of the UNIA. Garvey repeatedly made it clear, however, that no formal religious organization would be designated as the "official" religion of the Association, and there is no evidence that Ford left the UNIA because of this policy. In fact, there seems to have been some interest in Judaism in UNIA chapters around the country. For instance, considerable prominence was given to the speech of a rabbi, Dr. Rudolph Isaac Coffee (white), a Jewish philosopher who addressed the Oakland, California, UNIA Division on the topic "America and Africa." According to the report,

> The noted philosopher dealt impressively with the white man's interpretation of Christianity; and how false it is to the true conception and teaching of the Christ Jesus. The Fatherhood of God and the brotherhood of man were thoroughly analyzed and explained and the commandment, "Love thy neighbor as thy self" was meant for all mankind irrespective of color, race or creed! [51]

Coffee, who was indeed a prominent Jewish philosopher, had editorialized earlier in the Chicago Sentinel, asking how it was possible that Negroes in America could respect a church which was divided on the basis of color, opining that "the day of supine acquiescence is ended," and that Negroes were becoming increasingly class conscious. [52] Presumably the reason Coffee had taken an interest in the UNIA was the excitement generated by the explorer Jacques Faitlovitch, who discovered the Falasha Jews in Ethiopia and who had recently begun efforts to raise funds in America to assist this impoverished group of Black Jews. A month before his Oakland address, Coffee had written another editorial in the Sentinel reporting in detail on Faitlovitch's efforts and strongly encouraging Chicago Jews to support "these brethren, not with charity and alms, but with money to organize schools, hospitals and other necessary institutions." [53]

Further interest in Judaism among UNIA chapters is evident in the report of a Philadelphia Division meeting, at which the leader of the local Black Jewish congregation, Prophet F. S. Cherry, was principal spokesman. The report sent to the Negro World stated,

> On Sunday, February 21 at 3 P.M., the Philadelphia Division No. 162, had a wonderful Mass Meeting at Morris Chapel Baptist Church. The

> principal speaker of the evening was Prophet
> Cherry, who spoke from the depths of his heart
> to his congregation. The meeting was a delight-
> ful one, and all went away fully satisfied.[54]

Unfortunately, the substance of his talk is not recorded, so
we do not know whether the subject was the UNIA, Black
Judaism, or both of these. Ford and Cherry are the only
two names of Black Jews directly linked to the UNIA. The
repeated use by Garveyites of the Jewish people as a model
for racial self-development, the numerous "Black Zionist"
themes which permeated Garveyite thinking, and especially
the interest in the Falasha Jews generated by Faitlovitch and
others in the early 1920s, all conspired, however, to spark
a mutual interest by each of the two organizations in the
other.[55] In terms of the spectrum of opinion within the UNIA
concerning both the Black Church and religion in general, the
Black Jews sided with those atheistic and agnostic members
who perceived the Black Christian clergy as a grave menace
to racial progress; though they would not, of course, have
agreed to generalizing this criticism to religion per se.

Other Churchmen in the UNIA

As would be expected, there were comparatively few
Black clergymen in predominantly white denominations who
were Garvey supporters, since a fundamental tenet of the
UNIA was Black control of Black institutions. Occasionally,
though, one finds men such as William Walter Lucas, the
prominent Methodist Episcopal leader from Atlanta (and a
member of his denomination's Foreign Mission Board),
speaking on behalf of Garvey. In one of his Liberty Hall
speeches, for instance, Lucas characterized the UNIA as
"the greatest mass movement of Negroes in the world."[56]
Other Methodist clergymen who spoke at UNIA meetings on
behalf of Garvey include a Reverend Ivy of New Haven, Connecticut; Rev. McMahon of Knoxville, Tennessee; a Reverend
Robinson of Columbus, Ohio; and Dr. C. N. Grandison, the
president of Bennett College, Greensboro, North Carolina.

The following churches had one or more clergymen
who were Garveyites or at least who spoke favorably at local
UNIA meetings on behalf of the UNIA: the Christian Church,
the Church of Christ, the Congregational Church, the Emanuel
Holiness Church, the Pentecostal Church, the Presbyterian
Church, and the Universal Spiritualist Church.[57]

The only religious group which as an organization officially endorsed the UNIA was the Church of the Living God, a small Black Pentecostal sect which has been characterized as "Probably the first 'black supremacy' religious movement in America."[58] At the church's annual convention, meeting in New Haven, Connecticut, the Church of the Living God not only endorsed the UNIA but also voted to send a special offering to the UNIA International Convention which was being held the next week in New York. Leaders of the church, as identified in the Negro World article carrying the story, included Prince C. Allen, The Prophet; Elder Stephen I. Lee; Bishop R. H. Parker; and Elder Phillip Bishop.[59]

Finally, members of the Ethiopian Coptic Church who were Garvey supporters included the Reverend S. B. Barbour, Philadelphia, Pennsylvania; Bishop Edwin H. Collins, New York, New York; and Rev. Joseph Josiah Cranston of Baltimore, Maryland. The latter had been a signatory of the 1920 Declaration of Rights.[60]

Retrospective: Clergymen in the UNIA

What can be said in summary about this large and diverse group of men and women whose biographies have been detailed? Perhaps the single most striking factor is the diversity of the group itself. Every independent Black denomination with a membership of more than twenty-five thousand in 1920 had clergymen who were actively working on behalf of the UNIA, as did many of the smaller independent Black denominations. In addition, there were a small but significant number of clergy who were members of predominantly white denominations, including the Methodist Episcopal, Protestant Episcopal, Congregational and Presbyterian churches. The pastors came from every geographic region of the United States except the Pacific Northwest, which had an extremely small Black population in the 1920s.

There was also considerable diversity in terms of educational background, with several UNIA supporters holding earned doctorates; numerous other clergymen having been awarded honorary doctorates; but with by far the largest number of ministers having studied at one of several Black denominational colleges or seminaries, especially Wilberforce, Morris Brown, Virginia Theological Seminary, and Livingstone. In addition, there were a number of clergymen for whom no formal educational training at the B.A. level is

indicated, and presumably many of these had been called to
the ministry without receiving formal education. The diversity of educational, geographic and denominational backgrounds
for the clergy associated with the UNIA is itself significant,
for it reflects the diversity and multiplicity of the mass membership which the Association as a whole was able to attract.
In some cases the clergy were able to lead their congregations to sympathy and support for the UNIA, and in other
cases it was members of the congregation who were the active supporters of the Garvey program and who were able to
convince their pastors of the importance of supporting that
program.

There are also notable similarities among Garveyite
clergy which emerge when one examines the group as a whole.
Garveyite clergymen tended to be avid supporters of African
missionary endeavors. Several of the ministers were members of denominational foreign mission boards: Junius C.
Austin, William H. Moses, J. D. Brooks, and W. W. Lucas.
Other individuals were nationally known for their support of
African missions, including W. W. Brown, the "father of
African Baptist Missionaries," Lelia Walters, John E. Bruce,
and R. R. Wright, Jr. In addition there was a considerable
list of missionaries in Africa who supported the UNIA, among
whom we can count W. H. Thomas, R. Harten, H. H. Jones,
I. S. Vanderhorst, J. Francis Robinson, William H. Heard,
Emily Christmas Kinch, S. E. C. Lord, P. E. Batson, I. E.
C. Steady, and Francis Wilcom Ellegor.

A second rubric under which a significant number of
Garveyite clergymen can be characterized is that of "social
gospelers." Indeed, to the extent that the Social Gospel embodied a rejection of the exclusive focus of Christian concern
on the world to come and a demand that attention be paid to
the immediate human issues of survival, justice, and concern for the physical as well as spiritual needs of one's
fellow man, it could be said that every clergyman who supported the UNIA was an advocate of the Social Gospel. In
the narrower sense of the word, however, among those who
had studied the theological writings of Gladden, Rauschenbusch, and others, and who had been influenced by the efforts
at reconstruction of the city typified by Jane Addams and
others, there were a number of clergymen who were directly
influenced by the Social Gospel. Among these can be counted
J. R. L. Diggs, William Yancy Bell, R. R. Wright, Jr.,
Arnold Hamilton Maloney, and W. W. Brown as well as Garvey champion Reverdy C. Ransom. This list includes only

those who were directly influenced in their theological training by the Social Gospel. Further investigation into the background of other clergymen would doubtless provide many additional names to add to this list.

Further, Garveyite churchmen had a tendency to be involved with a variety of racial protest organizations prior to their association with the UNIA. Among these organizations one might mention the National Equal Rights League (supported by, e.g., J. R. L. Diggs and J. G. St. Clair Drake); the Afro-American Council (e.g., John E. Bruce); the NAACP (e.g., T. W. Anderson, David R. Wallace, Arnold H. Maloney and doubtless many others); and the Philadelphia Colored Protective Association (William H. Moses, J. W. H. Eason, and R. R. Wright, Jr.).

Finally, one can not help but note the network of inter-personal relations, cutting across denominational lines, which bound many--especially the most well-known religious leaders among the Garvey movement--to one another. The Episcopalian Arnold H. Maloney, for instance, reveals in his autobiography that he was a lifelong friend of George Alexander McGuire; that as a student in New York City he had listened with admiration to the sermons of AME preacher Reverdy C. Ransom; that his friendship with the Baptist Junius C. Austin antedated their involvement in the UNIA; and that having left the Episcopal ministry he was able to utilize his contacts in the AME Church to secure a teaching position at Wilberforce University during the years of his most active involvement in the UNIA. William H. Ferris has already been cited as a "well-connected" Garveyite who, as literary editor of the Negro World, was able to put to good use his experience at the A.M.E. Church Review and the AME Book Concern, his easy association with members of the AME Bishops' Council, his knowledge of AMEZ church leadership, and his personal friendship with Baptist leaders such as William Moses. Moses, in turn, was a long time friend of Junius C. Austin, had worked with R. R. Wright, Jr., in Philadelphia organizing the Colored Protective Association, and was well acquainted with prominent New York clergymen such as W. W. Brown, William Yancy Bell, and J. R. White.

The list could go on and on, and with additional research into manuscripts, biographical and autobiographical accounts, and newspapers of the period, it is a certainty that innumerable additional personal associations will be discovered.

It would seem that sufficient documentation has been adduced, however, to show that among a considerable portion of the educated and articulate Black clergy of the early 1920s there was a network of informal association and personal friendships that had existed over a number of years; that these friendships were undergirded by a shared interest in missionary efforts in Africa which were perceived as a task devolving in a special way upon men and women of African descent. They were further reinforced by a widely held conviction that the Gospel which they served contained an important message for the social as well as the individual existence of man; and finally those friendships were cemented by participation in a variety of voluntary associations formed over the years to augment the work of individual churches and denominations in achieving certain goals for the race as a whole. For a brief but most fascinating and exciting period of time in the early 1920s the organization which brought this diverse group of clergy together with a much more heterogeneous group of social, political, economic (and even some anti-religious) radicals was the Universal Negro Improvement Association.

NOTES

1. Fox, Guardian of Boston, pp. 110-112.

2. Alexander Walters, My Life and Work (New York, 1917), pp. 166 and 172.

3. See, for example, AME Bishop C. S. Smith's letter to the editor in The World's Work 41 (March 1921), 435-36. On Bruce generally, see also Peter Gilbert, ed., The Selected Writings of John Edward Bruce: Militant Black Journalist (New York, 1971).

4. Bruce, "Introduction," in Walters, My Life, p. 11. Emphasis added.

5. Ibid.

6. Hill and Kilson, Apropos of Africa, pp. 173-74.

7. Speech of John E. Bruce comparing Islam and Christianity with respect to Negroes, in John Bruce Papers, Item 2009, Schomburg Collection, New York Public Library, quoting at p. 5.

8. Bruce was one of Garvey's earliest supporters in the United States and had served as American correspondent for the African Times and Orient Review, a London based journal "Devoted to the Interests of the Coloured Races of the World." Garvey had worked briefly for that paper prior to founding the UNIA in 1914. On Bruce, see Vincent, Black Power, pp. 99-100, and the biographical sketch in Who's Who of the Colored Race (1915), p. 47.

9. NW 12:8 (April 8, 1922), p. 2.

10. NW 12:18 (June 17, 1922), p. 7. During the time she was an active Garveyite Mrs. Walters performed numerous official and unofficial duties with Bruce, such as serving as judge at a Fourth of July carnival. Cf. NW 10:22 (July 16, 1921), p. 1. By no means were all her friends Garveyites. Mrs. Alvista Perkins, niece of New York lawyer and educator Edward Austin Johnson, recalls, in a personal reminiscence with the writer, having listened to Sunday afternoon conversations at her uncle's home in which Lelia Walters, a frequent house visitor, was ridiculed for having joined the UNIA bandwagon. Mrs. Perkins's memory was that Lelia Walters had little trouble in disposing of her critics with her quick wit and considerable verbal abilities.

11. See above, chapter 4.

12. "The Menace of Garveyism," The A.M.E. Zion Quarterly Review 34 (1923), 47-49.

13. John E. Bruce, "The Passing Show," NW 15:15 (November 24, 1923), p. 4. AME Zion clergymen who were active in local UNIA Divisions include Rev. Leo Johnson, Oakland, California; Rev. E. R. Bryant, Braddock, Pennsylvania; Dr. Duncan Jones, Brooklyn, New York; and Rev. H. B. Gantt, Los Angeles, California.

14. Biographical details are found in Who's Who in Colored America (1927), p. 12. Richard Bardolph, who lists Bell as one of the "most conspicuously mentioned" Negro churchmen in the years 1900-1936, makes special note of his militant attitude against racial injustice and attributes this to parental influence.

Bardolph writes, "Bishop Bell traces his early racial attitudes to several influences. His high-spirited grandfather exhorted the household to isolate themselves from whites and in no case to work for them, and his parents harbored equally strong hostilities....

By the time he went to college his hostilities were steadily disciplined by his religious feelings and a resolute quest for balance between self-restraint and self-respect, but fresh shocks disturbed the equipoise the youth fought to achieve." The Negro Vanguard (New York, 1961), p. 152.

15. William Y. Bell, "The Christian Spirit in Race Redemption," delivered in Liberty Hall, August 1923. NW 14:26 (August 11, 1923), pp. 2, 8.

16. Ibid., p. 8.

17. Ibid.

18. Ibid. Bell was elected bishop of the CME Church in 1938 and served actively in that post for twenty-four years.

19. NW 14:23 (July 21, 1923), p. 4.

20. NW 11:26 (February 11, 1922); NW 14:26 (August 11, 1923), p. 8; Amy Jacques Garvey, Garvey and Garveyism, p. 154. Other CME clergymen who were identified in the Negro World as active on behalf of the UNIA include Rev. B. B. Nelson of Poplar Bluff, Missouri; one Dr. Lewis of Sapulpa, Oklahoma; and Rev. J. W. Kinchloe of Santa Monica, California.

21. See for example the letter to the editor of the Living Church (January 29, 1927), p. 436 by George Freeman Bragg, Jr., in which he documents the statistical shift in Black Episcopal membership from South to North. Bragg reports that there were 3,011 colored communicants in seven southern states in the mid-1850s, which number had increased to a mere 7,196 some forty years later. Comparable figures for the six listed northern states in the same interval were 1,975 and 19,511. The influx of West Indian Anglicans into the United States accounts for the bulk of this increase.

22. Wallace Thurman, Negro Life in New York's Harlem
    (Girard, Kansas, 1928), p. 55. A character in one
    of Thurman's novels drew a somewhat more vivid
    portrait of that same church, and at the same time
    suggested another characteristic of Black Episco-
    palians. The dark skinned protagonist of the novel,
    Gwendolyn, had just arrived in New York City and
    with her new found friend Emma Lou was attempting
    to find a hospitable congregation. "When she and
    Emma Lou began going around together, trying to
    find a church to attend regularly, she had immediately
    blackballed the Episcopal Church, for she knew that
    most of its members were 'pinks,' and despite the
    fact that a number of dark-skinned West Indians,
    former members of the Church of England, had forced
    their way in, Gwendolyn knew that the Episcopal Church
    in Harlem, as in most Negro communities, was dedi-
    cated to the salvation of light-skinned Negroes." The
    Blacker the Berry (New York, 1929), pp. 233-34.
         It is somewhat ironic to note that Marcus Garvey
    was uniformly denounced by the Black intelligentsia
    for having introduced a "completely extraneous" color
    consciousness into the American scene when he made
    reference to the light complexion of the intelligentsia.
    One scholar, who repeats this criticism of Garvey's
    "mistake," footnotes without apparent awareness of
    contradiction a personal reminiscence in which a Ne-
    gro doctor from Chicago had remarked that the UNIA
    actually stood for "Ugliest [Blackest?] Negroes in
    America." E. Franklin Frazier, Black Bourgeoisie
    (New York, 1962), p. 105 and n. 14. One may as-
    sume that color consciousness among American Ne-
    groes was not something invented by Marcus Garvey.

23. Bragg was the principal organizer around the turn of
    the century of an informal association of Black Epis-
    copal clergymen designated the Conference of Church
    Workers among Colored People. He used his weekly
    church bulletin, the Church Advocate, to keep mem-
    bers abreast of problems and developments important
    to Black Episcopalians. A biography of this fas-
    cinating church leader is long overdue. On the Con-
    ference of Church Workers, see Bragg's Afro-Ameri-
    can Group, chapter 20.

24. Arnold Hamilton Maloney, The Adequate Norm: An
    Essay on Christian Ethics (n.p., 1914).

25. Arnold Hamilton Maloney, Amber Gold: An Adventure in Autobiography (Boston, 1946), pp. 117-19. For additional biographical details, see Who's Who in Colored America (1927), p. 136.

26. Bragg, Afro-American Group, p. 280.

27. Maloney, Amber Gold, p. 124.

28. Ibid., pp. 133-35. I have been unable to locate a copy of this report.

29. Ibid., p. 140.

30. Ibid.

31. The Annual Catalogue for Wilberforce University for the academic year 1923-24 lists Maloney as Professor of Psychology, noting also that he was awarded an honorary D.D. from Morris Brown University in 1922. Course offerings listed in the Psychology Department for that year included "Social Psychology," "Criminal and Legal Psychology," and "Racial Psychology."

32. Arnold Hamilton Maloney, Some Essentials of Race Leadership (Xenia, 1924), pp. 11-13.

33. Ibid., pp. 65 and 68. Emphasis added.

34. Chapter 15, "A Plea For Unity of the Negro Church," ibid., pp. 108-115 at pp. 113-15. The text of this speech, delivered in Liberty Hall, Harlem, is also reprinted in NW 12:21 (July 8, 1922), p. 5.

35. NW 26:1 (August 10, 1929), p. 3.

36. Letter dated June 22, 1922, in NW 12:20 (July 1, 1922), p. 5. It is intriguing to speculate that Bennett may have been the "sick friend" whom Maloney visited on his way to New York for his anticipated ordination into the AOC. Bennett himself appears on the list of "Hierarchy of the AOC" with the title of "Primate," some twenty years later. See Orthodox Messenger 2 (1942), p. 9.

37. Cited in Amy Jacques Garvey, Garvey and Garveyism, p. 55. Mrs. Garvey incorrectly identifies Miller as

a member of the "Presbyterian" Episcopal Church.
On Miller, see biographical sketches in Who's Who
in the Colored Race (1915), p. 192 and Who's Who
in Colored America (1927), pp. 141-42.

38. NW 8:11 (May 1, 1920), p. 4 and NW 10:20 (July 2,
1921), p. 1.

39. NW 12:25 (August 5, 1922), p. 3.

40. On Hudson, cf. NW 30:6 (September 5, 1921), p. 5.
Wallace's speech is described in NW 21:26 (February
5, 1927), p. 8.

41. Details are provided in Delilah L. Beasley, The Negro
Trail Blazers in California (Los Angeles, 1919),
pp. 11, 159, 190.

42. Who's Who in Colored America (1930-32).

43. See above, chapter 1.

44. Albert Ehrman, "Black Judaism in New York," Journal
of Ecumenical Studies 8 (1971), p. 104. Additional
biographical information is available in Sidney Kobre,
"Rabbi Ford," The Reflex (January 1929), pp. 25-29.

45. Howard Brotz, The Black Jews of Harlem (New York,
1964), pp. 11, 12.

46. Vincent, Black Power, pp. 134-35. Vincent persistently
confuses Arnold Josiah Ford, the Rabbi, with James
A. Ford, an AOC clergyman. These were two different men.

47. Ruth Landes, "Negro Jews in Harlem," Jewish Journal
of Sociology 9 (1967), p. 180.

48. Who's Who in Colored America (1930-32). Emphasis
added.

49. NW 17:1 (August 16, 1924), p. 3.

50. Pittsburgh Courier 17:32 (August 7, 1926), p. 2.

51. NW 13:23 (January 20, 1923), p. 9.

52. Rudolph I. Coffee, "Democracy in Religion," Sentinel 44 (December 9, 1921), p. 7.

53. Rudolph I. Coffee, "The Falashas," Sentinel 48 (November 17, 1922), p. 9. The American Pro-Falasha Committee was organized in the U.S. in 1922. On Faitlovitch, see The Universal Jewish Encyclopedia (New York, 1942), pp. 233-34. Howard Brotz notes that Faitlovitch himself visited Arnold J. Ford's congregation to see if there were any connection between this group and the Falashas whom he was seeking to help. Brotz reports that Faitlovitch concluded that Ford "was misled," but that the visit had a considerable effect on Ford, for whom "the very knowledge that there were people in Ethiopia whom the Jewish community recognized as Jews and who were called Falashas immediately became their most treasured insight." Black Jews, p. 49. E. U. Essien-Udom notes in his study of Black Nationalism (Dell Publishing Co., Inc., 1964) that A. J. Ford studied for a time at the University of Southern California, p. 55.

54. NW 31:6 (March 5, 1932), p. 3.

55. Wentworth A. Matthew, who assumed the rabbinate of the congregation when Ford left, also had a high regard for Garvey. Brotz remarked, in fact, that "the race leader whom Matthew most admires, next to Booker T. Washington, is Garvey." Black Jews, p. 101. It should be pointed out that though most writers whom we have cited indicate that Ford was the founder of the Harlem congregation of Black Jews, this opinion is not uniformly held. Roi Ottley, for instance, in an article based on interviews with Matthew, reported that it was the latter, whose "father was a Falasha, or African Negro Jew, and his mother a Christian, a native of the West Indies," who was the founder. Ottley writes, "As chief rabbi, he is eminently prepared to lead his people. Shortly after he and his mother settled in St. Kitts, B.W.I., he left and came to New York, where he entered a Christian theological school. After he heard the 'call' to Judaism--a period he recalls as the most thrilling of his life-- he enrolled at the Rose of Sharon Theological Seminary in Cincinnati, an institution run by the Falashas. He returned to Harlem in 1919 and organized the congregation of Commandment Keepers. Five years

later he went abroad to study Jewish theology at the
University of Berlin, on a scholarship obtained for
him by an influential white rabbi. In his absence,
Rabbi Joshiah [sic] Ford, a Negro immigrant from
Barbados, carried on his work until 1927 when he
returned to his flock and rabbinical chores." "The
Black Jews of Harlem," Travel 79 (July 1942), p.
21. Ottley's chronology corresponds to the information we have cited earlier from the 1930-32 Who's
Who, where it was stated that Ford was "called
to" (a presumably already existing) congregation
in 1924.

56. NW 12:21 (July 8, 1922), p. 7. Lucas apparently left
the Methodist ministry shortly after making this
speech.

57. The individuals and the churches to which they belonged
are as follows:

Christian Church	Rev. M. Frederick Mitchell
	Los Angeles, California
Church of Christ	Rev. J. E. Anderson
	Danville, Illinois
	Rev. S. Thompson
	Washington, D. C.
Congregational	Rev. J. Thompson
Church	Rev. P. R. DeBerry
	Raleigh, North Carolina
Emanuel Holiness	Rev. L. E. Belgrave
Church	New York, New York
Pentecostal Church	Rev. Sidney H. Solomon
	Glenwood, Pennsylvania
Presbyterian Church	Rev. L. E. Fairley
	Raleigh, North Carolina
	Rev. Dr. E. Everett Lewis
	Gary, Indiana
	Rev. F. D. Nance
	Norfolk, Virginia
Universal Spiritualist	Dr. J. R. White
Church	New York, New York

58. Vinson Synan, The Holiness-Pentecostal Movement in
the United States (Grand Rapids, Michigan, 1971),
p. 176. See also Elmer T. Clark, The Small Sects
in America (New York, 1949), pp. 120-21.

59. NW 12:25 (August 5, 1922), p. 14.

60. On Cranston, see NW 9:12 (November 6, 1920), and NW 10:20 (July 2, 1921), p. 10.

CONCLUSION

"The rhetoric of Garveyism," according to a recent study, "was unabashedly religious, although deliberately nonsectarian."[1] That remark goes almost to the heart of the matter. Garveyism was most emphatically "deliberately nonsectarian," as is evidenced by the painful controversy between George Alexander McGuire and Marcus Garvey over the institutional form that the UNIA as a religious or quasi-religious organization ought to take. As has been demonstrated in chapter three, that argument was settled along lines determined by Marcus Garvey and reflected not only his own preferences but also the reality of the UNIA constituency, composed as it was of active members of divers Black denominations.[2] With evident pretensions to nationhood in Africa and on behalf of Africa's Diaspora children, the UNIA had in principle to be able to make room for every variety of believer, both Christian and non-Christian.

At the same time, the Universal Negro Improvement Association was "unabashedly religious," and, as has been shown in chapter one, a rich variety of religious rituals and symbols were developed to inculcate and embody the deeply held beliefs which bound its members together. These rituals and symbols were often novel and imaginative, and though at times they tended (as in the case of the baptismal ceremony) to a level of specificity that bordered on sectarianism, for the most part they avoided this danger.[3]

A question arises, however, with respect to the connotation of the word "rhetoric" in describing the religious aspects of the Garvey movement. If one assumes the positive definition, "skillful or artistic use of speech," there is no doubt that this is an apt characterization. If one assumes the pejorative meaning of rhetoric as the "artificial" use of language, and thereby interprets the religious character of the UNIA as but a self-conscious ruse devised to seduce

195

members into participation in the Association's activities,
then this writer would have to dissent. As was argued in
chapter two, Marcus Garvey took seriously the religious
character of the movement he founded, and he articulated
a remarkably well developed and internally consistent theological framework by which to interpret the meaning of his
people's history and their destiny under a God who was
working on their behalf. The themes were not new. Rather,
they were drawn from a long tradition of Black religious reflection upon the experience of a people, and it is precisely
this which made Garveyism as a religious movement attractive to clergymen from so wide a range of denominational
backgrounds. Garvey's distinctive contribution was to cast
the movement in the appropriate institutional form which he
himself characterized as "one great Christian confraternity
without regard to any particular denomination," and which
has here been called a form of Black civil religion.

NOTES

1. Emory J. Tolbert, "The Universal Negro Improvement
   Association in Los Angeles: A Study of Western
   Garveyism" (Seminar Paper: University of California
   at Los Angeles, unpublished), p. 53. See also To-
   bert's Ph.D. dissertation by the same title, (University of California, Los Angeles, 1975).

2. The universal association which Garvey formed was explicitly not constructed on the model of a sect; indeed,
   sociologist of religion Ernst Troeltsch's "church type"
   of association (in which the religious institution is co-
   terminus with society itself, and is an all-embracing
   institution within which politics, economics and limited
   religious diversity take shape), is a much more apt
   analogy than is his concept of "sect" in describing the
   character of religion within the UNIA. See Ernst
   Troeltsch, Social Teachings of the Christian Churches
   2 (New York, 1960), Conclusion, for a summary discussion of his typology of religious institutions.

3. As suggested in chapter three, the baptismal ceremony
   can cut both ways in its church or sect type of orientation. In the Troeltschean framework, infant baptism
   is a classic "churchly" characteristic in which one is
   "born into" the religious community rather than volun-
   tarily choosing membership.

WORKS CITED

Books

Bardolph, Richard. The Negro Vanguard. New York: Vintage Books, 1961.

Barrett, Leonard E. The Rastafarians: A Study in Messianic Cultism in Jamaica. Rio Piedras, Puerto Rico: Institute of Caribbean Studies, 1968.

Beasley, Delilah L. The Negro Trail Blazers of California. Los Angeles: [n. p.], 1919.

Bracey, John H., Jr.; Meier, August; and Rudwick, Elliott, eds. Black Nationalism in America. Indianapolis: The Bobbs-Merrill Company, Inc., 1970.

Bragg, George F., Jr. History of the Afro-American Group of the Episcopal Church. Baltimore: Church Advocate Press, 1922.

Brotz, Howard. The Black Jews of Harlem: Negro Nationalism and the Dilemmas of Negro Leadership. New York: The Free Press of Glencoe Press, 1964.

Brown, William Montgomery. The Church for Americans. New York: T. Whittaker, 1895.

_____. The Crucial Race Question OR Where and How Shall the Color Line Be Drawn? Little Rock: The Arkansas Churchman's Publishing Co., 1907.

_____. My Heresy: The Autobiography of an Idea. New York: The John Day Company, 1926.

Burkett, Randall K. Black Redemption: Churchmen Speak

197

for the Garvey Movement. Philadelphia: Temple University Press, 1978.

_____, and Richard Newman, eds. Black Apostles: Afro-American Clergy Confront the Twentieth Century. Boston: G. K. Hall & Co., 1978.

Cherry, Conrad C. God's New Israel: Religious Interpretations of American Destiny. Englewood Cliffs: Prentice-Hall, Inc., 1971.

Clark, Elmer T. The Small Sects in America. Revised edition. New York: Abingdon Press, 1949.

Constitution and Book of Laws Made for the Government of the Universal Negro Improvement Association, Inc., and African Communities League, Inc., of the World. New York: Universal Press, July 1918; revised and amended August 1922.

Cronon, Edmund David. Black Moses: The Story of Marcus Garvey and the Universal Negro Improvement Association. Madison: University of Wisconsin Press, 1969.

Cruse, Harold. The Crisis of the Negro Intellectual. New York: William Morrow & Company, Inc., 1967.

Cullen, Countee. Color. New York: Harper & Brothers, 1925.

Drake, St. Clair. The Redemption of Africa and Black Religion. Chicago: Third World Press, 1970.

Essien-Udom, Essien Udosen. Black Nationalism: A Search for an Identity in America. New York: Dell Publishing Co., Inc., 1964.

Fauset, Arthur Huff. Black Gods of the Metropolis: Negro Religious Cults of the Urban North. Philadelphia: University of Pennsylvania Press, 1944.

Ferris, William H. The African Abroad: or His Evolution in Western Civilization; Tracing His Development Under Caucasian Milieux. 2 vols. New Haven: The Tuttle, Morehouse and Taylor Press, 1913.

Ford, Arnold Josiah. The Universal Ethiopian Hymnal. New York: Beth B'nai Abraham Publishing Co., n.d.

Fox, Stephen R. The Guardian of Boston: William Monroe Trotter. New York: Atheneum, 1970.

Frazier, E. Franklin. Black Bourgeoisie. New York: Collier Books, 1962.

_____. The Negro Church in America. New York: Schocken Books Inc., 1966.

Fullinwider, S. P. The Mind and Mood of Black America: 20th Century Thought. Homewood, Illinois: The Dorsey Press, 1969.

Garvey, Amy Jacques. Garvey and Garveyism. London: Collier-Macmillan Ltd., 1970.

Garvey, Marcus. Philosophy and Opinions of Marcus Garvey. Edited by Amy Jacques Garvey. 2 vols. New York: Atheneum, 1969.

_____. Selections from the Poetic Meditations of Marcus Garvey. Edited by Amy Jacques Garvey. New York: n.p., c.1927.

_____. Speech of Hon. Marcus Garvey ... Delivered at 71st Regiment Armory Tuesday Night, August 1st ... Before the Third Annual International Convention of the Negro Peoples of the World. [New York: n.p., 1922.]

_____. The Tragedy of White Injustice. Edited by Amy Jacques Garvey. New York: n.p., 1927.

Gilbert, Peter, ed. The Selected Writings of John Edward Bruce: Militant Black Journalist. New York: Arno Press, 1971.

Greene, Harry W. Holders of Doctorates Among Negroes. Boston: Meador Publishing Company, 1946.

Haynes, Elizabeth Ross. The Black Boy of Atlanta. Boston: House of Edinboro, Publishers, 1952.

Hill, Adelaide Cromwell, and Kilson, Martin, comps. and eds. Apropos of Africa: Sentiments of Negro American Leaders on Africa from the 1800s to the 1950s. London: Frank Cass & Company, Ltd., 1969.

Hill, Robert A., comp. The Black Man: A Monthly Magazine of Negro Thought and Opinion. Millwood, N.J.: Kraus-Thomson, Org., 1975.

Johnson, James Weldon. Along this Way: The Autobiography of James Weldon Johnson. New York: Viking Compass Edition, 1961.

_____. Black Manhattan. New York: Alfred A. Knopf, 1930.

Jordan, Lewis Garret. Negro Baptist History, U.S.A. 1750-1930. Nashville: The Sunday School Publishing Board, National Baptist Convention, n.d.

Kornweibel, Theodore, Jr. No Crystal Stair: Black Life and the Messenger, 1917-1928. Westport, Conn.: Greenwood Press, 1975.

Locke, Alain, ed. The New Negro: An Interpretation. New York: Arno Press, 1968.

Lyman, Stanford M. The Black American in Sociological Thought. New York: Putnam, 1972.

McGuire, George Alexander. Appendix to The Crucial Race Question OR Where and How Shall the Color Line Be Drawn?, by William Montgomery Brown. Little Rock: The Arkansas Churchman's Publishing Company, 1907.

_____. The Universal Negro Ritual containing Forms, Prayers, and Offices for use in the Universal Negro Improvement Association together with a Collection of Hymns Authorized by the High Executive Council Compiled by His Grace, Rev. Dr. George Alexander Mc-Guire, Chaplain General Approved by His Excellency, Marcus Garvey, President General and Provisional President of Africa. n.p., 1921.

_____, comp. Universal Negro Catechism. n.p., 1921.

McKay, Claude. Harlem-Negro Metropolis. New York: E. P. Dutton & Company, Inc., 1940.

_____. A Long Way from Home. New York: Lee Furman, 1937.

Maloney, Arnold Hamilton. The Adequate Norm: An Essay on Christian Ethics. n.p., C. E. Pawley & Company, 1914.

_____. Amber Gold: An Adventure in Autobiography. Boston: Meador Publishing Co., 1946.

_____. Some Essentials of Race Leadership. Xenia, Ohio: The Aldine Publishing House, 1924.

Markham, Violet Rosa. The New Era in South Africa. London: Smith, Elder, & Company, 1904.

Martin, Tony. Race First: The Ideological and Organizational Struggles of Marcus Garvey and the Universal Negro Improvement Association. Westport, Conn.: Greenwood Press, 1976.

Mays, Benjamin E. The Negro's God as Reflected in His Literature. New York: Atheneum, 1969.

_____, and Nicholson, Joseph William. The Negro's Church. New York: Negro Universities Press, 1969.

Mead, Frank S. Handbook of Denominations in the United States. 5th ed. New York: Abingdon Press, 1970.

Meier, August. Negro Thought in America: 1880-1915. Ann Arbor: Ann Arbor Paperback, 1966.

Moses, William Henry. The Colored Baptists' Family Tree. Nashville: Sunday School Publishing Board of the National Baptist Convention, U.S.A., 1925.

_____. The White Peril. Philadelphia: Lisle-Carey Press, Foreign Mission Board of the National Baptist Convention U.S.A., [1919?].

Ottley, Roi. "New World A-Coming": Inside Black America. Boston: Houghton Mifflin Company, 1943.

_____, and Weatherby, William J., eds. The Negro in New York: An Informal Social History 1626-1940. New York: New York Public Library, 1967.

Phillips, Porter W. W. W. Brown, Host. New York: Fleming H. Revell Company, 1941.

Powell, Adam C. [Sr.]. Against the Tide: An Autobiography. New York: Richard R. Smith, 1938.

Ransom, Reverdy Cassius. The Pilgrimage of Harriet Ransom's Son. Nashville: Sunday School Union, n. d.

Rauschenbusch, Walter. Christianizing the Social Order. New York: The Macmillan Co., 1912.

Shepperson, George, and Price, Thomas. Independent African: John Chilembwe and the Origins, Setting and Significance of the Nyasaland Native Rising of 1915. Edinburgh: The Edinburgh University Press, 1958.

Synan, Vinson. The Holiness-Pentecostal Movement in the United States. Grand Rapids, Michigan: William B. Eerdmans, 1971.

Terry-Thompson, Arthur Cornelius. The History of the African Orthodox Church. New York: Beacon Press, 1956.

Thurman, Wallace. The Blacker the Berry. New York: Arno Press & the New York Times, 1969.

_____. Negro Life in New York's Harlem. Girard, Kansas: Haldeman-Julius Publications, 1928.

Troeltsch, Ernst. Social Teachings of the Christian Churches. Vol. 2. New York: Harper and Row, Publishers, 1960.

Vincent, Theodore G. Black Power and the Garvey Movement. Berkeley: Ramparts Press, 1971.

Walters, Alexander. My Life and Work. New York: Fleming H. Revell Company, 1917.

Watson, Emory Olin, ed. Yearbook of the Churches, 1924-5. Baltimore: n. p., 1934.

Who's Who in Colored America: A Biographical Dictionary of Notable Living Persons of Negro Descent in America. Vol. 1, 1927. Edited by Joseph J. Boris. New York: Who's Who in Colored America Corp., 1927.

Who's Who of the Colored Race: A General Biographical

Dictionary of Men and Women of African Descent. Vol. 1, 1915. Edited by Frank Lincoln Mather. Chicago: By the Author, 1915.

Wilmore, Gayraud S. Black Religion and Black Radicalism. Garden City, N.Y.: Doubleday & Company, Inc., 1972.

Woodson, Carter G. The History of the Negro Church. 2nd ed. Washington, D.C.: The Associated Publishers, 1945.

_____, ed. The Works of Francis J. Grimké. Vol. 4: Letters. Washington, D.C.: The Associated Press, Inc., 1942.

Wright, Richard Robert, Jr. The Bishops of the African Methodist Episcopal Church. [Nashville:] A.M.E. Sunday School Union, 1963.

_____. Eighty-Seven Years Behind the Black Curtain. Philadelphia: Rare Book Company, 1965.

_____, ed. Centennial Encyclopaedia of the African Methodist Episcopal Church. Philadelphia: A.M.E. Book Concern, 1916.

Articles and Miscellaneous Materials

"The American Church Institute for Negroes." Southern Workman 35 (1906), 470.

Becker, William H. "The Black Church: Manhood and Mission." Journal of the American Academy of Religion 40 (1972), 316-333.

Beckwith, Martha Warren. "Some Religious Cults in Jamaica." American Journal of Psychology 34 (1923) 32-45.

Bellah, Robert N. "Civil Religion in America." In The Religious Situation: 1968, pp. 331-393. Edited by Donald R. Cutler. Boston: Beacon Press, 1968.

Bragg, George Freeman, Jr. "Letter to the Editor." Living Church (January 29, 1927), p. 436.

Coffee, Rudolph I. "Democracy in Religion." Sentinel 44 (December 9, 1921), 7.

_____. "The Falashas." Sentinel 48 (November 17, 1922), 9.

Cromwell, John W. "First Negro Churches in the District of Columbia." Journal of Negro History 7 (1922), 64-106.

Diggs, James Robert Lincoln. "Negro Church Life." Voice of the Negro 1 (1904), 46-50.

Drake, St. Clair. "The Negro Church and Associations." New York, June 1, 1940. (Mimeographed research memorandum.)

DuBois, W. E. Burghardt. "Back to Africa." Century 105 (February 1923), 539-548.

_____. "The Black Star Line." Crisis 24 (September 1922), 210-14.

_____. "Marcus Garvey." Crisis 21 (December 1920), 58-60; 21 (January 1921), 112-15.

_____. "The U. N. I. A." Crisis 25 (January 1923), 120-22.

Ehrman, Albert. "Black Judaism in New York." Journal of Ecumenical Studies 8 (1971), 103-114.

Elkins, William F. "Marcus Garvey, the Negro World, and the British West Indies: 1919-1920." Science and Society 36 (1972), 63-77.

Forbes, George Washington. "Garvey's Plight--The Pity of It All." A. M. E. Church Review 40 (1923), 50-51.

_____. "Marcus Garvey and His League of Nations." A. M. E. Church Review 37 (1921), 166-67.

_____. "Within the Sphere of Letters." A. M. E. Church Review 35 (1918), 122-23.

Franklin, Vincent P. "The Philadelphia Race Riot of 1918." Philadelphia Magazine of History and Biography 99 (1975), 336-50.

Frazier, E. Franklin. "Garvey: A Mass Leader." Nation 123 (August 18, 1926), 147-48.

Garvey, Marcus. "Intelligence, Education, Universal Knowledge and How to Get It." Lesson Guides prepared for the School of African Philosophy. (Mimeographed.)

Gregg, John A. "Africa and a Way Out." A. M. E. Church Review 37 (1921), 205-213.

Kent, George E. "The Soulful Way of Claude McKay." Black World 20 (November 1970), 37-51.

Kobre, Sidney S. "Rabbi Ford." The Reflex (January 1929), 25-29.

Landes, Ruth. "Negro Jews in Harlem." Jewish Journal of Sociology 9 (1967), 175-189.

McKay, Claude. "Garvey as a Negro Moses." Liberator 5 (April 1922), 8-9.

Matthews, Carl S. "Marcus Garvey Writes from Jamaica on the Mulatto Escape Hatch." Journal of Negro History 59 (1974), 170-76.

"The Menace of Garveyism." The A. M. E. Zion Quarterly Review 34 (1923), 47-49.

Ottley, Roi. "The Black Jews of Harlem." Travel 79 (July 1942), 18-21+.

Plummer, H. Vinton. "The U. N. I. A. as I See It--Then and Now." The Spokesman 2 (May-June 1927), 10+.

Randolph, A. Philip. [Editorial.] Messenger 5 (January 1923), 561.

[Ransom, Reverdy Cassius.] "Back to Africa: A Militant Call." A. M. E. Church Review 37 (1920), 88-89.

_____. "The Golden Dream of Negro Nationality." A. M. E. Church Review 40 (1923), 44.

_____. "A Quadrilateral View of the Attitude and Outlook for Negroes Throughout the World." A. M. E. Church Review 38 (1921), 82-85.

"Richard Robert Wright." [Obituary.] Journal of Negro History 32 (1947), 529-530.

Rushing, Byron. "A Note on the Origin of the African Orthodox Church." Journal of Negro History 57 (1972), 37-39.

Smith, Charles Spencer. "To the Editor of the World's Work." World's Work 41 (March 1921), 435-36.

Tolbert, Emory J. "The Universal Negro Improvement Association in Los Angeles: A Study of Western Garveyism." Ph.D. dissertation, University of California at Los Angeles, 1975.

White, Gavin. "Patriarch McGuire and the Episcopal Church." Historical Magazine of the Protestant Episcopal Church 38 (1969), 109-141.

Williams, Daniel T., ed. "The Perilous Road of Marcus M. Garvey: A Bibliography." In Eight Negro Bibliographies. Comp. by Daniel T. Williams assisted by Cecil S. Belle. New York: Kraus Reprint Co., 1970.

Williams, Preston N. "Towards a Sociological Understanding of the Black Religious Community." Soundings 54 (1971), 260-270.

Wright, Richard Robert, Jr. "What Does the Negro Want in Our Democracy?" Reprinted in A Documentary History of the Negro People in the United States, 1910-1932, pp. 285-293. Edited by Herbert Aptheker. Secaucus, New Jersey: The Citadel Press, 1973.

INDEX

Compiled with the assistance of Janice P. Merz

207